ASCENDANCY TO OBLIVION

Michael McConville read Modern History at Trinity College, Dublin. During the Second World War he served as a Royal Marine Commando officer in Yugoslavia and Italy. From 1950 to 1961 he worked in the Malayan Civil Service. He was subsequently a diplomat, serving in Ceylon, Haiti, Canada and Yugoslavia, among other places. He retired from the Diplomatic Service in 1977, at which time he was Consul-General in Zagreb. He lives in Somerset.

ALSO BY MICHAEL McCONVILLE

Leap in the Dark
The Burke Foundation
Tales from the Mess
More Tales from the Mess
Tell it to the Marines
Small War in the Balkans

ASCENDANCY TO OBLIVION

The Story of the Anglo-Irish

Michael McConville

PHOENIX
PRESS

5 UPPER SAINT MARTIN'S LANE
LONDON
WC2H 9EA

A PHOENIX PRESS PAPERBACK

First published in Great Britain
by Quartet Books in 1986
This paperback edition published in 2001
by Phoenix Press,
a division of The Orion Publishing Group Ltd,
Orion House, 5 Upper St Martin's Lane,
London WC2H 9EA

A CIP catalogue record for this book
is available from the British Library.

Printed and bound in Great Britain by
Clays Ltd, St Ives plc

ISBN 1 84212 271 1

AUTHOR'S NOTE

In the early stages of the roughing out of the framework of this book
it became clear that there would be a problem of definition. Who
were the Anglo-Irish? Were they, as the label suggests, everyone of
mixed English and Irish blood who lived in Ireland? Or were they, as
a narrower interpretation has it, a particular caste, the product of
historical circumstances, who during the eighteenth, nineteenth and
early twentieth centuries were dominant in Irish affairs and were
distinguishable by their politics, their culture and their religion from
the 'native' Irish? And if the second alternative is correct, how did it
come about that a fair proportion of the dominant caste were
ethnically of Norman, Gaelic Irish, French Huguenot and Dutch
origin while some of the 'native' Irish were of almost undiluted
English stock?

The best way to resolve these complexities, it seemed to me, was to
start at the beginning, when nobody at all lived in Ireland, and to
trace the origins and motives of successive immigrations. They all
contributed to the racial hybrid of modern Ireland. All of them
passed through England, Scotland or Wales on their way over. In
that respect almost all Irish men and women are Anglo-Irish. The
attitudes, triumphs and failures of the group to which the name is
more usually applied can be better understood against the background of those who came before them.

I have relied extensively upon published sources. I am particularly
indebted to the authors of those listed in the select bibliography. My

grateful thanks also to the National Gallery of Ireland and to *Bord Failte* for permission to reproduce the plates in the illustrated section.

ASCENDANCY TO OBLIVION

FOREWORD

The Anglo-Irish were an unusual colonial caste that for a little more than two hundred years, out of the five thousand during which Ireland has been inhabited, dominated the ordering of the island's affairs.

Their power was at its zenith for the whole of the eighteenth century. Before then, for five hundred years, attempts to govern Ireland in the interests of England had been made inconsistently, resisted erratically, and were only partially successful. After the eighteenth century, for the whole of the nineteenth and the beginning of the twentieth, the Anglo-Irish remained dominant, confident of their abilities and of their future in the country as people qualified inherently to lead it.

By the 1980s they have, as an entity, as good as disappeared. They are numerically decimated and politically neutered. The children of such of them as have remained in independent Ireland are scrupulous in emphasizing their Irishness, and coy about recalling the Anglo element of the racial equation. The likelihood is that in about two more generations the residue will have been so diminished by assimilation and emigration that the Anglo-Irish will have become little more than a folk memory, and an unpopular one.

The aim of this book is to record where they came from and why; what they did and why; and how and why they went into decline. Their story is explicable only when it is set in the context of other races who came to be in Ireland, and of the contribution they made

1

to the genetic pudding. Simplistic views, cherished by some romantics, of a seven-hundred-year-long struggle between the English nation and the Irish nation, at the end of which Irish courage and virtue were triumphant, do not stand up to examination. The Anglos were not entirely Anglo, and the Irish were not entirely Gaelic Irish. Alliances and allegiances were inconstant.

In the years of their ascendancy the Anglo-Irish constituted a small, élite oligarchy, professing a minority Protestant religion in an overwhelmingly Catholic island of modest intrinsic value, but of strategic importance to the contestants in a succession of European wars of little relevance to Ireland. To these, Ireland was a necessary incidental, not a principal. The role of the oligarchy was in essence defensive: to protect Britain's western flank by denying the use of Ireland as a forming-up position for amphibious operations by European Catholic powers hostile to Protestant England. The method chosen for meeting this requirement was total occupation and control. Along with its achievement went rich pickings, cheerfully grabbed at.

The Anglo-Irish exercised the authority delegated to them from London with a haphazard mixture of arrogance, high-mindedness, insensitivity, selfishness, elegance, venality, charity, devotion to duty, cruelty, artistic sophistication, stupidity, eccentricity, clear-headedness, kindliness and political myopia. They governed Ireland usually not very well, sometimes abominably badly, and in some respects better than the present generation of Irishmen gives them credit for.

Their domestic legacy is of political and racial resentment (much of it formalized, unjustified, its origins ill-understood); some superb Georgian architecture; cultural and educational establishments – Trinity College, Dublin, the Royal Irish Academy, the Royal Dublin Society – the equal of any, anywhere; an infrastructure of cities, towns, roads and railways upon which the economy of modern, independent Ireland has built; and the political framework of a parliamentary democracy supported by a professional civil service which, with only slight adaptation, has (at least so far) proved the type of government most favoured by the great majority of adult citizens of the Republic. The legacy also, of course, includes the English language, still in almost universal daily use despite a prolonged, forlorn official programme for the survival of Irish.

2

The wider contribution of the Anglo-Irish to posterity is, for a relatively small and historically transient group, astonishingly rich. To letters they gave Swift, Burke, Goldsmith, Sheridan, George Moore, Oscar Wilde, W.B.Yeats, George Bernard Shaw and Samuel Beckett. To soldiering, Wellington, Roberts, Wolseley, the Goughs, any number of Victorian and First World War generals, the bulk of the British military leadership in the Second World War – Alanbrooke, Dill, Alexander, Gort, Montgomery, Auchinleck – a post-war Chief of the Imperial General Staff, Templer, and an impressive assembly of winners of the Victoria Cross.

A random, not comprehensive, trawl in other waters yields Bram Stoker who wrote of Count Dracula, Shackleton who explored the Antarctic, the Harmsworths who revolutionized British newspaper publishing, Castlereagh and Burke in British politics, a sizeable proportion of the administrators of the Indian and Colonial empires, Bishop Berkeley in philosophy, William Orpen in painting, the entire strength of the original Irish international rugby fifteen, and innumerable owners and trainers of victorious horses at Aintree and Epsom.

Their versatility was not always applied to stimulate the conventional approval of their contemporaries. Wolfe Tone, Lord Edward Fitzgerald, Robert Emmet, Thomas Davis, John Mitchell and Charles Stewart Parnell were Anglo-Irishmen who led the Irish opposition, violent or constitutional, to British rule. At a less ideologically elevated level, the Anglo-Irish, notably during the eighteenth century, provided in disproportionate numbers a spectacularly uninhibited array of gamblers, lechers, duellists, spendthrifts, drunks, crooks and miscellaneous loonies.

Now to the beginning.

CHAPTER ONE

At Newgrange in County Meath, near the village of Slane by the River Boyne, there is a complex passage grave set in a burial mound. The main chamber, and its approach tunnel, are lined with large blocks of ornamented cut stone. Above the entrance, sixty-two feet from the chamber, is an aperture known to archaeology as a roof-box. The roof-box was disregarded as a puzzling and probably irrelevant hole in the structure until 1967, when its significance was identified by a gifted academic from University College, Dublin. The burial mound faces the south-east. If the sky is clear at the time of the winter solstice, 22 December, the rising sun shines through the roof-box and illuminates the shallow hollows of stones upon which had been laid the bones of the dead, previously in part cremated.

The archaeological evidence puts the date of the devising and construction of this ancient cemetery at about three thousand years before the birth of Christ. Similar passage graves have been found in other parts of Ireland, forty of them in areas of the Boyne valley near to Newgrange. Little is known of who made them. Whoever they were, they were clearly a people with a sophisticated knowledge of architecture, masonry, astronomy, mathematics and the effective organization of manual labour, who showed a scrupulous reverence for their dead.

Other findings elsewhere in Ireland demonstrate that these aboriginal pre-Celtic Irishmen were fishermen and food-gatherers who customarily lived on the banks of rivers and lakes. The first of them must have arrived in the country not long before the Newgrange passage grave was built. Before then, Ireland was uninhabitable. In common with the rest of northern Europe it was under a thick crust of ice. It was not until the climatic modifications of five thousand years ago that the island, then a bulbous peninsula linked by a causeway to western Scotland, became an attractive proposition for human settlement and exploitation.

Of all the ingredients in the Irish racial compound only these early settlers would have stood a chance of mounting a successful defence against charges of colonialism ('esp. derog.: alleged policy of exploitation of backward or weak peoples': *The Concise Oxford Dictionary*), should the General Assembly of the United Nations have been operational at the time. When they arrived, there was nobody available for them to exploit. They doubtless exploited each other, as has been the universal human habit down the ages. But for centuries they were left to do it in domesticity, until they were faced about seven hundred years before Christ by the advance elements of a mass migration that would have breached the UN Charter on almost every count.

This influx was Celtic. Its membership was of Indo-Germanic origin, and those who came to Ireland were the leading fringe of a huge surge of human movement that slowly crossed continental Europe in a generally westerly direction. The term Celt, in modern times appropriated by resentful ethnic minorities and sectarian soccer clubs, was in essence linguistic rather than racial. It was applied, long after the first migratory shifts began, by Roman imperial historians who viewed with civilized austerity the travelling barbarian hordes (*Celtae*), sharers of a loosely common language.

The *Celtae* went upon their unpredictable expeditions in tribal groupings of aggressive intent, and were spectacularly destructive of such urban development as at the time existed and happened to attract their attention. Students of British imperial and colonial history will recognize without difficulty the attitude of the Romans to the *Celtae*. So will watchers of American Western movies. To Roman eyes the *Celtae* were not the supine, servile equivalent of 'wogs', despised for their anxiety to make themselves either agreeable or invisible. They were dangerous toughs with a disposition to fight, precursors in the imperial canonical series of the Pathans of the North-West Frontier, or the Plains 'Injuns' who so

5

discommoded the likes of General Custer.

The branch, or successive accumulation of waves, or agglomeration of blobs, of this mass western trek that found its way to the offshore Atlantic island of Ireland, brought its own customs, culture and tongue. The earliest Irishmen, after more than two thousand years of – so far as can be determined – undisturbed occupancy, ceased to be identifiable as a race. They were assimilated or destroyed by the Celtic invaders. Their artefacts remain, mostly expressed in stone, objects of much devoted and ingenious research by specialist scholars.

The new Celtic society in Ireland, separated by famously wild stretches of sea from the island of Britain and from the mainland of Europe, was for the next thousand years left in relative isolation to develop its own political, agro-economic and cultural institutions. The Romans, the most cohesive and efficiently expansionist nation of the era, first came to Britain in 55 BC and subsequently overran and colonized most of what is now England. But the strategic constraints imposed by distance and the capricious moat of the Irish Sea, left Ireland immune from Roman military attention, colonization, heavy-handed oppression and, arguably, the benefits of a civilizing tuition in Christianity, a written language understood throughout the known European world, advanced agricultural practices, the building of roads, municipal engineering and adequate provision for sanitation and warm baths.

The isolation was far from total. There was two-way trading, and two-way raiding, between accessible parts of Ireland and accessible parts of Scotland, Wales, the Isle of Man and Cornwall. It was, for example, an outside source, Welsh Christian missionaries, who first put into use a term that described generically the inhabitants of the entire island. The Welsh *Gwyddel* was translated to the Irish *Goidel*, later anglicized to Gael.

Few societies in history have been given the opportunity to evolve with only minuscule outside interference for so long as that of Gaelic Ireland – that of its destroyed predecessors being among the exceptions. It was a slow-moving evolution, conditioned by a respect for tradition coloured by legend, by the absence of external stimuli to encourage a reconsideration of the usefulness of practices

6

and attitudes that had served adequately for countless generations, and by the physical and climatic resources and limitations of a small island set in an incidental geo-political-cultural quarantine.

Gaelic Ireland's central weakness was that it stayed fragmented. It neither achieved nor aspired to anything resembling a national unity. It retained the tribal structure of its distant immigrant forebears. With local variations there was a common language, a common culture, common customs and a common tribal and social organization. But tribal self-interest was paramount. The fact that this totality was doomed unless the whole conglomeration of quarrelling groupings consolidated in resistance to outside dilution, incursion, and ultimately outright conquest, was not perceived until it was far too late to prevent the overthrow of the entire Gaelic system. When the invaders eventually arrived, Danish, Norman, English, they were first looked upon not as violators of the integrity of the national territory, but as a transitory local nuisance or as useful allies who could be enlisted to help discomfit hostile neighbours.

There was a further important, non-military, disability attached to this lack of national cohesion. There was no effective central government apparatus with which foreigners could negotiate realistically if they felt so disposed. Scotland and Norway, countries with populations of a size comparable to that of Ireland, were able in time to engage with some degree of credibility in rudimentary diplomatic dealings. Ireland never was.

The social and political lodestar of each of the quasi-independent tribal communities was a body of customary law, passed orally from one generation of erudite professional lawyers to the next. A man's legal obligations were defined in the context of what was expected of him in his dealings with his family and with the tribe, not, understandably, with the non-existent nation.[1]

Land, the source of all wealth to a pastoral and agricultural people, was tribal collective property. No one member, not even the tribal or regional king, had the right to dispose of it to anyone else.

---

[1] Thomas Davis (1814–45), who inspired much patriotic emotion with 'A Nation Once Again', verses later set to music and calling nostalgically for a return to ancient institutional glories, had it wrong.

7

Kingship was not directly hereditary. Replacement kings were elected from a panel of candidates chosen from prominent inter-related families within the tribe.

A developed class system prevailed. Leadership, in war or peace, was provided by the aristocracy from which the monarch was drawn. A professional middle class of Druids, judges, historians, poets and physicians gave specialized advice, analagous to that proffered by the present-day Civil Service, on sacred rites, law, health, precedents, commemorations and the rest. The proletariat was subdivided into the free and the slaves. The free owned cattle, grew crops and profited modestly from both. The slaves, battle captives later supplemented by victims, including Saint Patrick, of amphibious raiding parties making the most of the decline of the Roman Empire, slaved.

There were no towns. The Gaelic Irish lived in isolated family steadings. They gathered defensively behind earthwork, and later stone, fortifications when it became prudent to do so in time of war, and they assembled at the same places in times of peace for ritual celebration or divine placation.

Warfare between individual tribes, and between impermanent alliances of tribes, was recurrent. Its physical objectives were the acquisition or repossession of land, and the taking of cattle, a mobile, visible and countable expression of wealth. An obvious and increasingly frequent political objective in a territory with clearly defined coastal boundaries which at one time supported something like one hundred and fifty independent communities, was consolidation of groups of smaller entities into larger ones under a single leadership. The aim was sometimes achieved, but the achievement tended to lack stability. The successful contestant did not become the ruler of newly acquired subjects. His primacy was acknowledged, and tribute was paid to him in cattle, but domestic tribal affairs continued to be ordered domestically as they had been immemorially.

Another endemic source of strife was a product of the institution of elective monarchy. Defeated candidates did not necessarily accept, as twentieth-century politicians in parliamentary democracies are supposed to accept, that whatever the manifest unsuitability of the winner, he was none the less what the electorate thought that they wanted. Disappointed contenders were apt to register their objections to electoral verdicts by force of arms, thereby adding an element of dynastic intra-tribal civil war to the already proliferating inter-tribal ones.

The fighting (some of it stylized military posturing in the manner later perfected by the *condotierri* in Renaissance Italy), the cattle raiding and the enslavement of captives were accepted as a natural part of the texture of human existence. They were commemorated and embellished by the poets, whose job it was to sustain tribal morale and to promote the case for election to kingship of the particular candidate to whom the poets were attached. But although the warfare was often conducted with savagery – no more, and no less, than that being undertaken in other contemporary societies – the Gaelic Irish were by no means entirely preoccupied with bloodshed and plunder. They were an artistically inclined people, who cherished and honoured their poets, story-tellers and musicians. Their metalwork craftsmen created intricate ornamentation, worn by both men and women and displayed on the harness of horses. Their actions, personal and communal, were governed by a corpus of inherited and enforced law. Their spirituality was expressed in pagan forms, largely animistic, but demonstrating a belief that there was more to life than a short-term earthly tenancy during which wisdom coincided with cunning, and success lay in the ruthless acquisition of accessories to self-indulgence.

The most senior on the long list of innovators of English origin who, for better or worse, transformed Irish society is Saint Patrick. In the early part of the 5th century AD, when he was a boy in England, he was kidnapped by an Irish raiding party. He was brought to Antrim, and was held for seven years as a slave. He escaped back to England, where he was ordained a Christian priest. He returned to Ireland and preached Christianity, with success. The success was neither immediate nor total, and was not entirely his in that he was the dominant figure among many missionary collaborators, not an individualist proselytizer. But the success was sufficiently convincing to persuade Pope Celestine in 431 AD to nominate the first Christian bishop, Palladius, to an Irish see.

The advent of Christianity, aside from its more obvious manifestations in the rearrangement of Irish spiritual beliefs and values,

9

was the catalyst that determined the course of the next sixteen hundred years of Irish social, cultural and political evolution. Prior to Patrick's mission, both pre-Celtic and Gaelic Ireland had developed their distinctive characteristics within a framework of insular ignorance of, or indifference to, happenings in the rest of the known European world. Christianity brought Ireland for the first time into association with an international community with a shared religious faith. However imperfectly observed, and however imperfect the temporal activities of its adherents, that faith opened doors to ideas, practices, devices and institutions previously unimagined by the islanders.

The early effect was a cultural flowering of an intensity that gave Ireland an esteem in the eyes of foreigners, and an earned pleasure in its own achievements, that has not been approached since. The later effects, the product of distortions introduced by outsiders as secondary logical requirements for the attainment of non-Irish ends, are on dismal display in the latter half of the twentieth century in such locations as Belfast, Derry and South Armagh.

The most effective secular instrument to accompany the conversion of Ireland to Christianity was the Latin script, concise, serviceable and capable of mastery by any reasonably persistent scholar. Knowledge, whether legal, historical, technical or religious, had traditionally been handed down orally in Gaelic Ireland. *Ogham*, an imprecise system of lines of varying length set at right angles to a central vertical line, not unlike a primitive form of written semaphore, had come into limited use, but it was of restricted practicality and unpopular with a fundamentally conservative intelligentsia. There was conservative resistance to the new script too, and to the embodiment of introduced learning in Latin. But a realistic expediency, fostered by a growing appreciation of the value of monastic centres of scholarship, led inexorably to its universal adoption by the educated.

For three hundred years, during which a synthesis between ancient ways and imported religious and cultural influences evolved, Ireland flourished intellectually and artistically. Towns and cities, the bases upon which the lay and ecclesiastical organizations of Rome and its imperial possessions had rested, were still non-existent in Ireland. An adaptable Irish Church expanded the role of monasteries, sited wherever they could do the most missionary and educational good among dispersed rural populations, refined by the voluntary withdrawal of more contemplative monks to lonely and remote hermitages. Monastic scribes transliterated the gospels with a loving and lovely calligraphy and a heroic patience (the best-known of the surviving examples is the *Book of Kells*, housed now in the library of Trinity College, Dublin). Irish missionaries established overseas religious and scholarly communities, from Lindisfarne and Iona in Britain to the far side of the Alps, teaching and evangelizing among the pagan barbarians who had partially moved in to fill the vacuum left by the disintegration of the Roman empire. Students from all over Europe made their slow way to Ireland for instruction at what were effectively the forerunners of universities, such as the one at Glendalough in what is now County Wicklow. The royal schools at the court of Charlemagne were manned by Irish teachers. The era passed into legend, summarized and popularized as the time when Ireland was the Land of Saints and Scholars.

There was a sizeable degree of accuracy in the description, but it was over-succinct. It omitted reference to two modifying factors, one local and susceptible to Irish control, one external and generated entirely by external forces. The first was the old weakness, once tolerable, soon to be socially fatal, of national disunity. The number of independently led political organisms had been reduced drastically in number to four or five, but the traditional internecine strugglings for sectional supremacy still persisted parallel to the developing revolution in religious practice and cultural richness. The external factor was Viking expansionism.

The Vikings, Scandinavian adventurers who were boat-builders, navigators, warriors and sea-borne looters of distinction, initially found Irish targets both irresistible and unresisting. Ireland had had no experience of armed incursion from overseas since the arrival fifteen hundred years previously of the Gaelic Irish themselves. The artistic wealth generated by three hundred years of Christian culture was largely, and from the point of view of the predatory, conveniently, concentrated in monastic settlements. Since the monasteries also acted as primitive banks, and stored portable royal riches along with Church treasure, Viking forays prospered.

But these Norsemen were more than alarming and efficient plunderers who took what they wanted, destroyed what they did not, and departed. They set up advance bases, temporary at first, for

11

ship maintenance and the counting and distribution of booty. Operational convenience, and the value of shortened lines of communication to other Viking enterprises, rival or complementary, in the Orkneys, south-west Scotland, the Isle of Man, and northern England, led to the transformation of these impermanent encampments into defended settlements. Effective defence postulated short perimeters, which in turn made necessary the grouping together of buildings, residential and administrative.

For innumerable generations the Gaelic Irish had assembled together when under threat, but they had always dispersed to their rural steadings when the threat was lifted. The Norsemen had nowhere on land to disperse to. They stayed where they were. Urban Ireland was born. Dublin, Wexford, Waterford, Cork and Limerick, which between them now accommodate about two-thirds of the population of the Republic of Ireland, are all of Norse origin. They were lived in more or less exclusively by Norsemen for a period as long as the white man has lived in North America. The infusion of Norse blood, skills and attitudes into the hybrid which patriotic shorthand centuries later summarized as the Gaelic Order, is too often overlooked in the polemics.

Irish school history books celebrate the defeat of the Danes at Clontarf in 1014 by the High King Brian Bóroimhe (anglicized to Brian Boru), the most effective unifying ruler ever to be produced by Gaelic Ireland. But Clontarf was not the climax of a war between nations. Settled Danes from the Norse kingdom of Dublin, who had for several generations interbred with the Gaelic Irish, and who shared similar limited and local political horizons, fought alongside Brian as allies against invaders who according to patriotic history should have been their collaborative kinsmen. The fighting strength of the Gaelic kingdom of Leinster, which was stubbornly resistant to Brian's overlordship, joined forces with the overseas Danes. A genuine national consciousness, expressed either as a binding together among fellow-Irishmen, or more negatively as a unifying xenophobic resistance to aggressive strangers, was unheard of, unthought of, and would continue to remain so for the best part of the next eight hundred years.

Fifty-two years after Clontarf another branch of the Norse military migration invaded England from northern France. The Normans retained the hereditary Norse fighting zeal and valour, but refined it by adopting comparatively advanced military tactics, discipline and equipment, and by evolving a comparatively sophisticated political feudal system. An absolute monarch was the source of all property, wealth, honour and appointments, which he distributed to a subordinate aristocracy in return for hard cash and warlike support.

The Normans soon controlled England. It was in keeping with their restless ambition for the acquisition of new lands that in 1169 a body of armed Norman knights and their followers should arrive in Ireland. It was entirely in keeping with contemporary Irish political practice and philosophy that the Norman advance guard should have come by the invitation of an Irish regional king, who needed help in a complicated dispute that he was conducting with two other kings, and who saw nothing out of the ordinary in enlisting it extra-territorially from the most formidable fighting force available.

The inviting monarch was Dermot MacMurrough of Leinster. His domestic disagreements were with Rory O'Connor, the High King whose suzerainty Dermot declined to accept, and with O'Rourke of Breffny, whose wife Dermot had stolen. Dermot MacMurrough has gone down in the retrospectively compiled demonology of Irish chauvinism as the self-serving traitor who first let the English into Ireland, but it is an arbitrary, unjust and unrealistic judgement. Given the Norman record and Norman habits it was inevitable that they should have come to Ireland anyway and trounced any Irish military opposition.

The ones who came first were English only in the sense that they sailed from the island of Britain upon which they had imposed a foreign control for just over a hundred years. They were francophone travelling adventurers whose immediately previous preoccupation had been the subjugation of the Welsh Marches. A contemporary annalist records Dermot's departure from Ireland in search of these new allies not as an iniquitous example of betrayal, but as a lamentable absence. And if O'Connor, O'Rourke or any other Irish king of the era had felt the need for outside help and had identified, as astutely as MacMurrough, the Normans as a source of such help, there is no reason to think that they would have acted differently. What none of them could have foreseen was the durability and longevity of the Norman presence, and the permanent

13

influence that it was to have upon the island.[2]

Although in practice the original Norman encroachment was by independent-minded soldiers of fortune with an eye to the main chance, there was a tenuous thread of English constitutional legitimacy to the undertaking. It had been authorized by King Henry II of England, who as a forward-looking contingency planner had earlier negotiated with the Papacy a provisional endorsement of any expansion of his dominions to Ireland that he considered desirable. Pope Adrian IV had obliged with a papal bull, *Laudabiliter*, that entrusted Henry with the task of putting to rights the unsatisfactory moral and generally irreligious attitudes prevalent among the Irish. There is controversy about the authenticity of this bull. No duplicate exists in the Vatican archives. Pope Adrian was the only English pope, ever. There have been subsequent allegations of collusive English trickery, forgery, and a range of similar ecclesiastical and diplomatic irregularities.

Genuine or spurious, the papal bull was of little relevance to the realities. Its lack would not have inhibited a Norman incursion, sponsored by a Plantagenet king who had to be constantly alert to the threat to his authority in England posed by recalcitrant and insubordinate barons, and who was pleased to see potential domestic opposition diminished by the engagement of some of it in ventures elsewhere. When the king did eventually come to Ireland he did so not to take formal possession of new territories won in his name and in the name of England, but to ensure that the winners of them were not so overcome with self-satisfaction at their successes that they should establish a rival independent Norman-Irish kingdom.

And the successes had been very substantial indeed. Norman determination, skill at arms and adaptability took them inexorably to all the most strategically dominant and agriculturally fertile corners of the country. They were ferocious in imposing their will, but unprejudiced in their assessment of what they found attractive, and what they did not, in existing Irish society. The original wave of Norman interlopers duly made their constitutional obeisances to

[2] The influence can be identified, for example, in the political leadership of twentieth-century Ireland. Since the creation of the Irish Free State in 1922 there have been eight heads of government. Of these, five – Cosgrave, Costello, Lynch, the younger Cosgrave and Fitzgerald – have Norman names. Of the remaining three only Haughey is a Gaelic-Irish name. De Valera is Portuguese and Lemass is Huguenot.

14

Henry when he arrived with a force of sufficient strength to underline his expectation that his supremacy was to be acknowledged. A similar fealty was pledged by a variety of Gaelic Irish chiefs and by the hierarchy. But whatever good intentions were inspired by these ceremonial orthodoxies, they were, at least in part, soon overlaid by the isolation, exigencies and charms of contemporary Irish rural life.

A theoretically centralized royal government, set up in Dublin, could transmit as royal writ instructions initiated in London. But it soon became clear that in most of Ireland, beyond the closely controlled Pale around the capital, governmental edicts were subjected to as much selective interpretation and indifference by the king's Norman lieges as they were by the Gaelic Irish chieftains. A complementary cause for government concern was the disconcerting realization that as time went on many Norman leaders were effectively *becoming* Gaelic Irish chieftains. They married Irish wives, adopted Irish speech and Irish customs, and in the much-quoted phrase became *hiberniores hibernis ipsos*, 'more Irish than the Irish'; so did a substantial number of successive generations of settlers brought in from England to exploit the new lands, to provide reliable manpower for the new towns and manors, and to contribute the commercial and technical expertise required for the smooth running of the new colony.

The new colony did not run smoothly. Until the religious Reformation of the sixteenth century, which introduced a new and even more disruptive factor into the polity of Ireland, the country's affairs proceeded in a series of kaleidoscopic patterns that were constant only in their inconstancy and that ranged between the uneasy and the chaotic. The one fixture was Dublin Castle, the centre of English government, and the Pale, the area of English-controlled lands abutting it. The Pale comprised several counties in which English settlers settled, English laws prevailed, and the English language, evolving from Norman-French superimposed upon Anglo-Saxon, was spoken. The Pale's boundaries bent, gave, and recovered in irregular conformity to irregular events beyond the periphery. But even when Irish pressure was at its highest there remained a solid block of cultivated territory occupied by English-orientated inhabitants who, if not always uncritically acquiescent in what they were told to do by Dublin Castle, usually recognized that self-preservation was a powerful motive for doing it.

Beyond the Pale, English rule was patchy and inconsistently enforced. Feudal theory had it that in exchange for the royal grant of lands, the holder would administer and defend his acquisition in the royal interest. During the early phases of the expansion most of the grantees met this obligation, but distance from the central authority, primitive channels of communication, and absorption in the practicalities of life, soon began to erode respect for the niceties of constitutional legality. Loyalty to the crown, and the honouring of feudal commitments, increasingly depended upon how closely royal rights coincided with private interests. The Fitzgeralds of Desmond in Munster, their kinsmen of Kildare in Leinster, the Butlers of Ormonde – who were almost constantly in armed dispute with the Kildare Fitzgeralds, the De Burgos of Ulster – who without title sequestrated large areas of Connacht and gaelicized their name to Burke – all of these gradually evolved into independent chieftains managing their territories with a high-handed indifference to Dublin.

There was sporadic, sometimes incessant, fighting between them: between the Normans and the Gaelic Irish, between combinations of some Normans and some Irish against combinations of other Normans and other Irish. The periods of precarious peace were marked by extensive degeneracy, a term with a then more restricted meaning than it later came to hold, but one that excited much the same abhorrence among the purists. It embraced inter-racial marriage, the use by the Norman-English of the Irish language and their adoption of the Irish custom of fosterage, by which alliances between powerful families were strengthened through the mutual exchange of children for upbringing. A broad spread of other undesirable habits included the use of Irish-type saddlery and the playing by less privileged retainers of 'the games which men call "Hurlings", with great clubs at ball upon the ground, from which great evils and maims have arisen'. In most of Ireland beyond the Pale, and in parts of the Pale itself, degeneracy, particularly inter-racial breeding, moved steadily from a subject for official censoriousness to the norm of everyday life.

The Gaelic Irish were untroubled by notions about the importance of preserving a genetically unadulterated racial heritage. They had already interbred with Danes, and they did so assiduously with

Normans and the following waves of supporting English settlers. They held to their traditional loose organization of tribal groupings and opportunist alliances, and fought for, against, and with the Norman lords, the garrison from the Pale, and an irregular succession of expeditions mounted from England, sometimes under royal leadership, with the intention of establishing order and transforming Ireland into the prosperous and well-conducted colony that it clearly had the potential to become, if only someone could work out how to transform it.

There were some, temporary, English successes. They were followed invariably by a return to one form or another of the old, shapeless, ill-controlled *status quo*. The hesitations and inconsistencies of English policy were further compounded for protracted periods by dynastic warfare in England, reflected not very strongly among the English in Ireland by partisan fighting between supporters of Lancastrian or Yorkist claimants to the throne, motivated less by emotional loyalties than by calculations of envisioned private gain.

A formal event that followed the accession of Henry VIII in the early sixteenth century illustrates compactly the manner in which the qualities and attributes of those leaders charged with helping to govern Ireland in the king of England's name had evolved. The proclamation of Henry as king was read to the Irish parliament, a rudimentary assembly but none the less representative of the hereditary ruling caste of English Ireland. Only one member, the Butler Earl of Ormonde, could understand it. It was translated into Irish for the benefit of the rest.

Since the future directions (plural, they were many) that Ireland was to take were ultimately determined by Henry's personal embracing of the Protestant faith, it might be as well to make a summary appraisal of the condition of his Irish inheritance. And since contentious sectarian Christianity, genuine, cosmetic or opportunist, was in the ensuing centuries to become indistinguishable from political and pseudo-ethnic divisiveness, it might also be as well to do the appraising against a measuring board which all branches of the Christian religion consider valid. Markings can only be arbitrary and made in the light of recorded information.

The first two of the Ten Commandments are concerned with the

17

worship of graven images and the taking of the name of the Lord in vain. It is possible that in early Tudor Ireland there survived isolated pockets of Druidical adherents, but if so they were of no communal significance. Nor was the taking of the Lord's name in vain, which was doubtless as prevalent then as it is now. There is little evidence about the degree to which the Sabbath day was maintained as both restful and holy, but it is clear that both restfulness and holiness went by the board when military urgencies supervened. Fathers and mothers, designated for honouring under the fourth Commandment, were presumably honoured about as much as they are in the present day, but fathers in particular were at risk when the question of who was the most suitable man to control tribal destinies arose.

The last six thou shalt nots on the list were, in the collective Irish ethos of the times, treated with theoretical respect and in practice disregarded on a heroic scale. They covered, after all, what was almost a complete inventory of the objectives of the country's entire adult population. Killing, committing adultery, stealing, bearing false witness against neighbours, coveting other people's wives, houses, lands, servants, handmaids, oxen (read longhorn cattle), asses (add horses), were what the persisting strife in Gaelic Ireland, as modified by Norman technological and philosophical inno-vations, had traditionally been about. (For that matter, it was what the history of almost everywhere else has traditionally been about, allowing for local adaptations. But in view of later, much later, attempts at a rearrangement of the Irish pack into neatly identifiable teams of the Good versus the Abominable, it is worth pointing out that Original Sin, or human frailty, or whatever synonym is currently fashionable, is not a monopoly of one side in any particular controversy.)

The holders of these accommodating interpretations of the moral imperatives of the religion to which everyone nominally subscribed, and by which many genuinely believed their actions to be guided, were distributed demographically in loosely classifiable groupings.

The Pale's population came largely, but not exclusively, from stock later to be known as Old English. So did that of a handful of walled towns, mostly of Norse provenance – Cork, Limerick, Waterford, Galway and Kilkenny. Each had its royal charter, its minor equivalent of the Dublin Pale, and its recurrent apprehensions about what the natives outside the gates would try next.

The countryside at large was divided asymmetrically between mingled semi-autonomous territories of varied, and varying, extent. Some were controlled by Norman lords of (by now) mixed blood, whose headquarters were in stone-built castles. Others were controlled by Gaelic Irish chiefs who in many cases imitated the Normans and built castles of their own. These Gaelic leaders and their followers were also of mixed blood. Earlier Danish and Norman infusions had been supplemented by an additional source, the Gallowglasses, Scoto-Scandinavian mercenary soldiers of disciplined efficiency who had been imported as a counter to the earlier Normans, and who like so many people who come on a visit to Ireland, had stayed there.

In one area only, the northern province of Ulster, the old Gaelic system remained undiluted by outside genes and practices. Ulster was geographically remote from Dublin, topographically difficult to conquer, and led by a succession of O'Neill and O'Donnell chieftains of notable ability and tenacity.

Until the sixteenth century, English kings were designated as 'Lords' of Ireland. In 1541 Henry VIII declared himself to be King of Ireland as well as of England. He did some forceful preliminary clearing of the ground by breaking the strength of the Kildare Fitzgeralds, who apart from controlling vast tracts of territory, had for several generations held the office of Deputy, the nominated English governor of Ireland. Not surprisingly, this approved dynastic monopoly of delegated power had bred dynastic pretensions that were no longer acceptable to a monarch determined upon the unambiguous exercise of his prerogative. Royal moves and Geraldine counter-moves, complicated in the spirit of the times by suspicion, opportunism, warfare and the slaughter of non-combatants, culminated in the death in the Tower of London of the Earl of Kildare, and the execution at Tyburn of five of his brothers and of his eldest son, Silken Thomas. The next royal initiative led, in the first instance, to less shedding of blood. It also, almost inadvertently, laid the rather shaky foundations upon which the future ascendancy of the Anglo-Irish was built.

The policy of 'Surrender and Re-grant' was originally conceived as a forthright attempt to impose administrative tidiness upon a constitutionally unworkable ragbag. Land was wealth, and wealth meant power. In feudal theory all land was ultimately the property of the crown. But by the middle 1500s, four centuries of partial occupation of Ireland by the Normans, characterized by intermittent anarchy, forcible annexations, and the conviction that possession was ten-tenths of the law, further confounded by the totally different system by which the Gaelic Irish held their hereditary lands, had reduced to near-impossibility any hope of the orderly control of public affairs. Neatness, it was decided, could be restored only by the surrender of landholders' titles, followed by the prompt issue of new titles to the same landholders, with standard conditions listing obligations and privileges.

There was general compliance. To the landholders of non-Gaelic extraction, the Norman magnates in large areas of Leinster, Munster and Connacht, and the English lords of the Pale, the measure was at its worst no more than a bureaucratic inconvenience. They had always lived, at least notionally, under English law and there was nothing foreign to them in this particular manifestation of it. The Gaelic Irish chieftains, to whom the requirement also applied, were equally disinclined to be troublesome about it. Either through inability to understand its full implications, or because of calculations of personal and filial advantage, they complied – and in so doing acquiesced in the destruction of the basic component of a Gaelic order that had lasted for two thousand years.

The lands that the Irish chiefs surrendered were not theirs to surrender. They were communal tribal property. In return for the documentary transmission of something that they did not own, the Irish chiefs were given a hereditary title, enforceable by English law, to its feudal occupancy. They accepted this arrangement, in their own words, and in translation, 'most willingly and joyously'. If they realized that the corollary of acknowledging the crown as the ultimate owner of land conferred upon subjects, was that the crown could take away again what it had once bestowed, they made no recorded protest. It was an oversight that was to furnish a legalistic validity to much stylishly justified theft.

The process of repossessing Irish lands as a penalty for the 'misbehaviour' of an Irish chieftain, and re-allocating his territory to 'planters' more amenable to the requirements of the English government, took a long time to evolve. Early experiments were *ad hoc* responses to local tactical stimuli. During the middle 1500s, in the reign of Henry's Catholic daughter Mary Tudor and her consort Philip of Spain, the errant O'Connors and their tributary followers in Laois and Offaly were dispossessed. Laois was redesignated the Queen's County; Offaly the King's County. The territory was distributed among Old English settlers from the Dublin Pale, and the outlying defences of Dublin benefited accordingly. In Antrim a small embattled English enclave struggled fitfully to withstand the harassment of its evicted Irish predecessors. These colonies were improvisations. Colonization became a matter for serious consideration as a policy only in the last third of the century, during the prolonged reign of Queen Elizabeth I.

Until this time the religious upheavals generated by the Protestant Reformation in England had no real counterpart in Ireland. There were those of both faiths who held strong convictions. There were some unedifying conversions, not least among the clergy, made with an avaricious eye to the main chance. But personal preference still largely prevailed. There might have been some uneasiness, but few of those with a constitutional obligation to support the crown saw any inconsistency in the retention of their traditional faith while pledging fealty to a ruler who had rejected it. Disagreements, resentments and rebelliousness were the stuff of temporal self-interest, not of spiritual exaltation. The Old English lords of the Pale, for example, the Eustaces, Dillons, Plunketts, Nugents, Brabazons and the rest, remained Catholic but had more to gain from the new English Protestant dispensation than they had from their co-religionist hereditary enemies the Gaelic Irish. The Norman-Irish magnates, with a much greater infusion of Gaelic blood in their systems than the Pale lords, reached their decisions and calculated their balances of advantage on different grounds, but until the late sixteenth century religion was not a major consideration to them.

The international reaction to the consolidation of English Protestantism was more profound. The counter-reformation was spirited and sophisticated. It suffered from the usual deviousness and mutual mistrust among its devotees, but when the battle lines were mustered Protestant England was at risk. Catholic France and Catholic Spain, when not at each other's throats, were the most dangerous contenders for the task of destroying the new English heretic society, for reconverting its survivors, and for acquiring its

21

wealth. The Papacy, then a lay state as well as the ancient and inspirational centre of Christendom, set the tone for what was expected of the crusaders in the Holy War. The repetitive papal message was neatly encapsulated in an exhortation by Pope Gregory, after he had provided two thousand soldiers of doubtful value to accompany James Fitzmaurice on a liturgically blessed military adventure to Munster in 1579: 'If these men do not serve to go to England,' pronounced His Holiness, 'and there unseat the heretic queen, at least they will serve to go to Ireland and there commence the attack, for the state of all Christendom dependeth upon the stout assailing of England.'

The English disinclination to be stoutly assailed, and the stoutness with which they set about assailers, is a national characteristic of long provenance. Any worthwhile analysis of the European Catholic threat, and the steps necessary to contain it, inevitably centred upon the need for either a compliant or a subservient Ireland. Ireland had been notably neither for five hundred years. Elizabethan advisers were slowly, and contentiously, examining the problem, when a chain of events, prompted almost inconsequentially by the latest round in a Norman-Irish feud of long standing, led to the identification of what seemed to be a possible solution. It was a solution that was shrouded in enormous slaughter, suffering and devastation.

Given entrenched attitudes, the condition of European politico-religious rivalries, and the geographical situation of Ireland, it was as good as inevitable that the level of endemic violence in the country would rise markedly. It is characteristic of the anarchic ambience of the times that the trigger which precipitated the overthrow of the Gaelic order and its replacement by the rule of an alien oligarchy, was a private fight conducted by private armies about land rents. The principals in this affair were two of the three most powerful Norman-Irish leaders in the country, Gerald Fitzgerald, the four-teenth Earl of Desmond, and Thomas Butler, the tenth Earl of Ormonde.

Both the original Irish Butler and the first Fitzgerald came to Ireland with King John. The Fitzgeralds in everything but name were kings of Munster. The lands that they controlled covered

22

over 1,500 square miles, and included, apart from Munster, substantial areas of Connacht and Leinster. The ruler of these domains, Gerald, who was as ruthless as he was absolute, directed his affairs from his base at Askeaton on the Kerry shore of the Shannon. Its architecture was Norman, its customs Irish.

The Butler stronghold was Kilkenny Castle. Their lands in Leinster and Munster abutted the Pale, and Ormonde was more susceptible to English influence than was Desmond. But Ormonde was when he chose as much an Irish chieftain as was Desmond.

Desmond, at least nominally, was a Catholic. Ormonde, unusually among his Norman-Irish contemporaries, was a Protestant. Both acknowledged the suzerainty of the crown, and both had experience, of different kinds, of England. Desmond as a boy had been imprisoned in the Tower of London, in which his grandfather had died. Ormonde had been brought up at the English court. He had Boleyn relatives, and was a cousin of Queen Elizabeth, whom he had known well as a child. In the context of his dispute with Desmond there was an oddity about another Ormonde relative. His mother was Desmond's second wife.

Neither Ormonde nor Desmond looked upon their allegiance to the crown as an impediment to their independent right to conduct private warfare as it had been conducted by their forebears for centuries. This was a miscalculation.

The queen, to their surprise, expressed extreme vexation when she heard that two of her most prominent Irish lords had mobilized large elements of their Gaelic supporters and engaged in a violent affray to settle a trivial disagreement. The fight had been on the Blackwater River in Waterford. Ormonde, leading a force of O'Kennedys, Burkes and MacGillapatrics, had triumphed over Desmond and his O'Sullivans, MacSheehys, MacCarthys and O'Connors. The casualties numbered more than three hundred Geraldine dead, and among the wounded and captured was Gerald Fitzgerald, the Earl of Desmond himself.

Both leaders were summoned to London by an angry queen – 'No sword shall be drawn in this realm but the Queen's, which shall touch only the guilty.' Ormonde's followers brought Desmond on a stretcher. Desmond was once more put into the Tower of London to await trial. Ormonde was paroled, after admonishment.

Desmond's captivity was less than onerous. His wife and one of

23

his sons joined him. So, for meals, did a hundred or so of his retainers, including musicians and poets, who travelled to London at the Desmond expense. But the expense was crippling and had to be curtailed. The close family remained, but Desmond's continuing relative comfort did not assuage his hurt pride nor compensate for the deprivation of freedom to an autocratic individualist. Meanwhile the courtiers discussed what to do with a man whose potential for originating major trouble was even greater than his outstanding record of doing so.

After nearly two years of tolerable but frustrating imprisonment, Desmond was paroled to house arrest in the establishment of Warham St Leger, a London merchant with Irish interests. This improvement was offset by a shortage of money. There was a further geographical improvement in 1568 when Desmond was permitted to move at will through an extended area around the River Thames. Then his wish to be back where his power lay, coupled with his fierce resentment, tempted Desmond into a trap.

Martin Frobisher, later to win fame as an Elizabethan seadog and scourge of the Dons, offered to smuggle Desmond by ship down the Thames and back to Munster. Desmond accepted, went to the agreed wharf, armed and in disguise, and was arrested. Frobisher had been an *agent provocateur*. Desmond was charged with breaking parole and treasonable conspiracy.

He was offered a chance of saving his life and he took it. He renounced his title, forfeited 'voluntarily' his immense landholdings, and accepted a small pension. One of the conditions of his pardon was that he should continue to live in St Leger's London house during the queen's pleasure. The queen's pleasure lasted for four more years. During that period the first colonization of Munster was put in train.

The original Munster Plantation was the first English venture into genuine colonialism. It predated the founding of the New England settlements in North America by fifty years. The preceding four centuries of English involvement in Ireland had been opportunist, or in response to unpredicted events, or allowed to develop haphazardly through lethargy, indifference or incapacity. The Munster enterprise was planned. It was badly planned, as its outcome was to demonstrate, but for the first time ever forethought was given to the problems that would face settlers of English origin in a sequestrated territory of rich potential value where the original inhabitants could be assumed to be hostile.

Both the ethos and the available resources of the era demanded that the settlement should be effected through private enterprise. Common sense suggested that the planters should be men of military as well as agricultural experience, so that they could simultaneously make private profits, help to swell the treasury through taxation, and be capable of looking after themselves with minimum calls upon a royal army that was at once spectacularly inefficient and expensive to run. A sanctimonious and rather unreal preoccupation with legal niceties contributed a last element to the piece. The ideal candidate to fit the job description would be a country gentleman of adventurous disposition who had once been a soldier and who could put up an adequately plausible claim to a land title in Munster.

One presented himself almost immediately. Sir Peter Carew might reasonably be described as the prototype Anglo-Irishman. He had more rough edges than most, if not all, of his successors, but then most prototypes do. Later there were softer, gentler, and more urbane specimens of the breed, but Carew had qualities that were not unfamiliar in the Anglo-Ireland of generations to come. He was physically tough, as ruthless as any Gaelic or Norman Irish chief, almost illiterate, energetic, cantankerous, accident-prone, and he had a good lawyer.

The lawyer's name was Hooker. He worked in Exeter, near where Carew lived, and he had a passion for old documents. He became the chronicler of the first Munster Plantation. Before becoming so he made himself the ingenious interpreter of a set of obscurely illegible deeds that according to the Hooker advocacy established Carew's hereditary right to the ownership of large expanses of the forfeited Geraldine lands. Cheered by these findings, Sir Peter sent Hooker to Dublin Castle for further research. Hooker made short work of this, and within a month had equipped his employer with a pedigree sufficiently convincing to induce him to go to London to persuade the queen and her counsellors that he was the man, qualified by birth and experience, to found the new nation of Englishmen in Ireland.

Whether or not the queen was impressed by the dynastic evidence on offer (an important bit of which, Hooker recorded, 'was very old and had been trodden under the foot, and by that means the letters were almost worn out') she endorsed the Carew colonization scheme. Carew returned to the English West Country to make his preparations. He was not reticent about the procedures that he had adopted to engineer the royal approval, and there was an outbreak of imitative ancestral research among the squirearchy of Devon, Cornwall and Somerset.

Authorizations to participate in the colonization went to, among others, Sir Richard Grenville, years later to go down fighting in the *Revenge* with his entire ship's company off the Azores, rather than surrender to the Spanish; Sir Humphrey Gilbert, the half-brother of Sir Walter Raleigh (Raleigh himself was later to leave several indelible marks, including the introduction of the potato, upon Ireland); and Sir Warham St Leger, in whose house the Earl of Desmond had been confined in London. Enlisted by these leaders, and assembling at the English western seaports of Bristol, Chester, Plymouth and Mount's Bay, were the requisite number of yeoman, artisan, labouring and soldiering volunteers, most of them unaware of what lay ahead and filled with optimism about their material prospects.

The various components of this loosely cohesive expedition made their separate ways to Waterford, Cork and Youghal. Carew, the pioneer, wasted no time in hurrying to Dublin, where he advanced his claims, supported by Hooker's version of the evidence, to the Dublin parliament, a body of limited legislative power but considerable scope for delaying or modifying what it disliked. Surprisingly, for a collection of landed proprietors whose own self-preservation was bound up in honouring the legitimacy of existing titles, and who might have supposed that to acquiesce in the dismantlement of the estate of their most extensively endowed confrère could only establish a precedent with distressing undertones for themselves, they neither delayed nor modified. Carew was confirmed as the rightful owner of the barony of Idrone in County Carlow, half of a hitherto unheard-of entity described as the kingdom of Cork, and of an assortment of other broad areas in the heartland of the Desmond country. Almost without exception these lands were already occupied, as they had been immemorially, by the Gaelic Irish.

As the headquarters of his new development enterprise Carew

26

chose Idrone. Carlow was closer to the central government in Dublin and was more fertile and less wild than the remote fastnesses of his acquisitions in south-west Munster. There was also the advantage, or so it seemed at the time, that the Idrone lands abutted the possessions of the Ormonde Butlers, who were increasingly showing evidence of their loyalty to the crown. By the beginning of the autumn Carew's new settlement in Idrone was on its way to an illusory permanence. The resident Kavanaghs were being chased away, land was being parcelled out among the newcomers, rudimentary farmsteads were being built, and occasional peel towers were going up for warning and defence.

Farther to the south and west Warham St Leger and Richard Grenville were establishing their own plantations near the city of Cork. Humphrey Gilbert and his associates were at work farther west still, beyond the River Blackwater. With local adaptations the cycle followed by all these communities was identical: eviction of the Irish, distribution of land, construction of the first buildings, clearance and cultivation.

The ease with which these radical disruptions of the way of life of an ancient society were effected, demonstrated yet again the fundamental weakness, disunity, of Gaelic Ireland. Tribal rivalry and sectional feuding still took as much precedence as resistance to armed confiscation of the source of the race's wealth. A co-ordinated Irish guerrilla harassment of the first Munster Plantation would have killed the project, and most of its projectors, within a few weeks of its inception. There was considerable harassment, but none of it was co-ordinated. There were instances in which the Irish accepted English help in the prosecution of feuds against old enemies. At other times, one part of a tribe, including the Idrone Kavanaghs, anxious to avoid English reprisals, fought another part intent on avenging themselves upon the English intruders.

The settlements went ahead towards moderately peaceful prosperity. The seeds of their ruin were probably sown at the beginning, but the germination of the one that led to the ultimate damage was the responsibility of the founder, Sir Peter Carew himself.

The Carew vigour and incisiveness were, as has earlier been hinted at, unmatched by subtlety or sensitivity. He was a stranger to nuance and compromise, a black and white classifier uninterested in shades of grey. As he saw it, his mission was to underpin personal

27

aggrandizement by forcing upon Ireland civilized values honoured in Tudor England. His response to any challenge was to take instant remedial action, without pausing to work out the possible consequences of what he was doing. He applied these simple principles to a cattle-raiding initiative mounted by Ormonde's brothers, Sir Edmund and Sir Edward Butler.

To modern minds, as to Sir Peter Carew's, cattle-raiding is no more than one of the many varieties of robbery. In the Ireland of the times, with its ambivalent rules of conduct, cattle-raiding was something of a popular sport, an interesting adventure spiced by danger and the chance of a quick profit. The Butler brothers, from their Kilkenny bases, jointly rounded up some cattle that belonged to neighbours of long seniority, and then extended their operations into Carlow. Carew's curious title deeds had put him into ownership of lands that had formerly been Butler property. The Butlers helped themselves to the beeves on these pastures, met some opposition, killed a few luckless opponents and set fire to a church.

All this was deplorable, but no more so than many another everyday incident of the times. Carew, unfamiliar with entrenched Norman-Irish practices, chose to interpret the Butler high spirits as a malevolent affront to his authority. He at once instituted a campaign of armed reprisal. There were no half measures about it.

With a force of English militia from the Idrone settlement, dispossessed Kavanaghs eager to ingratiate themselves with the new local management and, most sinister of all, Irish mercenary *bonnachts* of no fixed allegiance, Carew set off after the Butler brothers. They were bewildered by what seemed to them an extravagant response to a routine irregularity, and withdrew to Kilkenny. Undeterred by the thought that he was invading territory that was the property of Thomas, Earl of Ormonde, the outstanding loyalist of his day and cousin to the queen (he was currently in Whitehall trying to negotiate for himself a fair share of the Desmond territorial plunder), Carew pressed onwards to Kilkenny town.

His troops, soon out of hand, destroyed, looted, burnt and raped as they went. Kilkenny itself was an oasis of English-style civility, a mercantile mediaeval enclave dominated by the Ormondes' castle and the Gothic magnificence of St Canice's Cathedral. Carew's rabble stormed into the town, incinerated the merchants' houses, wrecked the cathedral, overran the castle's defences, ransacked

Ormonde's personal possessions and pillaged the cathedral treasury. There were extensive massacre and rape. One of the rape victims, according to one report, was Sir Edward Butler's wife.

Sir Edward Butler was among those captured. Had Carew been capable of making a rational assessment he might now have concluded that he had avenged himself, with compound interest, upon the cattle-rustling Butler brothers; that the ill-disciplined horde that he led was out of control; that things in general had gone farther than enough; and that it was high time to give some thought to the effect that all this mayhem was likely to have on the complex interplay of forces elsewhere in Ireland.

If any of these ideas crossed Carew's mind he soon disposed of them. His next move was to chase the other Butler brother, Sir Edmund, from one castle to another, until he finally cornered him in Clogrennan Castle. Butler evaded capture there, but the garrison and its accompanying women and children were slaughtered. Butler was taken a few days later. Carew had, in parlance yet to come into use, achieved his strategic objective. Both the cattle thieves were in his custody. He may even have thought that he could go home to Idrone and resume life where he had interrupted it. If so, this option was denied to him. He had started the snowball rolling down the hill and nothing he could now do could impede its momentum.

In his immediate vicinity of Kilkenny/Carlow a growing and murderous opposition accumulated. There were the dispossessed who saw the chance to exploit the chaos that Carew had generated around him. These took out their vengeance in pitiless ambushes against his returning, disintegrating army, debilitated by casualties and desertions, floundering through bog and forest. Outraged Butlers joined in the attacks, supported by their hereditary enemies, the Kildare Fitzgeralds, cousins to the Desmonds, cagily loyal to the crown but appalled by the havoc-ridden progress of an authorized crown agent who seemed to be a self-destructive lunatic.

Further afield, in the south-west, the old Gallowglass Mac-Sweeneys and MacSheehys, the hibernicized Burkes, the Norman-Irish Roches and Barrys and the Muskerry MacCarthys, rose in unison to destroy the Munster Plantation before they too were subjected to the lethal caprices of planters such as Carew. Settlements were raided, settlers were slaughtered. In the south-east, a combined Butler/Kildare Fitzgerald marauding party descended

29

upon the Enniscorthy Fair in Wexford and carried away a huge booty in horses, cattle, gold, silver and imported tradeware.

In the midst of this confusion a fresh and dangerous Irish leader entered formally into the fray. From the English point of view he was dangerous on two counts. James Fitzmaurice, the Earl of Desmond's cousin, was both a formidable soldier and a clear-thinking political realist who had identified a unifying cause that could bring together all those opposed to the new settlements. Fitzmaurice denounced the Acts of Uniformity and Supremacy that gave legal sanction to the established Protestant Church in Ireland. He linked the elimination of the settlements with the restoration of the Catholic Church.

The Fitzmaurice intervention, and the military skill, cruelty and deviousness that he brought with it, added further gall to the perils already undergone by the southern and south-western settlers. The coastal towns of Cork, Waterford and Youghal, long occupied by Old English adherents of the crown, were soon under siege. They were thronged with settler refugees, far from welcome. Their cattle and horses had been slaughtered, their farms had been burned, and those who had escaped massacre had been driven and whipped naked, men and women, through the devastated countryside. Mutual hatred was pervasive.

In London it was appreciated that not only the Munster Plantation but the whole of Ireland was at risk, and with it the maritime defence of England against Catholic Europe. The remedy devised was partly political, largely military. Ormonde was ordered back to Ireland with instructions to detach his family and their large following from the insurgents. The crown commanders, Sidney and Perrot, were authorized to conscript the loyal (i.e. Old English) population into the army and 'to prosecute any rebel or rebels with sword and with fire', an injunction to pitilessness that was followed with a grisly enthusiasm.

The ensuing campaign of pacification and counter-defiance was as brutal as any so far seen in Ireland, where brutality on the field of action was the norm. The butchery of prisoners, wounded and unwounded, was a well-established commonplace. Sidney, entrusted with the clearance of the roads joining Cork, Limerick and Dublin, and with no troops to spare to garrison nodal points already cleared, anticipated interference by killing every Irishman found bearing arms. He used large trees as mass gallows. He burnt cabins, slew cattle and burned crops. Humphrey Gilbert, brave as a lion in battle, decorated the approach to his headquarters in Kilmallock with rows of heads mounted on spikes. ('I never heard or read of any man more feared than he is among the Irish nation,' said his half-brother, Sir Walter Raleigh, appreciatively.) When, during Gilbert's absence in England, Kilmallock was captured by Fitzmaurice, there was a three-day orgy of looting followed by the burning of the town to ashes and its subsequent occupation by wolves.

There were few fixed engagements in this form of warfare. Skirmishes, ambushes, pursuits, exemplary destruction, reprisals, torture and the slaughter by both sides of non-co-operative civilians endured repetitively until 1573. Fitzmaurice, trapped with a few surviving followers in the barren hills of Kerry, was starved into surrender. He came out and submitted to Perrot in Kilmallock. His submission was accepted and he was not put under constraint. A few days later he was in France.

Military victory had indisputably gone to the English. But military victory is useless unless it contributes to the achievement of a political objective. The overriding one, the denial of south-west Ireland as a base for any foreign power intent upon invading England, had, at least temporarily, been met. Very little else had. The first Anglo-Irish settlers had been massacred or dispersed, their farmsteads destroyed, their lands a wilderness. Munster was plagued by famine. Instead of the taxes from the Plantation paying for the upkeep of the additional forces needed to buttress English rule in Ireland, the expense of the campaign had left both the English and the Irish treasuries on the edge of bankruptcy.

There was a last manifestation of the waste and futility of the past few years. Desmond, whose arrest and subsequent forfeit of titles had set in motion the whole calamitous sequence, was released and restored to his former eminence. The calculation in Whitehall was that since the experiment of occupation and direct rule had been a failure, the only alternative was a return to the *status quo ante bellum*. A bonus was thought to lie in Desmond's known distaste for

31

his cousin Fitzmaurice, at large in France, and rightly judged to be still a threat.

Desmond's first act on his return to his castle at Askeaton left no doubts about his interpretation of his restored powers. Within a few weeks he had hanged or driven away the few English officials who remained, brought under control every townland in his territory, and restored the property and privileges of the Catholic Church. There was fury in Dublin Castle and in Whitehall, but for the time being the English had had enough of Irish wars. They were acquiescent.

So ended the first attempt to establish a wholly English colony in a major area of rural Ireland. Most of its executants were dead or discouraged. The erratic and irascible Sir Peter Carew, bewildered by the confusion in Irish affairs, went stolidly back to Devon and had little further to do with Ireland. He retained his ownership of Idrone, where his son was killed in a later rising. A few others, Perrot, St Leger, Raleigh, Humphrey Gilbert, were to be heard of in the Irish context again. So, before long, was the exiled James Fitzmaurice.

CHAPTER TWO

In 1579 James Fitzmaurice was in Rome, trying to persuade the Holy Father to provide some troops for a Catholic crusade in Munster. Fitzmaurice had already suffered courteous diplomatic rebuffs from the French and the Spanish over this request, both of whom had followed enthusiastic approval of the idea with a disappointing reluctance to do anything about it. Pope Gregory was more accommodating, but was insistent about the limits beyond which he would not go. There was some worldly bargaining. The pontiff knocked Fitzmaurice's bid for six thousand soldiers down to two thousand papal mercenaries, but raised the force to four thousand when Fitzmaurice suggested including two thousand jailed Italian bandits, who were subsequently paroled for the purpose.

Fortified by a papal blessing, equipped with a papal banner depicting the head of Christ ringed by thorns, and accompanied by an English Jesuit named Nicolas Sanders, this unlikely military formation made its way to Lisbon, where the bulk of it met with an unusual setback. Before it could arrange for its onward transport to Ireland it was conscripted into the army of King Sebastian of Portugal and taken off to invade Morocco, where almost everyone in it was killed in action.

This bizarre fiasco left only Fitzmaurice, Sanders, Cornelius O'Mulrian the Bishop of Killaloe, and the papal banner immediately available for future Irish operations, and illustrates in miniature the difficulties and misunderstandings attendant upon international military co-operation at the time. It also presaged in the manner of a stencil the difficulties that in the centuries ahead were to face many an exile determined to liberate his countrymen from the toils of a situation that he thought he understood, assisted by allies that he believed would measure up to their commitments.

Wolfe Tone in the late eighteenth century misjudged the domestic mood of Ireland and was over-ambitious in his assessment of what France would do to help his endeavours. Roger Casement made the same mistakes in the early twentieth century, again misjudging the mood and placing his reliance upon Germany, with similarly unsatisfactory results. Both Tone and Casement were, as it happened, Anglo-Irishmen, and both paid for their miscalculations with their lives. So, eventually, did Fitzmaurice in the late sixteenth century, but not before he had helped to create even more human misery than had flowed from the First Desmond War.

The weaknesses in the Fitzmaurice position are, in retrospect, readily apparent. He was out of touch with developments in Munster. In order to muster allies he was using as an argument the need to give the Munster Irish the freedom to practise their faith. With Desmond restored, they were already practising it. As with Tone and Casement centuries later, he was exaggerating to his potential backers the extent of domestic support to be expected when he landed. He also assumed, without first confirming it, that Desmond himself would give practical expression to his endorsement of the enterprise. His single-mindedness clouded his appreciation of the fact that absolute monarchs, even ostentatiously Catholic ones with a sympathetic turn of phrase, had their own problems, and were not disposed to put Fitzmaurice high on their scale of priorities until he had demonstrated by his actions that he had something to offer that could be exploited in their own interests. As an experienced soldier, he might have shown some reserve at the naïveté of the papal belief that a nation of the vigour, resourcefulness and ferocity of Elizabethan England would be incapable of dealing with a scratch military body, half of which was drawn from Italian prisoners released on probation.

But if Fitzmaurice's judgements were suspect, his determination was constant. He raised another small force, seven hundred strong. This time it consisted of Spaniards, Flemings, Italians, Portuguese, a few Irishmen and a handful of Catholic English. With Father Sanders, as papal nuncio, and Bishop O'Mulrian in attendance, Fitzmaurice sailed from Corunna in the spring. Unsurprisingly, the elevated religious motives of the expedition had no more influence upon the temporal behaviour of its members than the Christian principles proclaimed by the Protestant English in Ireland had upon theirs. The crew of a ship from Bristol that blundered into Fitzmaurice's little fleet were captured and thrown over the side. The force's landfall in Dingle Bay was followed by the erection of the papal banner, prayers of thanksgiving for safe arrival, and the looting and destruction by fire of Dingle town. Sail was then set for Smerwick harbour, at the western end of the Dingle peninsula, where a base defended by earthwork fortifications was established. The Smerwick fort was destined to be the site of one of the most controversial atrocities in a campaign that was replete with them.

Reactions to the arrival on the Kerry coast of this body of international liberators were mixed and labyrinthine. The Earl of Desmond, whose support had been assumed, was disinclined to give it, at least until he had clear indications of who was to win what seemed likely to be a prolonged contest. Desmond was getting no younger. After the hardships and deprivations of his earlier exile he had finally achieved what he had always set his heart on achieving, the undisturbed exercise of personal power, in the manner of his ancestors, in his vast hereditary territory. He had a natural dislike for the English, but for the past few years they had left him to his own devices. He had a personal dislike for his cousin Fitzmaurice, who had now upset an acceptable equilibrium. Desmond temporized. He maintained contact with Fitzmaurice and at the same time passed to English officials information and assurances of his loyalty to the crown. Inevitably he was soon mistrusted by both sides. He did not call out his followers in support of Fitzmaurice, but he took no action when some of them went to Fitzmaurice on their own initiative. Two of those whose initiative was unambiguous were Desmond's younger brothers, Sir John and Sir James of Desmond.

Although the English authorities in Ireland had had ample advance warning of the Fitzmaurice incursion from sources within the sophisticated Elizabethan intelligence service in Europe, they were unprepared for it when it materialized. The queen's notorious parsimony where Ireland was concerned, and her competing preoccupations elsewhere, had left the Dublin government with an insufficiency of troops. Urgent calls for help went to Whitehall, and in the meantime two emissaries of long Irish experience, Arthur Carter and Sir Henry Davells, were sent to Munster with instructions to investigate, negotiate, and generally procrastinate until Dublin Castle had at its disposal an army large enough to dispose of Fitzmaurice and, if necessary (as seemed probable), Desmond.

Carter and Davells duly hurried to Munster, met Desmond, and went with him to inspect from a safe distance the partially completed fortifications at Smerwick. In Davells' assessment they could be overrun by an early assault, in combination with an attack on those of Fitzmaurice's ships still present, to be led by another Devon seadog, Thomas Courtenay, who was lying offshore with an improvised flotilla of English ships. Davells reminded Desmond both of his duty and of his recent protestations of loyalty. Desmond was evasive and unco-operative. After much inconclusive discussion and a few indeterminate exchanges of shots with the Smerwick garrison, they dispersed to their separate destinations. Desmond returned to his stronghold at Askeaton; Davells and Carter, still playing for time, retired to a lodging house in Tralee.

Davells was unusual in the Irish wars of the times in that both English and Irish respected him for his integrity, humanity and generosity. He had in the past urged sense upon the bull-headed Carew, and had repeatedly acted almost as a father to Sir John of Desmond, upon whom he had bestowed great affection and wise advice. John and his brother James now led a party of their followers to the lodging house in Tralee, by night. Davells and Carter were in bed. John ran Davells through with a sword. James cut Carter's throat. The bodies were posthumously beheaded.

Desmond's insistence that he had no responsibility for this squalid barbarity carried little conviction among the English administrators. Waterhouse, the Chief Secretary in Dublin Castle, told Whitehall that Desmond's conduct was dishonourable, that 'this rebellion is the most perilous that ever was begun in Ireland', and that the despatch of the English troops already asked for was a matter of greater urgency than ever. The Second Desmond War, as convoluted and as destructive as the first, had progressed beyond its preliminary manoeuvrings.

Remarkably, the Earl of Desmond was successful for some time in preserving a nominal detachment from the tragedy that rapidly developed around him. His followers aligned themselves with Fitzmaurice by the hundred. His brothers Sir James and Sir John had already demonstrated convincingly where their sympathies lay. Desmond continued to preserve the fiction, or possibly the hope, that he could stand aside from the turmoil, neither influencing it nor being influenced by it.

While soldiers slowly gathered in England, and Dublin Castle relied increasingly upon the loyalty of the Ormonde Butlers and the Kildare Fitzgeralds, dissension, unconnected with policy or the definition of objectives, broke out in the Fitzmaurice camp. The contentious issue was discipline. One of Sir John of Desmond's men raped and murdered a camp-following woman. Fitzmaurice ordered the hanging of the offender. John was dismissive of this high-handed response to what he clearly regarded as a minor misdemeanour, and defended his man. Fitzmaurice, enraged, rode out of John's camp with a small party, probably intending to join Sanders.

Near Castleconnell, Fitzmaurice's horses showed signs of exhaustion. He forcibly confiscated a plough horse belonging to a peasant. The peasant angrily reported the theft to his lord, who as it happened was Theobald Burke, a robust defender of his own, a Protestant with no love for Fitzmaurice's cause, and a firm supporter of the English connection. Burke mustered a group of retainers, saddled up, and rode out to settle accounts with the recusant horse-thief who had trespassed upon his land.

An irritable parley at a small stream, with Fitzmaurice straddling his horse in the middle of it and Theobald Burke insulting him from the bank, led to the discharge of a musket by one of Burke's following. Fitzmaurice was hit, and rushed his horse at Burke. Fitzmaurice killed Burke, and then fell from his horse. There was a fracas which ended in the flight of the Burke faction. Victory was followed almost immediately by the death of Fitzmaurice. The shot from the musketeer had been fatal.

It was an inconsequential affray of a type that, like the Butler cattle raid that set off the First Desmond War, was almost commonplace in contemporary Ireland. Its distinguishing mark was the pure chance that Fitzmaurice had chosen to take the horse of a spirited ploughman who gave allegiance to one of the few Protestant

37

English supporters still extant in Munster, and a notably touchy one at that. Fitzmaurice's dying instructions offer a grim commentary upon the savagery with which the struggle was conducted. His body, he ordered, was to be dismembered. The head was to be buried separately from the trunk, both in unmarked places. Otherwise, he feared, the English would disinter his remains and put them on triumphal public display. His wishes were obeyed, but ineffectually. A few days later his body was strung up in the market place in Limerick. It was put to sporadic use as a target for crossbow training.

The death of Fitzmaurice changed little. Sir John of Desmond inherited his command. The English slowly collected more troops. They were led by Nicholas Maltby, a ruthless and energetic commander whose tactics included the murder and torture of as many non-combatants as he could find, in a calculated move to force Sir John to come into the open to protect civilians or risk losing popular support. Maltby devastated large tracts of country. There were major engagements at Springfield and Monasternenagh, the first an overwhelming Irish victory followed by the customary massacre of wounded prisoners, the second a hard-fought near-draw, technically an English win in that they remained in possession of the field and were thus able to take their turn at massacring Irish wounded. A rare product of the whole sordid conflict resulted from Monasternenagh, an expression of professional admiration from a soldier on one side for those of the other: 'These rebels came as resolutely to fight as the best soldiers in Europe could,' wrote Sir William Stanley, after experiencing the wild courage of a Gallow-glass assault.

Chivalrous appreciation of martial accomplishment was un-matched by mercy for enemies, assumed enemies and innocents luckless enough to be in the wrong place at the wrong time. Mass murder, rape, pillage and desecration continued to be the standard behaviour of both sides. The Earl of Desmond's delicately poised aloofness became increasingly precarious when Maltby, convinced that Desmond's regular protestations of loyalty simply shielded the machinations of an arch-conspirator, set out to provoke him into unambiguous rebellion.

38

The provocation was gross, the response plaintive but non-violent. Maltby's soldiers advanced upon Desmond's castle of Askeaton, killing and burning as they went. They peppered the walls with musket shot, plundered Askeaton Friary, where Desmonds had traditionally been buried, broke into the tombs, and distributed what was left of the corpses of bygone Fitzgerald noblemen and noblewomen along the river bank in view of the castle walls. One of the bodies dishonoured was that of Desmond's wife Joan, recently dead. She was also Ormonde's mother.

Desmond's reaction of disgusted rage still did not go beyond the literary. He wrote bitterly to Ormonde and to Sir Henry Sidney, complaining of Maltby's malicious barbarism and rehearsing his own recent demonstrations of loyalty – they included handing over Bishop O'Healey and two others for torture and death.

Ormonde's distress at the insult to his mother did not dent his allegiance. He remained an uncompromising queen's man. He was used as part of the mechanism for applying pressure to Desmond. Ormonde and Desmond met, to discuss an ultimatum. Unless Desmond surrendered his two chief strongholds of Askeaton and Carrigafoyle, captured and handed over his brothers James and John of Desmond, and added Father Sanders to the delivery, Desmond would be charged with high treason. Desmond offered Sanders, but rejected the first two conditions. It was made clear to him that it was all or nothing. The terms were not negotiable.

A last government message, instructing Desmond to present himself to the Lord Justice and the Council, and offering him exile in England, resolved the issue. On 3 November 1579, Desmond, old, weak, disillusioned and manoeuvred into reluctant rebellion, rebelled. He had to be helped into his saddle. He rode towards the mountains of Kerry.

Despite his frailty Desmond was a very effective rebel. His name and prestige were sufficient to rally those not altogether convinced of either the rectitude or wisdom of aligning themselves with Fitzmaurice and his successor, the bloodthirsty Sir John of Desmond. A new legitimacy and an enhanced hope of success were now attached to the enterprise. In Munster the last waverers, the O'Sullivans and MacCarthys, took to arms, and supported Sir John in the terrorization of English-held towns and of the few survivors of the Plantation. There was more burning and more killing. The Earl himself led the assault on the town of Youghal, built and endowed by his own family, and supervised its plunder, the slaughter of its menfolk and the firing of its buildings. The stone walls were razed, the women were distributed by lot for the amusement of the attackers, and the force moved on, laden with loot, to join Sir John in the south-west.

Far to the east, in Wicklow, the Kavanaghs rose up and set about the English towns in the plain through which ran the main line of communications between Dublin and Waterford. In Dublin reports came in of the destruction of Tralee and Kinsale, of disaffection that seemed to be touching even some of the previously reliable Catholic lords of the Pale, and of reverses such as the overrunning of the major English base at Limerick and the transformation of its garrison to besieged uselessness in the citadel. There were alarm, recrimination and an added shrillness in the recurrent calls to Whitehall for more help.

Slowly, the reinforcements from England were assembled and despatched. Urgency was added to their commitment by reports that the Spanish were about to take the field in Munster, reports that were premature but believed by both sides. Atrociousness reached new depths after Pelham, the Lord Justice, was authorized by the queen to grant pardons to any rebels who surrendered, except the Desmond leaders and Father Sanders. The measure had more to do with economy than with mercy. Its arithmetic was based on the calculation that it was cheaper to entice rebels into submission than to hunt them down in endless military chases. But Pelham devised a refinement of his own to the concession. Under 'Pelham's Pardon', surrenders were accepted only when the surrenderer could offer evidence – a cut-off head was the most usual – that before submission he had killed a rebel of more importance than himself. There were many who complied. Often the heads produced were those of men of little rebel significance, sometimes of men with no connection with the fighting at all.

In the Pale, Lord Baltinglass, a Catholic zealot who had been to Rome, came out in support of Desmond. Unlike his fellow Pale Lords, he found it conscientiously impossible to continue to reconcile his Catholicism with allegiance to a Protestant queen.

40

Baltinglass got little backing from the Catholic population of the Pale, and none at all from the other Pale lords, but he found it in plenty among the O'Byrnes and O'Tooles of the Wicklow mountains to the south of Dublin. Their destructive forays inspired a punitive expedition led by Pelham's successor, Grey. It was a ponderous progress, hampered by Grey's failure to realize that heavy body armour and chain mail, advisable for fighting on the plains of Europe, were a conspicuous handicap against fast-moving mountain men defending a hilly wilderness with which they had been familiar all their lives. Grey's soldiers blundered on, losing men steadily as they went, until they were finally and decisively defeated in the wild, rocky valley of Glenmalure. The survivors, including Grey, made a forlorn and disorderly retirement to Dublin Castle. Their abandoned wounded were butchered by Gallowglasses.

Grey profited from the disaster of Glenmalure. He was an adaptable commander, and he adopted new methods, as determinedly ruthless as those of Pelham. When Grey, with a re-formed army, went to Munster he never lost a battle. Desmond by then had withdrawn to West Kerry. A force of 'Spaniards', mostly Basques and Italians sent by the Papacy and commanded by Spanish officers, had at last arrived in Dingle. In the absence of co-ordination, or even effective liaison, with Desmond, it had made its way to the earthwork fort at Smerwick, built by the international levies who had landed with Fitzmaurice two years previously.

In early November English ships under Admiral Winter blockaded the peninsula. Grey's troops reached Smerwick on the following day, exhausted by hard marching, and held in control by disciplinary measures as ferocious as Grey's reprisals upon his Irish enemies. Guns from the fleet were put ashore and manhandled into position in front of the fort. The garrison was pounded by cannonfire. Its casualties grew in number. An agreed signal, that should have brought an attack by Desmond on the English rear, brought no response at all. The bombardment increased in intensity and effectiveness. The Spanish commander sued for terms. Negotiations continued intermittently for several days, with Grey adamant that there could be no conditions attached to surrender. The Spanish could lay down their arms or face progressive annihilation by gunfire and, since the fort had no proper water supply, by thirst.

The garrison surrendered with no guarantees of what would happen to them. What happened to them was that they were disarmed, stripped of their armour, marched back into the fort, and hacked to death by specially detailed parties of English soldiers, commanded by Captain Mackworth and Captain Walter Raleigh. Even by some of those coarsened into insensitivity by the abysmal practices of warfare as pursued in Ireland, Smerwick was regarded as an exceptional abomination. Raleigh is said to have made no mention of it for the rest of his life. Grey remained, at least outwardly, unrepentant. His action was backed by the English government. Grey's secretary, Edmund Spenser, later to write *The Faerie Queene*, to become the most distinguished English poet of his generation, and to be himself ruined by his association with Ireland, looked upon Grey's action as a strong-minded example of necessary severity. The massacre would dishearten rebels hopeful of European support. 'There was no other way but to make that short end of them which was made.'

The dreary, horrible attrition went on inexorably. There were fresh changes of allegiance, further reprisals and counter-reprisals, isolated instances of exceptional gallantry (Raleigh was prominent in one of these), and far from isolated reciprocal brutalities. Munster was despoiled and huge areas of it depopulated. The ghastliness of this form of warfare was supplemented by famine and plague. Father Sanders died of dysentery. Desmond's fortunes oscillated, sometimes buttressed by new support, sometimes falling through defections and defeats, always influenced by the unfulfilled hope of further, and next time decisive, European help.

The end was inevitable. English bravery, endurance and callousness were matched by the Irish. Irish numerical resources were greater, and Irish knowledge of the ground that was being fought over more intimate and experienced. English planning, organization, equipment, cohesion and adaptability were superior. Support for Desmond withered until he became a refugee on the run, hiding in remote woods and valleys, sustained by a handful of devoted helpers, their loyalty unimpaired by the prize money on offer for his head.

A combination of the lure of the reward money and a resentful thirst for personal vengeance brought about the finish. A Desmond foraging party, operating near Tralee Bay, broke into the house of a farmer named Moriarty. They helped themselves to all the food and clothing in the house, including the clothes worn by Moriarty's wife, and to several head of cattle. Moriarty, outraged on his return to find his house stripped and his wife naked and in distress, doubtless not uninfluenced by the thought that revenge could be complemented by profit, collected a small party and mounted a pursuit into the Slieve Mish mountains. It was a long, slow chase in November mist and rain, lasting for several weeks. A cabin in a glen was surrounded by night and assaulted at dawn. Desmond was inside. The attackers first broke his arm. Then they dragged him outside, decapitated him, and took the head to the English in Castlemaine. The reward paid was one thousand pounds.

It is a truism that misleading interpretations of bygone events tend to be made when later prejudices and convictions are attributed to past generations who did not share them. Gerald Fitzgerald, the fourteenth Earl of Desmond, was not, as later hagiographers were to claim, an Irish patriot who died fighting in an attempt to resist the foreign domination of his country. The concept would have been unrecognizable to him. He was a feudal Norman-Irish absolutist, for practical purposes an independent monarch, with a traditional acceptance of the legal and constitutional realities of his time and of their rightness and convenience. To him and his kind, there was no inconsistency between accepting the nominal authority of the English crown and exercising the authority of a Norman-Irish chieftain with Gaelic-Irish followers.

His tragedy, and the larger one that it imposed upon almost the entire population of Munster, was that both he and the society he led were rapidly becoming anachronisms in a larger European world that was moving in new directions while Gaelic Ireland stood still. There was much that was attractive about Gaelic Ireland. If there had not been, it would not have lasted almost unchanged for over two thousand years. But it was no longer possible for Gaelic Ireland to continue in isolation; and once it became unwittingly involved in the interaction between competing powers with new international ambitions and interests, with previously unheard-of politico-religious rivalries and with a dynamism and innovative flair that had passed Gaelic Ireland by, the attempt to maintain old institutions and old customs was doomed.

While other small countries – Portugal, Holland, England – were exploring the Americas and the Indies, discovering new commodities, establishing new trade patterns and generating new national wealth, Gaelic Ireland continued to raise, graze and raid cattle, to fight local fights, to celebrate old glories in poetry and song. Scientific curiosity, great art and architecture, stimulated no Irish Galileos, Michelangelos or Leonardo Da Vincis. None of this would have mattered in terms of social survival if there had been a realization that altered external circumstances were bound to impinge upon Ireland, and that some form of compromise with the new forces was essential to preserve at least something of the old order. There was no realization because no individual or institution was capable of it. Gaelic Ireland remained faithful to its inheritance of parochial myopia and racial disunity.

Desmond's death marked the close of a provincial civil war which had devastated Munster. His opponents had included his fellow Norman-Irish magnate Ormonde; Hugh O'Neill, Lord of Tyrone and the Gaelic-Irish chieftain of Ulster, the only truly Gaelic part of Ireland still remaining; and the Mayor of Cork, Sir Cormac Teig MacCarthy, a Gael of unbending loyalty to the crown. All of them allied themselves to the English. In the prevailing political and legal climate Desmond's death could have only one central consequence. The lands that had been Geraldine for four hundred years were once again forfeit. Their distribution, to (as the English saw it) trustworthy Irish, to surviving or inheriting proprietors of the First Munster Plantation, to developers and to new beneficiaries as reward for their services in the wars, was intended to ensure an extended peace. Much more systematic planning and preparation attended these new acquisitions than those of the likes of Sir Peter Carew a few years earlier.

CHAPTER THREE

There was prolonged legal examination of old titles, some going back for centuries, some of straightforward authenticity, some the ambivalent products of past Geraldine intimidation or fraud. The constitutional process of formal attainder of the dead Earl of Desmond, and the reversion to the crown of the largest expanse of land in Ireland held by one man, took the best part of three years. In the meantime surveyors surveyed, provisional allocations were made and lawyers argued expensively. Among the governments in London and Dublin, and the experienced commanders of the recent wars, there was little disagreement about what the purpose of the new settlement should be, or what overall shape it should take. It was to be a colony of Englishmen, organized in the manner of domestic English shires, with English gentlemen farming, developing and controlling their allotted estates, supported by labourers, craftsmen and specialists drawn from English immigrants. The commercial and defensive aims were seen as interlocking. This new society would, for the first time, bring efficient agriculture to some of the potentially most fertile ground in the queen's domains. It would be strong enough to keep what remained of the disaffected native Irish in their place. And, if the increasing flow of intelligence from Spain about Spanish plans to prepare a great Armada for the invasion of England were ever to achieve substance, the Munster settlement would ensure that at least one of the back gates to England could not be breached without a lively resistance.

The biggest shares went to the commanders, and to some of the senior officials in Dublin Castle, who had borne the burden of the warfare in both campaigns. There were 800,000 acres to be parcelled out. Names that were to be prominent in the Anglo-Ireland of succeeding centuries appeared for the first time on Irish land rolls. Sir William Herbert and Sir Edward Denny acquired great tracts of County Kerry. Sir Warham St Leger, in whose London house Desmond had been confined on parole before the First Desmond War, became the owner of his former house guest's property in a large part of County Cork. Beyond his distant boundaries his neighbours were the poet, Edmund Spenser, Grey's old secretary, and the tough old warriors Sir Thomas Norris and Hugh Cuffe. The Butler Earl of Ormonde, the Protestant head of a still largely Catholic family, got County Tipperary in its entirety, and thereby became one of the few links between the new planters and the Norman-Irish pre-Tudor society. Sir George Bourchier, Sir William Courtney, and Francis Barkley took most of County Limerick between them. Walter Raleigh, now in high favour with the queen, profited from her patronage to the extent of 42,000 acres along the River Blackwater, including Lismore Castle and the town of Youghal, wrecked a few years previously by Desmond. A knight-hood accompanied this munificence. An adjacent 12,000 acres went to another current royal favourite, Sir Christopher Hatton. He had never set foot in Ireland.

Even after these lions had taken their shares three-quarters of the sequestrated land remained to be disposed of – 600,000 acres in all. In London the Privy Council advertised the merits of colonization to gentlemen of the shires, emphasizing the opportunities open to younger sons and kinsmen of good families, urging them to repeople such parts of Munster as were now in the queen's possession, and to take with them to share the projected prosperity 'those of inferior calling and degree'. Some of the propaganda, notably a sheet that described 'the better sort of Irish' as very civil, hospitable, and honestly given, and to be forming themselves 'daily more and more after English manners', must have provoked a cynical laugh from veterans of the wars who recalled such examples of civility and hospitality as Sir John of Desmond's nailing a settler of the First Plantation to his own door. But few who read, or had read to them, this early piece of public relations had access to an old soldier who

46

might detect flaws in the prospectus.

Even so, the response was less enthusiastic than had been officially hoped for. Some adventurous younger sons came forward, but more preferred the known excitements of continental soldiering to the unforeseeable hazards of taking up land in a country with a deplorable reputation for ruining careers and shortening lives. A sizeable number of carpenters, masons, brewers and wheelwrights offered themselves, but again in insufficient numbers to fulfil the basic objective of the colony: the establishment of a self-sustaining English community, part garrison, part agricultural, in a confiscated territory that was a permanent strategic risk. Governmental insistence that 'the heads of every family shall be born of English parents, and the heirs female, inheritable to any of the same lands, shall marry with none but with persons born of English parents...' was to prove an aspiration rather than an enforceable proscription. There were never enough people, English born or born of English people, to go round.

Of the land that was taken up, some went to speculative investors who had no intention of submitting themselves to the possibility of physical danger in developing it. These either resold profitably to more stalwart characters willing to take a chance, or continued to live as absentee landlords in England and delegated their responsibilities to paid agents, thus setting a precedent that led to unhappy results in later centuries.

There was also a class of what in post-Civil War America, in circumstances similar to the post-Desmond War Ireland, would become known as carpet-baggers. The most enterprising of these, Richard Boyle, arrived in Dublin in 1588 with twenty-seven pounds, three shillings, a rapier, a dagger and one rather stylish set of clothes. He was a law student with an Oxford degree and a keenly developed mercantile instinct, possibly the first genuine businessman to reach Ireland. His limited capital was a minor handicap to a man of his talents. He bought Sir Walter Raleigh's entire holdings at a minuscule fraction of their true value, founded industries, lent money, changed money, entered into contracts for army supplies, had brushes with the law, advised governments, generated prosperity and conducted, when he could get away with it, some neat excursions into embezzlement. He was ostentatiously pious, and became the Earl of Cork, the progenitor of one of the great Anglo-Irish dynasties.

A kinsman of Boyle's, Lawrence Parsons, hard-working, opportunist and helped along by the unblushing nepotism characteristic of the times, was the first Parsons of a long line who were to play influential parts at significant moments in later Irish history. The first Irish Parsons soon became the second mayor of Youghal, in succession to Sir Walter Raleigh, whose enquiring and ambitious mind was considering faraway horizons. A Parsons brother who was a Lord Justice applied his inside knowledge and legal dexterity to the promotion of Lawrence from municipal to landed eminence, expressed in the acquisition of lands in Offaly forfeited by the Ely O'Carrolls. Lawrence Parsons built Birr Castle. His descendant, the Earl of Rosse, lives there now, one of the relatively few representatives of Plantation families still in possession of property allocated to them after the Desmond Wars.

Soldiers, administrators, carpet-baggers, younger sons of the English landed gentry and adventurers combined together, co-operatively or acrimoniously, in the transformation of about a quarter of the land surface of Ireland. They had a self-confidence and a cohesion lacking in most of their predecessors of the First Munster Plantation. Their Elizabethan vigour and resourcefulness set the standards, and possibly indirectly provided the inspiration, of later settlements beyond the seas that gave birth to the modern nations of the United States, Canada, Australia and New Zealand.

The former, Irish, landholders had been indifferent tillagers, not much concerned about communications, and tolerant of primitive dwellings that were adequate for their unexacting needs. They were cattle graziers, content with lush natural pasturage, unencumbered by wheeled vehicles, untroubled by the sparseness of roads so long as they could shift their herds along tracks or through valleys. The devastation of the recent wars had caused some modifications to the landscape, notably the clearing of forest in an attempt to reduce tactical opportunities for ambush, but essentially it had stayed unchanged for centuries. The changes now wrought by the newcomers have retained their outlines up to the present day.

Bog was drained. More forest was felled. Fields were cleared of rocks, and the rocks used to build surrounding stone walls. Roads were surveyed and constructed. Streams and rivers were bridged. Furze was burnt, land ploughed, crops planted, orchards established. Stone castles, some the reconstructions of ancient Norman and Irish castles, some entirely new, were built for the gentry. Houses, initially of timber and clay, later supplemented or replaced by stone and slate, were built by the retainers.

Trade began limpingly, and soon flowered modestly. The timber felled in land clearance was a useful export that met a growing overseas demand for pipestaves, components of the barrels in universal use for the movement and storage of portable goods before anyone thought of cardboard boxes and plastic containers. Early success in this form of commerce was followed by a systematic exploitation of Irish timber resources that has left modern Ireland one of the most treeless countries in Europe. An extensive trade, part legitimate, part contraband, developed between the port of Cork and continental Europe. Agricultural produce went on to the markets within Munster, and surpluses were sold to other parts of Ireland.

Development was accompanied by experiment and innovation. Plants and animals not indigenous to Ireland were brought in from outside. Raleigh, back briefly from an early foray to Virginia, brought with him the first potatoes to be seen on the eastern side of the Atlantic. He introduced to Ireland an easily grown root that was to sustain millions of Irish people for generations, and the failure of which through blight was to lead to the famine years in the 1840s. Another of Raleigh's North American souvenirs which had a far-reaching effect on the nervous cosseting, selective prosperity, and shortened life-expectancy of generations of Europeans as yet unborn, was tobacco. It is claimed with a mixture of pride and deprecation to have been first smoked in Europe in Raleigh's house, Myrtle Grove, in Youghal.

The clear successes of the Second Munster Plantation during its first twenty years of existence were offset by some reverses, one major alarm, and by a nagging source of concern to the deeper thinkers among the settlement's leaders. The reverses were defections by colonists. Some found the strangeness, the loneliness, the hard work and the uncertainties to be too much of a price to pay for the prospect of a higher level of prosperity than they would ever have achieved at home. They straggled back to an England that, whatever its personal drawbacks for them, was at least familiar.

Their departure, and the inability of the recruiters in England to attract enough settlers to meet the original manpower specifications prescribed by the authorities, led inevitably to a dilution of the principles laid down to govern the conduct of the settlement. With a shortage of 'persons born of English parents', and a growing amount of work to be done, it became commonplace for the shortfall in labour to be made up from the native Irish, who were locally available in abundance, physically strong and seemingly reconciled to the turn that events had taken. From the employment of casual labour, and an appreciation of its worth, it was a brief step to the integration of whole extended families into manorial comm-unities. This cohabitation (in every sense of the word; many a modern patriotic Munster republican must be a direct descendant of an Elizabethan English interloper) may have been economically advisable, and in terms of inter-racial understanding beneficial, but defensively it was a risk.

The risk became more worrying to the government during the alarm of 1588. The great Spanish Armada, whose preparation had been reported upon and monitored for so long, at last sailed to conquer England. It was defeated and dispersed by an English fleet, many of whose captains were English West Country seadogs with interests in the Munster Plantation. Its surviving ships took the long route home around the north of Scotland, and the north and west coasts of Ireland. Westerly gales forced twenty-six of them – or twenty-eight, if a persistent but unwritten legend of two others is accurate – ashore at a succession of places from the Donegal coast to west Kerry. Few of the crews were lucky. In the north the O'Neills and O'Donnells succoured some, but even there many were murdered and plundered by local inhabitants out of reach of their chieftains. Black Hugh O'Donnell had to be dissuaded from trying to sacrifice thirty Spaniards to the English in exchange for his son, held as a hostage in Dublin Castle. Hugh O'Neill, Earl of Tyrone, was the dissuader, and his reported words were prophetic. 'We and our posterity,' said O'Neill, 'might one day have to seek refuge in another country, as these castaways have done, and it would be a fitting revenge of Fate for betraying these poor creatures in their only refuge.'

In Connacht there was no succour and no pity. Those sailors not drowned while trying to swim to the shore were massacred when they reached it. The slaughter was instigated, and largely supervised, by English officials. Sir Richard Bingham, the Lord President of

Connacht, wrote unemotionally of the tally of his brother George who executed by hanging and clubbing 'seven or eight hundred or upwards, first and last, one way and another'. Sir Geoffrey Fenton approvingly counted eleven hundred Spanish corpses, drowned or clubbed, on the strands of County Sligo. The O'Malleys, acting independently of crown instructions, despatched the entire crew of Don Pedro de Mendoza as they struggled wearily to land near Clare Island. In Kerry, Lady Denny, temporarily taking charge in the absence of her landowner husband, ordered the summary hanging of thirty Spanish sailors who had been washed up on the foreshore of the newly acquired family estate.

It was merciless, revolting, effective and in keeping with the practices of the time. English or any other hostile sailors caught in similar circumstances upon a Spanish shore would have been dealt with identically. So far as the fortunes of Anglo-Ireland were concerned, and specifically where the well-being of the Munster planters was concerned, the routing of the Armada removed for the time being a fear that had hung over them all since they first came to Ireland.

Meanwhile another threat, nearer at hand but discernible so far only to the better-informed or more perceptive, was steadily developing.

One of the surprising things about the aftermath of Tudor warfare in Ireland was the liberality with which pardons were dispensed by English rulers to people who had been in rebellion against the crown. Legally rebellion was treason, and treason was punishable by death, in the particularly grisly judicial form of hanging, drawing and quartering. The term rebellion itself was more than a legal techni- cality, dreamt up by a dominant minority to give sanction to its vengeance upon patriotic insurgents who did not acknowledge the crown's right to rule. It was a monarchical and aristocratic age, and few societies in it were more monarchical and aristocratic than the conservative Gaelic Irish. It was not until the late eighteenth century, when the influences of first the American and then the French Revolutions were felt in Ireland, that the notion of national republicanism as an alternative to hereditary kingship was first thought about. Equally, in Tudor times there seemed nothing strange in Irish eyes in the fact that the monarch was based outside the country. Nation states everywhere were in their infancies. Irish nationalism as such did not exist. The recurrent rebellions were not aimed at overthrowing an alien monarchy, but at replacing the monarch's agents in Ireland by others more amenable to local or, at their largest, regional interests, as defined by a particular aristocratic autocratic leader.

For generations to come, the instigators of Irish rebellions habitually pledged their loyalty to the crown, while vigorously setting about the dismantlement of the crown's current assets. And when, as invariably happened, the rebels lost, those leaders who were still alive and had not gone into exile, submitted, reaffirmed their loyalty and asked for pardon. More often than not it was granted, usually, but not invariably, with a penalty attached of the forfeiture of land. There were some cases held to be so reprehensible that a pardon was out of the question – Desmond and Father Sanders, for example, would not have qualified and would not have been naïve enough to think that they might – but the criteria applied were expedient rather than moralistic or legalistic. What are now known as war crimes were not an issue. The yardstick was a rough assessment of the 'reformed' offender's capacity for causing future trouble in foreseeable circumstances. And foresight in Ireland was not an exact science.

The consequence of pardoning rebels on a large scale was that the original concept of the Munster Plantation as a monolithic block of English manpower, practice and reliability was not achieved. Aside from the large numbers of native Irish among the labour forces of various components of the settlement, there were broad tracts of land still inhabited by Irish septs who had been pardoned and confirmed in their continued right to occupy. Norman-Irish holdings, many of undiminished size, were intermingled with the new English ones and several were still in the hands of lords who had been active on the side of Desmond.

John Fitzedmund Fitzgerald, for example, the Seneschal of Imokilly, a cousin of Desmond's who had been one of the first and most effective of Fitzmaurice's supporters, remained in possession of 36,000 acres. (He was arrested as a precaution during the Armada episode and died in captivity in Dublin Castle.) Maurice Roche, Lord Fermoy, had when young and rash been out with Sir John of

Desmond until his more cautious father called him back again, yet he remained the proprietor of a large enclave surrounded by the lands of Edmund Spenser and his fellow settlers Cuffe, Keate and Hyde. There were others in similar circumstances. They naturally resented the new arrivals. Their resentment took the practical form of a certain amount of *ad hoc* physical harassment of the settlers' employees, while sophisticates such as Fermoy exercised their rights as reinstated loyal subjects to contest at law the authenticity of some of the titles held by the planters. This last ploy carried considerable weight. Although the legality of the transfers of most of the confiscated land was indisputable, there had been some confusion, some high-handed opportunism and a substantial incidence of calculated trickery, not least when unscrupulous entrepreneurs like the future Lord Cork put their fingers into the pie.

Had the settlement been able to progress in isolation, most of these frictions would probably have abated in time, through the normal human processes of compromise, and the normal legal processes of adjudication. But the settlement did not progress in isolation. Twenty years after its foundation it became lethally involved in the turmoil instituted by Hugh O'Neill, the Earl of Tyrone, the powerful and gifted leader of the Gaelic Irish of Ulster.

It was by now nearly four hundred and fifty years since the original Norman landing on the Wexford coast had inaugurated the entanglement of English and Irish affairs. In three-quarters of Ireland the English imprint was unmistakeable. The Dublin Pale and the major coastal towns like Waterford, Cork, Limerick and Galway ('Neither O nor Mac shall strut nor swagger through the streets of Galway': a municipal ordinance, 1581), as well as the Butler inland city of Kilkenny, had for centuries been English-speaking, English-administered under English law, with populations of overwhelmingly English origin. In Munster and those parts of Leinster beyond the Pale the Plantation was taking root, and the Gaelic Irish and hibernicized Normans seemed to be on the way to accommodating themselves to the new order of things. To the west lay Connacht, the least fertile and most sparsely populated of the four Irish provinces. Once the fief of the degenerate Burkes, *nés* de Burgo, Connacht had been tamed into acceptance of English authority by the implacable ferocity of (among others) Sir Richard Bingham, the Lord President who had orchestrated the massacre of the Armada survivors.[1]

One part of the country, the northern province of Ulster, had remained almost untouched by the English presence. The designation Ulster is nowadays much misused to describe in shorthand parlance the six counties of Antrim, Down, Armagh, Derry, Fermanagh and Tyrone, which constitute the territory of Northern Ireland, still an integral part of the United Kingdom. Historic Ulster had three more counties, Donegal, Cavan and Monaghan, that are now in the Irish Republic.

Ulster's immunity from English interference had largely been the product of geography. Unlike Leinster, it was not the nearest, most obvious and most central place for anyone from England to go to, and to develop into the hinterland of an administrative complex. In contrast to Munster, Ulster was the province most remote from continental Europe and least likely to be the scene of hostile foreign incursions. Whereas Connacht abutted both Leinster and Munster and was separated from them only by the Shannon, Ulster, also abutting Leinster and part of Connacht, was shielded by a necklace of lakes and mountains which were difficult to penetrate.

The dominant families in Ulster were the O'Neills of Tyrone (Tir Owen, the land of John) and the O'Donnells of Tyrconnel (Tir Connel, the land of Connel; broadly the modern Donegal). In the convention hallowed for centuries, the O'Neills and O'Donnells did not get on with one another. Under an inherited Gaelic Irish institution, Tanistry,[2] the heir to the current chieftain was chosen from a small panel of young, male, close blood-relations. From this there flowed much temptation to circumvent the nominated succession by getting rid of the nominated successor. Both these factors came to bear forcibly on the upbringing and attitudes of Hugh O'Neill.

---

[1] His descendants include the Lord Lucan who commanded the cavalry division in the Crimean War and was partially responsible for the débâcle of the charge of the Light Brigade at Balaclava; and another Lord Lucan, wanted by the Metropolitan Police and the popular press in connection with a sensational London murder in the 1970s.
[2] Under the present constitution of the Irish Republic, the Deputy to the Prime Minister is the Tanaiste. His physical survival prospects are more durable than were those of his predecessors.

Hugh's grandfather, Con Bacach O'Neill, had been the first of his patrimony to comply with the surrender and regrant policy of King Henry VIII. Con had been notionally transmogrified from a Gaelic chieftain, The O'Neill, into an English-type nobleman, the first Earl of Tyrone. Con's acceptance of this new dignity in no way impeded his continued exercise of ancient customs. His wife bore him a son, Shane. One of his many mistresses, Alison O'Kelly, a blacksmith's daughter from Dundalk, bore him a son named Matthew. This versatility was not unusual at the time, and would doubtless have been treated with sympathy, had not Con's enthusiasm for Alison O'Kelly ripened into a lasting attachment. When Shane and Matthew reached maturity, Con disinherited his legitimate son Shane and announced his preference for Matthew as his heir.

There followed a dynastic feud of intense, murderous severity. Shane imprisoned his father and left him to die in captivity. Shane hanged his half-brother Matthew, captured Matthew's elder son, Brian, and cut his throat. Shane's search for Matthew's younger son, Hugh, the final candidate on the list for extinction, was interrupted by what for Ulster was an unusual event. Dublin Castle was disturbed by the escalating instability among the O'Neills. Shane was judged too powerful to overthrow, and his displacement by the English would have added unpredictably to the chaos, but it was decided that a show of English force might help to lessen the tension. Sir Henry Sidney led English soldiers into Ulster. Militarily it was a sterile expedition, as it was intended to be, but there was an unanticipated consequence. Sidney found the young Hugh O'Neill tending horses near Dungannon, and took him away with him.

Sidney was, by contemporary standards, a humane man but his humanity in rescuing Hugh from his vengeful uncle was well laced with political calculation. The continuing existence of an O'Neill Tanist in English hands would, it was hoped, inhibit Shane from undesirable action. The chance to educate an O'Neill heir in English surroundings would, when the succession became due, provide an Earl of Tyrone equipped with a sophisticated polish unknown among Gaelic chieftains, and with a unique understanding of English ways of thought.

Sidney brought the nine-year-old Hugh O'Neill to his family seat at Penshurst in Kent. It was a civilized, cultured household, frequented by the great and talented. The boy met travellers, poets

55

and scholars. The queen's advisers came and went; Walsingham and Leicester, whose concerns were widespread and national; Ormonde and Perrot, whose preoccupations were with Ireland. In seven years' exposure to the customs, personalities and modes of thinking in one of the gathering-places of English power, the boy did indeed absorb a great deal of information. He was later to use it in the most successful campaign ever fought against the English by Gaelic Ireland, an enterprise that failed by the thinnest of margins and in its failure completed the disintegration of the Gaelic order.

Shane O'Neill was murdered in his tent by the O'Donnells when his nephew Hugh was sixteen years of age. Hugh left the splendours and comforts of Penshurst and returned to Ulster, grateful to the Sidneys on two counts. There was a genuine, natural gratitude for the saving of his life and for the consideration and kindness with which he had been treated. There was a more subtle, unexpressed gratitude for the insight that he had been given into the minds of men against whom he would sooner or later have to take decisive action.

First there was another form of action to be taken. Hugh did not succeed at once to the Tyrone earldom. Turlough Luineach was the new earl, with Hugh still subordinate as Viscount Dungannon. Turlough Luineach's devotion to the bottle suggested that accelerated natural causes would render an attempt at his assassination unnecessary, but there were other candidates with whom Hugh dealt remorselessly. The killing of Shane's children became an obsessive preoccupation, efficiently conducted over a period that coincided with the Desmond Wars in Munster.

Hugh, by now raised to the earldom, stayed aloof from the Munster rebels and indeed played a small but active part in their suppression. His protestations of loyalty to the crown were renewed as conscientiously as Desmond's had been before he was bullied into revolt, but the difference was that O'Neill was an entirely new phenomenon in Ireland, a Gaelic chief of ancient lineage who had the manners and suavity of an English nobleman. He mixed amiably with English officials, was given the deference due to his rank, and stimulated some controversy, quietened only after personal adjudication by the queen, when he married Mabel Bagenal, the young daughter of Sir Henry

56

Bagenal.[3] An English soldier of note, Sir Henry viewed the union with fatherly disapproval and in this, as a father, he was undoubtedly right. As an Elizabethan senior official he had no hope of sustaining his objections. Advantages of State took precedence over the happiness of young women, and in any case the new Countess of Tyrone seemed besotted with her dashing, courtly spouse.

Tyrone attracted further favourable English comment (Sir H. Bagenal presumably reserving his opinion) by modernizing his castle at Dungannon to a standard almost approaching that of Penshurst. He imported English craftsmen, and when the building was completed he stocked it with continental furnishings, paintings and tapestries.

All this evidence of the benefits of nurturing the son of a wild Gaelic Irishman in a cultured English household began to inspire in some English minds the hope that Tyrone, although of indisputably Irish blood, had become for practical purposes an imitation Englishman. He seemed one of themselves, a man to be relied upon to reshape Ulster society on the English model, an ally with whom a mutually beneficial accommodation of lasting significance could be reached. What did not become clear for some years was that Tyrone's boyhood sojourn in England had taught him more than urbane good manners. Among the other lessons that he had absorbed was the value of dissembling. He also had a deep respect for English military organization and weaponry, with particular reference to how they could best be adapted to use by the Irish of Ulster.

It is impossible to judge from this distance what Tyrone's precise motives were in arming and training in secret the most effective fighting force ever produced by Gaelic Ireland. Retrospective assessments, mostly coloured by the political outlook of individual assessors, fall into three groupings. The first is that his knowledge and experience of the English, combined with his developed capacity for analytical thought, had convinced him that English victory in Munster would be followed in time by a concerted attack on Ulster. Unless this attack was pre-empted by a well-planned drive against the English by the only Gaelic Irish province still intact, Gaelic

[3] Bagenalstown in County Carlow, named after the family, now has an alternative official Irish name but is still known almost universally as Bagenalstown.

57

Ireland would be destroyed for ever.

The second assessment is that O'Neill's preparations were precautionary. The fear of a major English attempt on Ulster remains, but its counter is attributed to different motives. What O'Neill really wanted, according to this argument, was peace, not peace in the exact sense, but to be left free of outside interference while he ruled as his ancestors had always ruled. The only way to preserve this traditional freedom of action was to provide himself with armed backing of such strength and efficiency that the English would be deterred indefinitely from moving against Ulster.

The third belief, widely popular in English circles of the time, was that O'Neill was a blood-crazed fanatic of Machiavellian deviousness who, while making himself superficially agreeable to the English, and winning their affection and confidence, planned to exterminate the lot of them in the same conscienceless manner in which he had disposed of the progeny of his uncle, Shane.

Of the three theories, one or other of the first two seems the more likely. But since this book is about the Anglo-Irish, and since subsequent Anglo-Irish actions were governed by Anglo-Irish attitudes, the content of the third should not be discounted even if its accuracy is questionable.

Hugh O'Neill's preparations, whether precautionary or offensive, were elaborate and included a range of innovations that were to transform the shape of warfare in Ireland. He smuggled in large quantities of muskets from Spain to supplement the traditional battle-axes and short swords. Before O'Neill, Irish fighting strengths had been recruited exclusively from one warrior class, the free. O'Neill extended the trawl to include the unfree, and thereby involved the entire Ulster population of military age in his force. Irish tactics had previously been notably unsubtle. Success had depended upon wild charges of fierce bravery. O'Neill, impressed by the steadiness and discipline shown by trained English pikemen, introduced an imitative uniformity among his own. In the past, Irish training, in so far as it had existed at all, had been rudimentary. The O'Neill training was detailed, comprehensive and prolonged.

Although these arrangements for setting up what amounted to a provincial army were conducted with rigorously enforced secrecy, and secrecy in an Ulster masked from the rest of Ireland by a barrier of hill and lake was easier to achieve than almost anywhere else in western Europe, it was inevitable that some word of the undertaking should spread. Hugh's way with suspected traitors and paid informers was as ruthless as it had been with his detested cousins, but suspicions fuelled by vague and unsubstantiated reports began to grow among English officialdom.

Hugh refused to be moved to premature action. He continued to associate easily with old friends in the English garrison in Newry, and with officials in Dublin Castle. He seemed to be in real danger of exposure when he was summoned to London to explain why he had ordered the killing of his cousin Hugh Gaveloch, one of the longer-lasting of Shane's sons. Hugh Gaveloch was under government protection, and an informer who had reported to Dublin O'Neill's dealings with the Spanish. O'Neill put up a defence of such masterly eloquence before the Privy Council that the investigation was abandoned. It ended cosily with O'Neill deploring the primitive condition of justice in Ulster and suggesting the early introduction of an English magistracy. The Council and he joined together in expressing their wishes for a quick resolution to all disturbances in Ireland, and O'Neill returned to Ulster, with a mild formal warning against his name but otherwise unharmed.

The suspicions continued. Hard evidence to sustain them remained absent. O'Neill's involvement in one of the more romantic excitements of Irish history, the escape of Hugh Roe O'Donnell from Dublin Castle, was regarded by some English officials as self-evident, but here again the bland dissembler had his tracks well covered.

In 1590, when Hugh Roe was fifteen years of age, he was kidnapped from a boat on Lough Swilly at the instigation of Sir John Perrot, then the Deputy. Perrot, the reputed bastard son of King Henry VIII, was a large, robust man whose ferocity with rebels was equalled by the persistence with which he stamped upon the more blatant peculations in the land transactions of the Munster settlers. He was in some respects the pioneer of an enduringly eccentric element in the long line of British colonial administrators. He believed that the natives should be brought to order, but once he had got them there he treated them fairly and recognized that there was much in their culture and customs that was admirable, and some that was worth imitating in the interests of what he saw as the common good.

Perrot had once caused serious disquiet in Dublin Castle and Whitehall by attempting to nip in the bud the Second Desmond War through personal combat. He sent a challenge to Fitzmaurice to fight it out with him, man to man, winner take all, a method of conducting public business which had considerable appeal to Gaelic Ireland and none at all to official Tudor England. Perrot turned out, mounted, armoured and armed at the designated jousting site. Fitzmaurice did not appear.

The kidnapping of the boy O'Donnell was a variant of the same approach to Irish problems. The Irish traditionally took or were offered hostages as sureties for acceptable behaviour. If, went the Perrot logic, the Irish did it why should the English not do it too? It was a train of thought that omitted a few niceties such as the sanctity of English law that Perrot was supposed to be upholding, but at least it worked in the short term. Black Hugh O'Donnell, the boy's father, stayed quiescent throughout his son's captivity. It was Black Hugh who had had to be restrained by O'Neill from bartering the lives of thirty Spanish survivors of the Armada against Hugh Roe's release.

The escape was a well-planned affair, and was followed by a superb example of endurance. Hugh Roe, and two boys who had been captured with him, Henry and Art O'Neill, were lodged in the Bermingham Tower of Dublin Castle. Through bribery or coercion, Hugh O'Neill contrived to arrange for the outlet to the privy to be left open on a January night. The outlet drained into the moat. The boys made their way down the drain, and were met by a small reception party of O'Hagans, foster-brothers of Hugh O'Neill. It was bitterly cold and snowing hard. Guided and escorted by the O'Hagans the three boys, who had been cooped up in a cell for three years on an indifferent diet and with little exercise, set out for the Dublin mountains to the west of the city. Once on the high ground they turned south and marched through an intense blizzard along ridge tracks towards the sanctuary offered by the O'Byrnes of County Wicklow. It was a journey of forty miles, over wild mountainous country and in appalling weather conditions. When they reached Glenmalure, where Grey's troops had been beaten ignominiously years earlier, the O'Neill boys collapsed from cold and exhaustion. Art O'Neill had frozen to death by the time he could be carried to the warmth of a friendly O'Byrne house. Henry O'Neill died later. Hugh Roe, aged eighteen, the only survivor, was spirited home to Donegal. Hugh O'Neill had a new ally, of proven determination and toughness, bound to him by gratitude.

Trafficking, bargaining, posturing, manoeuvring and plotting were incessant over the next few years. The English authorities in Ireland, beset by acute shortages of money and men, were left to make what they could of a deteriorating position by a queen with other matters on her mind. They did what they could to assemble intelligence and to counter increasingly threatening O'Neill initiatives by bluff and guile.

Hugh Roe O'Donnell duly inherited his father's mantle as Earl of Tyrconnel, and showed himself to be a perfect partner in the O'Neill machinations. O'Neill did the devious planning and intensified his preparations. O'Donnell provided enough cases of *force majeure* to establish his credentials as a danger to be taken seriously. He cheerfully accepted public responsibility for other armed ventures instigated by O'Neill, and left it to O'Neill to explain them away to Dublin Castle, which he did persuasively. The success of his persuasion depended to some extent upon the skill of his advocacy, but more of it was due to the resigned realism of his hearers. The Ulster coalition was becoming so powerful that there was clearly no chance of overthrowing it without a huge influx of additional military support from England. Of that there was no hope. The only practical policy was to try to contain it.

Hugh O'Neill at last demonstrated the fighting capacity of his clandestinely trained army in early 1595. The depredations of Hugh Roe O'Donnell had recently included raids on the string of English-garrisoned advance posts along the Ulster border. It was an undeclared form of warfare, and it met with an undeclared response, both sides preserving the fiction that not much out of the ordinary was in progress. Hugh Roe now surrounded the English fort in Monaghan. The English commander in Newry was Sir Henry Bagenal, whose fatherly forebodings about the unsuitability of Hugh O'Neill as a husband for his daughter Mabel had long since been vindicated. Mabel had died, in isolation and misery, unable to adjust to the rough and ready style of a man she had known as a model of the courtly virtues, but who on his own ground reverted to the habits of a tribal chieftain.

The loss of his daughter may or may not have added an edge to Bagenal's distaste for the Ulster Irish, but any commander in his position would have done what he did next. He fought his way to Monaghan with a column bringing supplies for the besieged garrison. The delivery was successful. On its way back to Newry, Bagenal's force ran into an ambush. Controlling the ambushers was Hugh O'Neill.

The engagement was at Clontibret. Bagenal himself and part of his command survived, but a complete English company was lost. There had been larger English reverses in recent Irish wars, but the significance of Clontibret went far beyond a local tactical defeat. O'Neill had at last made an unambiguous declaration of intent. This in itself was disturbing to the English, even if it amounted to not much more than confirmation of what had long since shifted from suspicion to assumption. What was really alarming was the skilful, confident manipulation by O'Neill of a body of the best-armed, best-disciplined Irish troops ever seen in Ireland. They made good use of the cover provided by ditches and forest, as Irish fighting men always had, but they also took on and beat the English in the open, where English organization and steadiness had generally prevailed in the past. The sight of Irish musketeers, mustered in formed ranks and firing controlled volleys, was disconcerting in itself and made more so by the fact that they were dressed 'in red coats like English soldiers'. The red coats and the drilled performance were products of another piece of O'Neill dexterity. He had sought and been granted six experienced English captains to train six one-hundred-strong companies for use against the queen's enemies in Ulster. It now appeared that the 'butter captains', so named because of the prevalence of butter in the Irish diet, had been tricked. A series of planned switches and substitutions had provided training for many more recruits than the six hundred initially covenanted for.

It was indicative of English weakness in the face of a danger that had been foreseen in principle but not in its unprecedented scope, that for three years after Clontibret they were incapable of either avenging their defeat or of restraining O'Neill. He went on to capture the fort at Monaghan. Hugh Roe mounted a raid into Connacht, and departed only after the English-ordained destruction of their own crops left nothing for anyone to eat. There were humiliating negotiations, followed by a truce. The wording of its terms included at O'Neill's insistence references to war and peace instead of the hallowed rebellion and pardon, a departure that enraged the queen. But the royal rage was unmatched by the supply of resources necessary to assuage it. *Ad hoc* compromise continued to be the only workable English policy.

During the three years prior to 1598, O'Neill offset cosmetic discussion with Dublin Castle by a warm correspondence with King Philip of Spain and sporadic acts of violence against English outposts on the Ulster border. In July 1598, the English at last responded in strength to the surrounding of one of their forts on the River Blackwater, which drains into the south-west corner of Lough Neagh. Sir Henry Bagenal, the son of O'Neill's angry father-in-law who had been beaten at Clontibret, set out from Armagh with four thousand foot, three hundred horse and four guns in support. O'Neill was waiting for them at a narrow ford on the River Callan. He had prepared his dispositions with care. The English advanced towards the ford, known as the Yellow Ford, in a long column split into six regiments. Bagenal was with the second. It was a slow progress, encumbered by the slow-moving wagons loaded with stores for the fort, and by the guns.

The two leading regiments were well into O'Neill's trap when a murderous fire was opened upon them by musketeers posted in trenches behind protecting high hedges. The survivors fought clear, but soon met more difficulties from musket men dug in ahead of them. The rear regiments tried to close up, and were in turn exposed to close-range accurate shooting, while their wagons and guns fell into concealed pits prepared for them on the road. Gaps developed between the regiments and were exploited by Irish skirmishers. Tangled fighting for most of the afternoon, co-ordinated on the Irish side by O'Neill, left to the individual initiatives of isolated commanders by the English, reached its climax with a well-timed assault by Irish pikemen. The explosion of two ammunition carts added further casualties and palls of smoke to the carnage. Bagenal was already dead. So were most of his officers and large numbers of his men. Wingfield, commanding the fifth regiment, was surrounded. Beating back repeated attacks, and unable to get any word of what was happening ahead of him, he decided that his only possible

63

course was to try to extricate those of the column still alive and fight his way back to Armagh. His retreat was harried all the way by the cavalry of Hugh Roe O'Donnell, specially placed for the purpose by O'Neill. The English cavalry provided a reasonably effective screen, and was the only English body to come with much credit through the most calamitous day in the history of English arms in Ireland.

In Armagh, Wingfield led his remnants to St Patrick's Cathedral. They barricaded themselves inside and were invested, but for the time being unharmed by the pursuing Irish. On the field of battle itself the butchery of wounded English prisoners was still in progress. There were some exemptions to the ritual: a number of Bagenal's captured soldiers were allowed to change sides.

The arithmetic of the battle casualties was as imprecise as was customary at the time. Estimates put the English losses from a force of about 4,400 at 2,000 dead, and 1,000 wounded. The four guns and all the supplies from the baggage train went to O'Neill, along with an enormous haul of captured weapons and equipment. But the extent of the Irish triumph transcended statistics. The moral effect was incalculable. O'Neill had demonstrated that an Irish army, properly trained and led, was capable of bringing to total detruction a well-armed and disciplined English force commanded by experienced leaders. It had never happened before during the four-hundred-year history of Anglo-Irish warfare.

Communications, by horsed courier within Ireland and by ships dependent upon inconstant winds overseas, were slow and un-reliable. The news of O'Neill's victory at the Yellow Ford reached different destinations at different times and provoked different reactions. There was jubilation in Spain and in the Vatican. King Philip described O'Neill as the Prince of Ireland. The Pope went one step further and ordered the manufacture of a gold crown to be used at O'Neill's coronation as King of Ireland. In London there was deep gloom at the defeat, exasperation at the expense that would have to be incurred to re-establish dominance, and a determination to re-establish it. The queen at last abandoned parsimony and authorized the raising of an English force of 25,000 men, the largest English army ever committed to Ireland. Its assembly, organization and provisioning would clearly take time. Until it was ready to move, what was left of the English armed strength in Ireland would have to deal as best as it could with any action O'Neill chose to take against those tied by loyalty, tradition or self-interest to the English crown.

O'Neill wasted no time in expanding what had been essentially an Ulster war into one that embraced the whole island. Hugh Roe O'Donnell took a body of Gallowglass and Donegal soldiers into Connacht, overran most of it, and in one major fight annihilated the English troops sent to contain him. Richard Tyrrell, of an Old English family but now one of O'Neill's more enterprising commanders, led 2,000 men towards Munster, pausing at intervals on his way to harry isolated English garrisons in Leinster and to bottle up Ormonde in Kilkenny. Once Tyrrell had reached Munster he immediately attracted new allies. The losers of the Second Desmond War came out *en masse* in his support.

The English settlers of the Second Munster Plantation were unprotected and unready. The province was depleted of English troops. The unwisdom of the settlers' earlier drift from the concept of an exclusively English colony into a patchwork of racially intermingled communities was soon demonstrated, bloodily. The resentments of the dispossessed Irish may have seemed to have dissipated, but they had remained strong. A Geraldine revival, largely spontaneous but led nominally by a nephew of the late Earl of Desmond, left behind it a huge swathe of slaughtered settler families, burning farmsteads, destroyed crops and maimed cattle. Cork, Waterford and Limerick held out, and became the sanctuaries for which English refugees aimed, but in most cases failed to reach. Of those who did, many had been stripped of their clothes, beaten, humiliated, often mutilated, on their journeys. A few isolated castles of exceptional defensive strength survived as English oases, under siege. They were packed with desperate survivors from surrounding farms and villages, recently prosperous and productive, now charred wreckage. Other great houses were simply razed to the ground, their portable valuables carried away for distribution among their attackers. Some of the leading settlers made successful escapes, but they lost almost everything. Magnates of consequence, proprietors of vast acreages, suddenly found themselves destitute. The Fittons, Bourchiers, Ughtreds, Goolds and Courtneys were among these penniless fugitives. So was the poet Edmund Spenser,

65

who managed to make his way first to Mallow, then to Cork, and finally by sea to England, where he died shortly afterwards in London.

Before he left Cork, Spenser, who apart from his status as a prominent landholder was the Clerk of the Munster Council, an office that gave him direct access to the royal court in Whitehall, wrote to the queen with an account of his experiences and impressions. He was understandably in a condition of mixed despair and fury. One passage in his despatch summarizes his personal views, and doubtless those of his surviving colleagues in the ruined colony. It was a reaction that was to determine the outlook of the Anglo-Irish for generations to come: 'The deviser of the settlement of Munster perhaps thought that the civil example of the English being set before the Irish, and their daily conversing with them, would have brought them by dislike of their own savage life to the liking and embracing of better civility. But it is far otherwise, for instead of following them, they fly the English, and most hatefully shun them, for two causes: first, because they have ever been brought up licentiously and to live as each one listeth; secondly, because they naturally hate the English, so that their fashions they also hate.'

Much the same sentiments of disappointment, rage and bewilderment were later echoed by colonizers the world over. With little redrafting the words could have been adapted for use by Americans (many of them of Irish origin) about Indians, Australians (also with a strong Irish component) about aborigines, French *colons* about indigenous Algerians, and for that matter members of Irish missionary orders distressed to find that their putative flocks inexplicably held a preference for cannibalism over Catholicism. Purveyors of what they consider to be superior values are seldom popular with the audiences they address and usually become arrogant and impatient. Neither quality invalidates their sincerity and determination.

The first of the English reinforcements to arrive were a detachment of 1,000 soldiers put into Cork by sea. They made the city invulnerable to attack, but were too few in number to be able to interfere in events outside it. O'Neill now controlled the whole of

Ireland with the exceptions of the Dublin Pale, where most of the Old English Catholic lords remained loyal to the crown, the fortified towns around the coast, and Ormonde's inland enclave of Kilkenny. The problem facing the English was less that of suppressing a rebellion than of reconquering a lost country. O'Neill, patient, wary, calculating, made no attempt to hurry matters to a premature conclusion. Spanish help was on its way of a size and ability far in excess of the sorrowful international conscripts who had been destroyed at Smerwick. Acting in the light of information from all available sources, O'Neill decided upon a policy of systematic consolidation, while he awaited the Spaniards who would combine with him to settle the issue. Within his reach was the realization of an achievement never before approached: the formation of a Gaelic Irish nation, united under one leader. It would undoubtedly produce some domestic dissidence but O'Neill was strong enough to deal with it. The greater threat of external interference also seemed containable. Queen Elizabeth was old and would soon die. Her almost certain successor, King James VI of Scotland, was the son of the Catholic Mary, Queen of Scots, executed by Elizabeth. James could be assumed to be more sympathetic to Gaelic Irish aspirations than was Elizabeth. In any case, the powerful protection of Spain would bring a standing reassurance.

Before the arrival of the Spanish, O'Neill had two new English commanders to contend with. The first was a court favourite, the Earl of Essex, whose expressed fire-eating intentions were easily countered by a manoeuvre at which O'Neill was adept. He proposed a parley. Essex agreed and conceded a truce. Essex was recalled and later beheaded. The truce was only one item in the charges against him.

The successor to Essex, Mountjoy, was of less malleable material. He had far greater resources at his disposal than had Essex. The new army was available. It had its weaknesses, but one of its strengths was the experience and individuality of its officers. Mountjoy was a reflective soldier who had made a deep study of his profession and was convinced that he had the measure of O'Neill. O'Neill had shown that led by him the Irish could beat the English in a set-piece battle fought on open ground, but the Irish had been incapable of taking the fortified towns. Their cavalry was inferior to that of the English. The Irish rode without stirrups and were thus deprived of the supports necessary for the correct use of the lance and sword in close fighting. Unlike the English, who could be supplied by sea, the Irish lived off the land. A wholesale destruction of crops and cattle would force them back to Ulster.

Mountjoy went methodically about his task. There was rural desolation on a larger scale than ever. Fighting was desultory and inconclusive. O'Neill was determined not to commit his full strength until the Spanish came.

The Spanish came in September 1601. Four thousand of them, under Don Juan Del Aguila, landed at Kinsale in County Cork. Their choice of landing place seems to have resulted from a last-minute decision taken when their ships were approaching the Irish coast. It ignored the stated Irish preference for disembarkation in Connacht or Ulster, and proved a bad selection. Instead of giving himself the freedom to move in concert with O'Neill, Del Aguila left his army in danger of being hemmed in upon the promontory where they had landed or having to fight their way out over ground not of their choosing. Mountjoy moved quickly. Within a short time of their landing the Spanish were effectively besieged in and around Kinsale.

O'Neill mustered his full forces to go to the Spaniards' aid. He reached Kinsale by Christmas. His troops were deployed behind Mountjoy's, who in their turn, with the Spanish in front of them and the Irish to their rear, found themselves in a state of siege. The Irish assault went in on the dark, rainy night of 3 January 1602. It was unco-ordinated with the Spanish and was an unqualified failure. O'Neill lost 1,200 killed, an uncounted but large number of wounded and 900 prisoners. In the barbaric fashion of the times Mountjoy hanged the prisoners. The Irish army withdrew in disorder and dispersed into fragmented groups. Hugh Roe O'Donnell, disheartened, left for Spain, where he was poisoned, almost certainly at the instance of the English. O'Neill fought on, but no longer with the aim of establishing himself as the head of an independent Gaelic Irish nation. His sights were set lower, upon personal survival. If he could continue to be a nuisance to the English he might be able to negotiate acceptable terms for his submission to them.

68

Foreign military help, as in Fitzmaurice's time, had been worthless. After the defeat and withdrawal of O'Neill's army Mountjoy offered Del Aguila the chance to go back unharmed to Spain with his soldiers. Del Aguila accepted, but not before he had contributed a civilizing innovation to Irish military history. Mountjoy's initial proposal had applied exclusively to Spaniards. Their Irish collaborators were to be handed over to the English. Del Aguila, who had evidence of Mountjoy's intentions in the form of nine hundred hanged Irish prisoners, refused an armistice unless its terms were applied to Spanish and Irish alike. Mountjoy conceded the point. Del Aguila's generalship has attracted much scorn from Irish historians, but he deserves high credit for this display of honourable humanity at a time and place in which it was scarce.

Hugh O'Neill persisted, until the spring of 1603, in a guerrilla war that extended to most of Ireland the horrors of death, starvation and destruction that had devastated Munster twice during the past quarter of a century: '. . . no spectacle was more frequent in the ditches of towns, and especially in wasted countries, than to see multitudes of these poor people dead with their mouths all coloured green by eating nettles, docks and all things they could rend above ground . . . These and very many like lamentable effects followed . . .' The description is by Fynes Moryson, an officer in Mountjoy's army. He viewed the Irish with the cynical bias of a soldier long engaged in fighting them, but he was clearly moved by the degradation to which they had been reduced.

O'Neill made his submission to Mountjoy at Mellifont Abbey in March. This time it was the English who supplied the devious urbanity. O'Neill knelt in front of Mountjoy, and then applied formally for pardon, first to the Irish Council and later to a delegation of the Irish parliament in Dublin. It was not until he had completed the ritual in Dublin Castle that he was told that Queen Elizabeth had died a week earlier. Had he known that James I, a Scottish monarch supposedly more favourably inclined towards Ireland, was on the English throne, O'Neill would certainly have delayed his submission, or negotiated it differently.

Whether this would have been in the interests of his country is a subject for speculation. He was an inspiring leader, a great soldier, a skilful and cunning diplomat. But there is nothing in his record to suggest that he considered Ireland more important than himself. Intervention by O'Neill in the Second Desmond War could have been decisive. He did not intervene. He was a callous killer of personal enemies in an age when personal rivals were killed callously. His subscription to this practice may be understandable, but it does not mark him out as a man who would have inaugurated a new era of lawful protection and individual freedom for Irish men and women. He continued a lost war after Kinsale, with dreadful consequences for the ordinary people of Ireland, in order to save as much as he could for himself from the wreckage. It was hardly the decision of a man with an overriding concern for the wellbeing of a people whom he had so nearly led to nationhood. The suspicion remains that in the O'Neill scale of values the achievement of a united Gaelic Ireland was of little interest unless it was accompanied by the essential corollary that he himself would be king of it.

Once he had completed the formalities required of an official penitent, O'Neill was allowed to return to Ulster. He stayed there uneasily until 1607. His last demonstration of his capacity for clandestine organization was a sad one. He could foresee no acceptable future for himself or for his kind in the new Ireland that was developing. Nor could Rory O'Donnell, Hugh Roe's nephew and successor as Earl of Tyrconnel. With a party of about a hundred followers, including women, children, priests and bards, the Earl of Tyrone and the Earl of Tyrconnel embarked quietly by night on a ship that O'Neill had arranged to slip in to a rendezvous on Lough Swilly. They sailed for continental Europe, never to return again to Ireland and never again to exert any influence upon what happened there.[4]

'The Flight of the Earls' did not in itself change much. The changes were already far advanced. But the voluntary withdrawal of Ireland's greatest Gaelic leader was a clear acceptance that the Gaelic order that had lasted for two thousand years was beyond hope of resuscitation. Some fragments of it survived for years to

---

[4] The descendants of Hugh O'Neill, himself the descendant of the Irish hero of legend, Niall of the Nine Hostages, still live and prosper in Spain. One of the sons of Graf O'Donnell von Tyrconnel, an Austrian nobleman, was posted as missing when serving in Russia as an officer in the *Wehrmacht* in 1942.

come. Its cultural legacy, or an amended version of it, persists to the present day. But for three hundred and more years after the earls' flight the dominant force in Irish affairs was English, as applied by the Anglo-Irish, with religion rather than race becoming increasingly the recognized badge of conformity.

CHAPTER FOUR

The spontaneous departure from Ireland of the two earls, who had between them been both the embodiment of traditional Gaelic leadership in Ulster and the proprietors under English law of vast areas of Ulster land, provided an unexpected opportunity for the elaboration of a scheme that was already being planned by Sir Arthur Chichester, the Lord Deputy in Dublin.[1] Chichester was a fair-minded realist who appreciated that short of genocide, which had never been considered as a policy although something closely approaching it had occurred in some parts of the country, there was no hope of lasting peace in Ireland unless the native Irish were left with enough land to satisfy their economic needs and to minimize the sense of grievance inevitable in a people defeated in war. Much of inhabited Ulster had been destroyed by the scorched-earth practices of both sides. Large parts of the province were untouched and undeveloped bogland and forest. Population numbers had been depleted drastically among both fighting men and civilians. Chichester wanted a new English Plantation in Ulster, but in its original form his scheme was based upon the premise that there was more than enough land available for everybody, resident Irish and imported English.

The Irish were to be considered first. After their needs had been

---

[1] Lord Donegal, who still lives in Ireland, is the blood successor to this English official who stayed.

72

allowed for – about one-third was calculated to be sufficient to support the relatively few who had survived – the balance would be shared among English settlers. The accession to the English throne of King James VI of Scotland had promoted the political union of Scotland and England, and since the south of Scotland was nearer to the north of Ireland than any part of England was, and since there had in any case always been an incessant two-way traffic of people across the narrow North Channel that separated Ulster from south-west Scotland, the 'English' would willy nilly be substantially, possibly predominantly, Scottish.

Had the Chichester plan been able to go ahead in conformity with its initial specifications it is at least possible that some tolerable variety of co-existence might have evolved between the original inhabitants and the newcomers. Two unforeseen happenings gene-rated a major modification that was to turn the Ulster Plantation into the most permanent of its kind, and to make twentieth-century politicians, British and Irish, wish wistfully that it wasn't.

The first unpredicted event was the flight of the earls. Their disappearance was judged to be the legal equivalent of a confession of guilt to conspiracy to renew their rebellion. Their lands became forfeit to the crown.

The second incident was an uncompromising reversion to old habits by Sir Cahir O'Doherty, a chieftain from the area of the River Foyle, whose acceptance and use of an English knighthood did not inhibit him from expressing his disagreements in a familiar manner. His response to a personal insult from the English governor of Derry was first to attack and capture the fort at Culmore, and then to attack and burn down Derry itself. Compared with what had gone before it was a minor uproar of only local significance and it was suppressed with customary thoroughness and brutality. But it provided debating ammunition for those who regarded Chichester as over-optimistic about the chances of the native Irish ever being other than recurrently rebellious, and who at the same time saw in the availability of the sequestrated O'Neill and O'Donnell lands an opportunity for profitable development. Commercial cupidity allied itself to administrative expediency. The Chichester concept gave way to something much more far-reaching. The first entry on the family tree, the branches of which would extend to the violence that has haunted Northern Ireland since the late 1960s, was pencilled in.

The Irish were not disregarded altogether in the revised arrangements, but they emerged at a poor second best. They would have
done even worse had their services not been extensively required to
provide the manual labour necessary for the new Plantation.

The new Plantation was not a homogeneous whole. Differing
solutions were found to meet differing circumstances in different
parts of Ulster. Down and Antrim, the two counties in the north-east
nearest to Scotland, moved into their new ownership through a
complicated business transaction that involved a persuasive piece of
blackmail, and connivance in high places. The victim, Con O'Neill,
held title to 60,000 acres of County Down. He was at the time locked
up in Carrickfergus Castle, suspected, or allegedly suspected, of
treason. Two Scottish entrepreneurs, of an ingenuity and deviousness that would have left the Earl of Cork blushing, came to visit
him. James Hamilton had a shifty background as a spy in the pay of
Dublin Castle. Hugh Montgomery was an Ayrshire laird. Their
proposition to Con O'Neill was that if he would transfer 20,000 of
his 60,000 acres to each of them, they would contrive to get him a
royal pardon. O'Neill rapidly decided that a sacrifice of 40,000
acres was an improvement upon hanging, drawing and quartering,
and concurred in the deal. The king obligingly gave his approval,
O'Neill was released, and Hamilton and Montgomery became
grandees with sufficient residual acumen to get their joint hands on
O'Neill's remaining 20,000 acres by more orthodox commercial
methods over the next few years.

Hamilton and Montgomery[2] would have been unlikely to last
long if they had been invited to explain themselves before a
Jacobean tribunal in line with the standards enforced by the modern
Department of Trade (there wasn't one). But they were efficient and
hard-working colonizers who transformed the almost derelict
wastelands that they acquired into models of contemporary agriculture, with settlers, plant strains and livestock brought in from the
Scottish Lowlands. Villages, churches and neat little houses soon
abounded. One of the embryo villages was Belfast.

To the westward of this distinctive replica of southern Scotland
the organization was less coherent and moved more slowly. The land

---

[2] Hamilton was the progenitor of the Dukes of Abercorn. Montgomery became the first
Viscount Montgomery of the Ards.

picked for colonization was allocated to three general categories of owner, with some overlapping between the categories. Some went to former soldiers in lieu of accumulated pay arrears, a method of settling overdue bills of considerable appeal to the leaders and employers of an army whose administration was in abysmal confusion, compounded by the corrupt practices of officers, paymasters, contractors (the Earl of Cork had his fingers deep into this particular till) and any other opportunists who could improve the shining hour.

Servitors, many of whom were also ex-soldiers, were the next beneficiaries. Servitors were those who could demonstrate satisfactorily to the government in Dublin that during the recent wars their loyalty and performance had been such as to qualify them for reward. It is difficult to imagine how applications from hopeful servitors were sifted in a society in which records were inadequate or non-existent, corruption among officials was commonplace, and the adjustment of professed enthusiasms in accordance with revised assessments of which side was likely to win was frequent; but however it was done, large numbers of servitors came safely through the selection machinery and moved in to their new properties in Ulster.

The third class of owner, and possibly the most significant in terms of lasting effect, were known as undertakers. The undertakers, like their predecessors in the second Munster settlement, were development agents. In return for benefits expressed in land or money or exploitation concessions, they undertook to manage all the details of the colonizing process, from the recruitment of settlers in England and Scotland to their transport and suitable establishment in Ireland. Under the terms of their contracts, undertakers were to supervise the expulsion of the native Irish from confiscated lands allocated for settlement, see to the building of stone or brick houses grouped together for defence, provide defensible communal structures and supply a proper amount of weapons and ammunition.

With variable co-ordination, the former soldiers, the servitors, and the undertakers, slowly took over large areas – usually the most fertile – of Armagh, Tyrone and Fermanagh, and lesser proportions of Cavan, Monaghan and Donegal. A special consortium of undertakers, organized by the city of London, took control of what had been the county of Coleraine, now renamed Londonderry.

75

The London joint-stock company, subscribed to by the various city guilds, secured a guarantee of the rights to profits from the fisheries of the Rivers Bann and Foyle, from church benefices and from customs duties. In exchange they agreed to stock the entire county with English settlers, and to develop and equip with permanent defences the towns of Derry and Coleraine. They began with a display of vigour and efficiency that reflected the maturity of the commercial skills that the city guilds had accumulated down the centuries. Two hundred craftsmen were shipped to Ireland, and at once went to work upon the expansion of Coleraine and of what Sir Cahir O'Doherty had left of Derry. Emigrants were assembled and despatched, farms and settlements were opened up, the nuclei of small towns were built (Draperstown and Salterstown, named after the London guilds that sponsored them, are still there), and the imposition of a new society upon an ancient land was generally set in train.

But the initial impetus began to diminish. Like the undertakers elsewhere in Ulster, and like the Munster planters of a generation earlier, the London consortium found it harder than expected to persuade potential emigrants that a fresh life in Ulster provided more attractions than staying at home or taking the greater step, now available and with a greater stake, of crossing the Atlantic to Virginia. With the exceptions of the Down enterprises of Hamilton and Montgomery, which were prosperous, well-run and fully subscribed in manpower, and with some other exceptions in a few other places, compromise became prevalent, as it had in Munster with disastrous long-term consequences.

Under the pure doctrine of the original plans for the plantation, which was not modified after the 'Flight of the Earls' and the O'Doherty episode, the properties of the native Irish were to be confined to explicitly designated localities in which those classified as 'deserving' were given grants of land that was to be sublet in the English manner and cultivated in a similarly English manner. There is little evidence to suggest that the native Irish of Ulster, deserving or otherwise, paid much attention to either English legal land practices or to the niceties of English agricultural procedures. They were hereditary cattle graziers, and they continued to graze cattle. But an increasing number of them, as before in Munster, were offered and took up employment in the Anglo-Scottish enclaves.

76

These stayed, worked, and interbred during thirty years of what in Ireland passed as peace, until Irish frustrations, compounded by the effects of internal frictions in England, broke out into another mass shedding of blood in 1641. By that time, the hatreds nurtured by varying adherences to three rival interpretations of the Christian religion added immeasurably to the sorrow.

CHAPTER FIVE

A tenet shared in the seventeenth century by responsible Catholic and Protestant theologians, with the power to get their thinking translated into practice, was that to recognize that some people might genuinely believe in a version of the Christian message which differs from one's own, and should therefore be allowed to follow their own consciences, was unreasonable. Tolerance of divergence from the truth was not virtuous. It was a sinful accommodation with heresy.

The application of this doctrine to Ireland took a considerable time to develop. It had not of course been an issue at all until King Henry VIII took England into Protestantism, and it was not much of one for many years after that. The Catholic Church in Ireland had for generations been in as much disarray as its counterparts almost everywhere in Europe. Its doctrines went largely untaught and its precepts unhonoured. There were avaricious bishops, and priests who married wives or took concubines. The Catholicism established in the Pale was essentially an English organization that operated separately from its Irish equivalent beyond the Pale. The Tudor confiscation of monastic property in Ireland led to the shedding of few tears among the laity. Their interest was in acquiring a share of the loot.

The Elizabethan adventurers who led the Munster planters were self-professed members of the Reformed Church, and some possibly took its teachings seriously. But they were commercially-minded

78

realists whose priority was profit. They might perhaps have felt something of a spiritual glow had there been a large-scale conversion of the Irish to Protestantism, but the greater part of the glow would have been kindled by the temporal consideration that the saving of souls was linked to an acknowledgement of the monarch as the head of the Church. Any right-thinking Protestant would think twice about putting himself into a state of rebellion against the crown if he had God to contend with along with the crown's representatives in Ireland. It would doubtless continue to happen, but less often. And fewer revolts would mean more stability which in turn would bring more prosperity.

It was in any case a hypothesis that was never put to the test. There were no large-scale conversions by the Gaelic or the Norman Irish to Protestantism. There were *some*, at all levels of the social strata including the clergy, and some notable magnates such as the Butler Earl of Ormonde and the O'Brien Lord Inchiquin, a descendant of Brian Boru, also made the change. But the overall incidence was small.

Given the prevalent apathy in Ireland about religion at the time, it is hard not to believe that if Protestant proselytes of genuine conviction had presented themselves in suffcient numbers, and had added to their spiritual message a postscript about the material benefits that could flow from an attachment to the new faith, the numbers would have been markedly higher. But ardent Protestant missionaries of this type did not exist. Church property was transferred from the Catholic clergy to the Protestant clergy, but the new incumbents were theologically unimpressive. They were all assiduous about drawing their pay, but few did much work, pastoral or liturgical. Some of them never set foot in Ireland, let alone in their dioceses.

In this situation, although religious labels provided a rough guide to where loyalties lay, they were not exclusive indicators. The Catholic Old English in the Pale were persistently loyal to the Protestant holder of the crown. Hugh O'Neill of the Ulster Catholic Irish supported the Protestant English against the Catholic Desmonds, before he himself, for reasons other than religious, began fighting the English. There were Gaelic leaders in the Desmond and O'Neill wars who made expedient changes of allegiance, and there were bands of Gaelic professional mercenaries who fought for whoever was likely to pay them most in cash or plunder.

During the latter part of the sixteenth century, ecclesiastical purists, on both sides of the doctrinal divide, began to apply a progressively effective influence upon their co-religionists, many of whom until now had been largely nominal adherents. The process accelerated as the seventeenth century passed through its first four decades. For the Catholics, the well-organized Society of Jesus, staffed by dedicated, intelligent and thoroughly educated enthusiasts, promoted throughout Europe a sophisticated campaign aimed at the restoration and preservation of Catholic values. Intramural abuses were attacked and eradicated. External divergences, enshrined in the teachings of Protestant reformers, were subjected to critical analyses and countered by an amalgam of intellectual argument and practical and spiritual support for societies and individuals who held to traditional practices.

Father Sanders, the English Jesuit who came to Munster with Fitzmaurice, was one of the pioneers of this movement. He had a multiplicity of successors. They were convincing because of the genuineness of their faith and the heroic zeal with which they taught it. Many of them suffered, or as they would have considered it, achieved, martyrdom. An inevitable outcome of their zealousness was that they infused a new fanaticism into worldly disputes.

To kill an enemy because he was by chance of birth the subject of a king or lord who was in contention with one's own king or lord was a custom of immemorial provenance throughout Europe. To be able to do so with the assurance that the deed was divinely blessed brought an enhanced ferocity to a tradition that had always been ferocious. The Thirty Years War on the continental mainland, notionally conducted by both sides for the love of Christ, was one of the cruellest and most destructive in Western history. Its ideological extension to Ireland took some little time.

On the Protestant side, the doctrinal zealots were the English Puritans and the Scottish Calvinists, the latter of whom were a powerful force among the Ulster planters. Their inspiration was less the Jesus of the Sermon on the Mount, the advocate of loving one's neighbour, than the wrathful and vengeful Old Testament Jehovah who smote His enemies. The enemies originally identified by the English Puritans were the king and his court, where sexual and fiscal morality was open to question, and whose doctrine of regal Divine

80

Right was objectionable in itself and even more so when its practice included demands for financial subsidies to meet objectives not underwritten by Old Testament prophets and iniquitously expensive to Low Church taxpayers. For the first forty years of the seventeenth century, Ireland's destiny was enmeshed in the development of this grumbling extraterritorial dispute. Ireland also contributed to it.

The Irish contribution came as a result of the Old English presence. They prevailed in a resolute loyalty to the kings, James I and his son, Charles I. Their retained Catholicism was an affront to the more intense among English Protestants, but its condonement was a continued financial necessity. The Old English were a standing guarantee that should the native Irish rise again, the nucleus of a locally recruited force would be available in Ireland to defend the English connection. Metropolitan English interests therefore required the maintenance of a tolerable balance between Old English religious susceptibilities and Old English monarchical loyalties. Over-zealous insistence upon conformity to the reformed faith would force upon the Old English a choice that they had so far been able to avoid. And if the choice did have to be made, there was little doubt that the majority of them, possibly nearly all of them, would have given precedence to Catholicism however much they would have regretted the need to abandon their king and sever their links with their English origins. In that case the only allies left to them would be their old enemies, the native Irish.

It followed that too much righteous pressure would not only deprive the metropolitan English and the new English Protestant settlers in Ireland of a cheap and effective component of their defences; at its worst it might bring about an active military opposition which in combination with the Irish could be lethally dangerous and ruinously expensive to counter. A fair measure of tactical sufferance, clearly distinguishable from ideological tolerance, was allowed uneasily to prevail.

In spite of this, there is no doubt that the Old English Catholics fell well short of immunity from harassment, considered in either religious or economic terms. Powerful individual men of conscience made clear their abhorrence of Popery and all that it stood for. 'The locusts of Rome', Lord Falkland, the Lord Deputy, described the Catholic clergy with a notable lack of ecumenism in the early 1620s, 'whose doctrines are as full of horrid treasons as many of their lives are full of horrible impieties'. But these prejudices, shared if less colourfully delineated by his successors, kept none of them back from a continuing process of negotiation with a still influential body whose leaders contributed nearly half of the membership of the Irish parliament. Statutory fines for failure to attend Protestant services went uncollected. The continued activity of most, but not all, of the Catholic clergy was tacitly condoned. There were sporadic instances of the suppression of Catholic institutions, one of which inspired a notable riot in Dublin, and there was consistent pressure from significant Protestants for more. But for nearly forty years, until the 1640s, the affairs of Ireland proceeded with a relative absence of violence.

Among and between the various groupings there were suspicion, hostility, bitterness and resentment. Yet by and large the man-oeuvrings were warily political. Every move, by every participant, had to be calculated in the light of the reaction that it would generate in England, where the ultimate power lay. And since from the time of the accession of King Charles I in 1625 there had been a steadily growing friction between the monarch and his parliament, Irish calculations became progressively more complex.

Irish interests were complex enough. By the late 1630s they fell into several categories, each with its own sub-divisions, and with considerable blurring at the edges. The Protestants were still in a small minority, but already they owned about one-quarter of the land, a proportion that was increasing as a series of new small plantations, the most successful of which was in Wexford, were developed. The Southern Protestants, some of them Norman-Irish and Gaelic-Irish converts, most of them descendants of Elizabethan planters, were on the whole loyal to the king in the dispute across the water. They subscribed to Anglicanism, mistrusted Protestant nonconformism, detested Catholicism, were avaricious in their pursuit of new land and wealth, and feared and despised the Gaelic Irish. The Southern Protestants also displayed a trait common to all colonists dependent for their survival upon the strength of a metropolitan power: an irritated cynicism about the motives and capacity of the governors, in their case the Lords Deputy, appointed by Whitehall to rule over them.

The Northern Protestant newly ennobled magnates, who because of the size of their land-holdings and their consequent wealth were as powerful as their Southern counterparts, shared roughly the same attitudes. But most of their tenants, the ordinary settlers, especially those of Scottish origin, were Presbyterian nonconformists who considered Anglicanism almost as objectionable as Catholicism (with good reason: Northern dissenters who refused conscientiously to attend Anglican services were subject to the same penalties that applied to Catholics and, lacking the tactical influence of the Southern Old English, were more likely to have them imposed). In so far as domestic Anglo-Scottish constitutional and religious rivalries spilled over into Ulster, the ordinary settlers gave their support to the Parliamentarians and Puritans. As in the earlier Munster settlements, many of the Ulster colonists had taken native Irish wives and had bred children of mixed origin. But these, almost without exception, had been absorbed into the imported culture and shared the views of the Protestant totality concerning the dangerous untrustworthiness of the Gaelic Irish.

Among the Catholic majority the Old English, as we have seen, were engaged in the tortuous process of trying to balance their adherence to the Catholic faith with their traditional loyalty to an English king who was a Protestant and whose Protestant subjects in Ireland were intent upon dispossessing them as soon as it was safe to do so. Like almost everyone else of English origin the Old English mistrusted the Gaelic Irish, but the Gaelic Irish were their co-religionists. Protestant pressures, even if comparatively muted, affected both groups. The two were inexorably being forced closer together by the recognition that they were jointly at risk.

During this period the Gaelic Irish remained largely quiescent. The more vigorous of them, the ones with an inherited aptitude for soldiering, went in their thousands to join the continental armies of Catholic powers, predominantly those of France and Spain. They were the founders of the distinguished military line of the Wild Geese, who for the next century and a half fought in every army in Europe in a series of campaigns that cost an estimated 2,000,000 Irish dead. The English authorities in Stuart Ireland – and in future reigns – did nothing to impede their departure. It was a convenient method of diminishing an always present threat that would have been multiplied immeasurably had the adventurers stayed in Ireland. Those Gaelic Irish who did stay demonstrated in 1641 how serious the threat was. Four decades of seeming resignation to their lot as despised outcasts restricted to the less productive parts of their own country or as menial dependants of newcomers who had forcibly annexed the best parts, came to an end abruptly on 23 October.

The 1641 Rebellion, unlike the Desmond and O'Neill wars, cannot be defined in simple terms of Irish dispossessed *versus* English expansionists. This revolt was something of a milestone in the evolutionary history of Irish insurgency. There were so many conflicting, inter-reacting and changeable forces at work, before, during and after the Rebellion, that the Rebellion itself viewed in retrospect looks like a badly fitting part in a badly assembled piece of machinery.

To extend this not altogether happy simile, the best way for anyone to understand how the machinery was assembled is to strip it down and study its components, in chronological order. By the 1630s King Charles I and the English parliament were in deadlock. The parliament was dominated by zealous Puritans, who disliked the established faith, the royal arrogance, the royal extravagance and the royal policies. Parliament had demonstrated its displeasure by refusing to pay for the last two.

The Calvinist Scots, who shared the English Puritan distaste for their joint king's activities, went one step further. They revolted. They signed a solemn Covenant and stood to arms. In 1639 the king's forces from England marched to suppress this revolt. It was an expensive enterprise, and it was in part financed by the Irish parliament, then a body of mixed Protestant and Catholic members, who voted £100,000 for the purpose.

For some time previously the Irish parliament had been discussing measures known as the 'Graces', promoted by Catholic members in a bid to secure their rights, and resisted by those Protestant members who were hostile to the concept of Catholic rights. The Catholic members, aside from a genuine belief that the best way to deal with an uprising by Scottish Calvinists was to squash it, had calculated that their co-operative fiscal gesture would be rewarded by the reasonably smooth passage of the 'Graces'. And so it might have been, but for the intervention of two of the Lord Justices, Parsons and Borlase, responsible at that time for the higher conduct of Irish government. Both were Puritans, both had sympathies with the Parliamentarians in the argument across the Irish Sea, and both held acquisitive ambitions about the large areas of land still in the possession of the Catholic Old English. Parsons and Borlase frustrated the 'Graces' by proroguing parliament before they could be adopted.

It was a clear signal to the Old English that the new men in power were intent upon the destruction of a community that had been the agent of successive English monarchs for nearly five centuries. The Old English were proud of their English ancestry, proud of their record of dedicated service to the crown, fierce in their loyalty to the king, and staunch in their adherence to the Catholic religion. They were digesting the implications of this manoeuvre by Parsons and Borlase, the latest in a cumulatively menacing series, when in October 1641, the Gaelic Irish of Ulster revolted.

Preparations for this eruption had been extensive, if ill-coordinated. Rory O'More and Sir Felim O'Neill were the domestic instigators. In Rome, Father Luke Wadding, the Head of the Irish Franciscan house, had negotiated assistance from the Pope and from Cardinal Richelieu in France. Whatever the good intentions of the leaders towards restraint, it was inevitable that the Ulster Irish would show little pity for the usurpers of their ancestral lands. The old, ghastly, familiar scenes of the destruction of the Munster settlements were re-enacted in Ulster. Planters were massacred. Houses and stored crops went up in flames. The numbers of men, women and children slaughtered were probably exaggerated by contemporary and later propagandists, but they were still high, perhaps as high as 10,000. They were entered into the tenacious memory of the Ulster Protestant community.

The English garrisons in Ulster were in many cases overrun. The surviving troops, and most of the surviving planter families, concentrated in such defended centres as Derry and Drogheda. In London, parliament voted money to suppress the rebellion, but there was a delay before the cash was forthcoming and in the event it was used to finance the as yet to be declared parliamentary war against the king. Another item of English parliamentary business, of more lasting significance for Ireland, was the swift passage of an 'Adventurers' Act', which provided for the confiscation of rebel-owned Irish estates and for their subsequent sale to subscribers known as Adventurers. An additional clause in this legislation forbade the offering of royal pardons to rebels.

For two months the Old English, torn by irreconcilable loyalties, and haunted by memories of past commitments, stayed aloof from the turmoil. Then, in December 1641, after many of their followers had left to join the rebels, and after it had been made even clearer to them by the likes of Parsons and Borlase that unless they abandoned their religion they would be classed as disaffected, they reiterated their loyalty to the king and rode off to join the Irish of Ulster.

The rebellion rapidly spread throughout the country. In Munster the English soldiers withdrew to the garrisons of Bandon and Cork, in the teeth of rebel operations mounted under the command of Lord Mountgarret, a Catholic member of the Ormonde Butler family. The king, backed by his near-mutinous English parliament, countered the defection of his loyal Old English subjects by engaging the services of his recently rebellious Scottish subjects. In April 1642, General Munro landed at Carrickfergus in County Antrim with a large Scottish force which was joined by the Ulster Scots and by Southern Irish Protestant sympathizers with the English Parliamentarians. The leaders of this last body were Lord Broghill, the son of the Earl of Cork who had done so well for himself out of his Irish commercial and other adventures, and Sir Charles Coote. At about the same time an anti-rebel contingent took the field in Munster under the command of Murrough O'Brien, Lord Inchiquin. A descendant of Brian Boru, Inchiquin was a Protestant, a fierce and competent soldier, and an illustration, if one were still needed, of the inadvisability of assuming that the sides taken by Irish disputants were necessarily governed by their family origins.

For the next few months there were marches, and counter-marches, and demonstrations of force, and minor sieges, and elaborate rhetoric. None of it was of much military significance. In the sad tradition of Irish wars (indeed, of all wars) the chief sufferers were the civilians who looked on while their cattle were sequestrated, their crops destroyed, their families beggared. A fresh twist to an already contorted situation came in August 1642. Charles I mustered his forces under the royal standard at Nottingham, and Civil War broke out in England. In Ireland loyalties were reassessed amid the usual calculations of where personal interests lay.

The alignment in Ireland resolved itself as follows. James, Earl of Ormonde, appointed Lord Lieutenant by the king, attracted to himself a substantial following of Irish Protestant royalists, who secured Dublin and its surroundings in the king's interest. Ormonde

86

was an intelligent, humane and tolerant man, a convinced Protestant but with Catholic brothers and nephews in loyal rebellion with the Old English. Ormonde's lodestars were a personal as well as a constitutional loyalty to the king, and a conviction that if Ireland were to prosper in peace the Protestant interest must be paramount, but not to the exclusion of a legitimate Catholic participation in public affairs.

The Lord Justices and the Irish parliament, which was now entirely Protestant because of the departure of the Old English, sided with the English parliament. Inchiquin and Broghill were soon in control of most of Munster. In north-west Ulster those Protestant settlers who had survived the massacres gathered together around two brothers of the Stewart family, and pledged themselves to parliament. Munro's Scottish army in north-east Ulster was under the orders of the English parliament and the Scottish Estates.

The Catholics, Gaelic Irish and Old English, set up their headquarters in Kilkenny. They formed a Supreme Council, in which each of the four provinces was represented. By October it had become the 'Confederate Catholics of Ireland'. An army for each province was established, with Rory O'More as the overall Commander-in-Chief.

There were early manifestations of dissension within both the political and military wings of the Confederacy. Unanimity prevailed about its prime objective, the restoration of the rights of the Catholic Church, a meeting of minds underpinned by episcopal threats of summary excommunication for anyone who failed to take an oath of association. Beyond that there were fundamental divergencies of principle. Old enmities did not stay latent. The Old English contribution to the philosophy covered demands for a general liberty of conscience, government by Catholic officials, restitution of lands confiscated for reasons of religion and the independence of the Irish parliament. The Gaelic Irish were not particularly interested in these details. What they wanted was their lands back, and the fostering of their native language and traditions.

The bickering did not diminish when in May two Irish commanders of note, with wide experience of fighting in continental armies, arrived from Europe to provide skilled military direction and to deliver arms and money provided by Cardinal Richelieu of France. Owen Roe O'Neill was a nephew of the great Earl of Tyrone.

Thomas Preston was from an Old English Pale family. The two had served alongside one another in European campaigns. The experience had generated mutual detestation.

Fortunately for the Confederation, military exigencies left the two with relatively little time to disagree in the council chamber. Owen Roe took over the command of the Ulster army. He showed himself to be of similar quality to his famous uncle. He was a stern disciplinarian, and an inspired trainer of troops. The Ulster soldiers were soon turned into the best at the disposal of the Confederacy.

Preston, with the Leinster army, was less successful. Ormonde, open-minded about most matters and willing to accept realistic compromises, was entirely inflexible over one point. He would not tolerate the flouting of the authority of the king. It was being flouted on a large scale by people with differing motives all over Ireland, and he could not deal with them all simultaneously, but when the opportunity arose for him to demonstrate that the king's representative meant to be obeyed he took it. Preston's army was disposed ill-advisedly and Ormonde saw an opening. He marched his Royalists into Wexford and routed Preston at New Ross.

Ormonde's versatility was then put to a further test by the arrival of secret instructions from England. The king's cause was not prospering. He needed military reinforcements. Ormonde was to try to arrange for these to be provided by the Catholic Confederation of Kilkenny, currently in rebellion, and one of whose armies had recently been beaten by Ormonde himself.

Ormonde was feeling his way to negotiating this tricky reshuffle of the cards when word of the royal intentions leaked to the Parliamentarians. Their outrage was genuine and their propaganda telling. Here was the king, who claimed to rule over his people by Divine Right, attempting to exercise his sovereignty by enrolling into his forces an army recruited from the savages who a short while before had massacred thousands of His Majesty's Protestant subjects in Ulster. Ormonde's instructions were abruptly rescinded. The king issued a diplomatic denial that he had ever contemplated such a thing.

International interest in the long-term politico-religious implications of the struggle was demonstrated practically in 1645 by the appointment to the Confederation of a Papal Nuncio. His name was Rinuccinni, and he brought with him an unbending will, a closed mind, a talent for Machiavellian intrigue and money from the Vatican and France. From the moment of his appearance in Kilkenny he engineered a hardening of attitudes. The intricacies of the origins of the contest were of small concern to him. He was interested only in the re-establishment of a Catholic Ireland, devoid of all heretics and committed to the restoration of the true faith throughout Europe. It was an aim that appealed to Owen Roe and to many of the Gaelic Irish. The Old English were more pragmatic about the realities of Irish life, but soon found that reasoned argument carried little weight when countered by threats of excommunication. The Rinuccinni intervention produced one inevitable effect upon the English of all shades of opinion: an insular resentment that a foreigner should have the impertinence to interfere in a domestic dispute.

In June 1646 Owen Roe O'Neill fought, and won brilliantly, the last great victory of Irish troops over English troops on Irish soil. The battle was at Benburb, on the same river as the Yellow Ford, where Owen Roe's uncle had routed Bagenal over fifty years earlier. Munro's Scots from north-east Ulster were attempting a junction with the Stewarts' settler army from the north-west. Owen Roe outwitted them, outfought them, routed them and inflicted 3,000 Protestant casualties. Preston marched to join Owen Roe. The chance of a successful exploitation of the victory was there for the taking. It was missed. Abrasive disagreements between the two commanders led to its slipping away.

A deterioration in the royal fortunes in England prompted a new royal initiative towards Ireland. Charles's defeat by Cromwell at Naseby had turned his thoughts again to the need for Irish help. Ormonde once more became the diplomatic intermediary. This time he was instructed to offer to the Confederacy a future Ireland in which Catholics would be exempted from taking the oath of supremacy, all laws applying religious penalties would be repealed, and the authenticity of all land titles held in 1628 would be confirmed.

Had these arrangements been on offer in 1641 the Old English Catholics would have had no cause to take to arms, and both Irish and English history might have taken a distinctively different turn. As it was most of the Old English leaders were prepared to accept them with postponed relief, but Rinuccinni thought otherwise. This proposed solution, which still left Protestants with a major measure of influence in Ireland, was to him both theologically and politically unacceptable. He applied his veto, with the customary sanctions attached for non-observance. Not enough of the Old English were excommunication-proof, reported Ormonde sardonically. The Confederate Assembly finally rejected the proposals in early 1649. Owen Roe was one of those firmly on the side of the Nuncio. The Gaelic Irish would have benefited from the increased religious freedom offered. They would not have recovered their planted lands.

It was in any case too late for the king to recoup his losses by suggesting concessions to the Catholic Irish. His days as holder of the crown were numbered. Cromwell and his Independents were increasingly dictating the course of English affairs. The collapse of the English Royalist cause was imminent. Ormonde studied developments carefully, made an assessment of what his duty called upon him to do, and surrendered Dublin to the Parliamentarians. He preferred, he said, English rebels to Irish rebels. Ormonde handed the Sword of State to Colonel Michael Jones upon his arrival in the capital with 8,000 Roundhead soldiers in train, and departed unobtrusively for France.

Even then, had Confederacy reactions been quick enough, and Confederacy organization good enough, there would have been a chance to pre-empt Jones before he was properly consolidated. Preston tried, but he was too late. Jones defeated him at Dangan. There were 3,000 Confederacy casualties. While Jones tidied up in Leinster, Inchiquin was doing the same for the Parliamentarians in Munster. In November 1647, near Kanturk, he routed a Confederate force led by Lord Taafe.

At this point, when the triumph of the Parliamentarians in Ireland seemed to be on the edge of becoming absolute, there was another unusual turn in what had already been a sequence of unusual turns. The arrogance with which Cromwell and his successful Independents conducted themselves in victory stimulated widespread reflection followed by extensive revulsion. Doubts about the wisdom of previous conduct affected almost everyone in the British Isles except the impermeably self-confident Cromwell and his formidable New Model Army. The Scots, the English Presbyterians, many of the Protestants of Ireland and Lord Inchiquin simply changed sides.

They became dedicated supporters of the king whom they had helped to bring down. This newly acquired loyalty became posthumous when King Charles was beheaded in January 1649, but the act of regicide, abhorrent to most in a monarchical age, itself helped to bring together old armed opponents.

Ormonde, reappointed Lord Lieutenant by the new king in exile, Charles II, returned to Ireland. Rinuccinni, disappointed that whatever happened next it would not be the emergence of an exclusively Catholic Ireland, returned to Rome. Owen Roe O'Neill, sympathizer with Rinuccinni's frustrated aspirations, stood aside. Broghill and Coote, among the first Protestant leaders in Ireland to nail their colours to the parliamentary mast, remained faithful to it. Amidst all the uncertainties and confusion, Ormonde led an attack on Dublin. He was a better statesman than soldier. Jones, with little difficulty, threw him back at Baggotrath.

It was at this point that Oliver Cromwell, the Lord Lieutenant and General for the Parliament of England, made his personal intervention into Irish affairs. It was brief, but decisive. It moulded the destinies of Ireland for centuries ahead.

A man who in his own country had recently won a civil war, decapitated his king, disestablished the Church of England, outlawed the monarchy and abolished the peerage, was unlikely to be bothered by the problems facing him in Ireland, however complicated they might seem. To assist their solution, he brought with him when he landed in Dublin on 15 August 1649, twenty thousand experienced and determined troops, all subscribers to a variety of fundamentalist religious sects that made no bones about the Old Testament requirement to exchange eyes for eyes and teeth for teeth. They were alarming because they combined total conviction in the correctness of what they were about to do with an evident ability to do it with profound efficiency. They were more alarming still because they came equipped with faulty information. They were unshakably convinced, as was Cromwell himself, that all Irish Catholics shared the responsibility for the massacres of the Ulster Protestants in 1641, and were thus proper candidates for divine vengeance, administered at second hand.

Cromwell's objectives were simply defined. He aimed first to

91

subdue the fragmented opposition that remained, and then to govern Ireland in the English interest, as interpreted by his new English Republican Commonwealth.[1]

An essential adjunct of the Cromwellian programme was the application of the Adventurers' Act (see page 85 above) which stipulated the confiscation of all lands held by rebels, their resettlement by nominated paid-up 'Adventurers', and a ban on the granting of royal, now transmuted to republican, pardons. A corollary of the negative act of not granting pardons was the positive one of wreaking vengeance upon the killers of the Ulster planters. There was no need to waste time in trying to identify these. It was a matter calling for indiscriminate reprisal.

Like the outstanding soldier that he was, Cromwell's preparations were thorough, his planning simple and logical, his troops at a high pitch of effectiveness and his movements swift. He started with Drogheda, a walled mediaeval town thirty miles to the north of Dublin. The defences were stormed and all resistance overcome. There followed a massacre of the defenders and of the townspeople, men, women and children. Estimates of the numbers killed vary erratically, and, as in the case of the Ulster massacres, some were later inflated for purposes of propaganda. The usually accepted figure is about 3,500.

Drogheda held an ancient royal charter, was a commercial centre, and had in bygone centuries accommodated sittings of the Irish parliament. It was a typical Old English Pale town, though larger than most. Its inhabitants, and certainly its leading citizens, must almost entirely have been of English descent, and proudly so. It is sadly ironic that Cromwell, in his avenging crusade to extract comparable payment for the shedding in Ulster by the Gaelic Irish of what he described as 'innocent blood', should, possibly without realizing it, have chosen as victims a community whose forebears had been one of the mainstays of English rule in Ireland for five hundred years.

His next target was Wexford, in the south-east of the country. Wexford, like Drogheda, was another town with a royal charter and

[1] Cromwell's republican administration of Ireland preceded the first independent Irish Republic, established by the government of Mr John A. Costello in 1948, by 299 years. There were constitutional differences.

was garrisoned by Old English Royalist troops. Attempts at a parley to negotiate a surrender failed, probably through muddle, but possibly, as Cromwell's critics later alleged, by devious design. Wexford was duly and ferociously taken by assault. The ensuing butchery of garrison and townsfolk was as comprehensive as it had been in Drogheda.

While Cromwell continued to seek out and destroy his enemies in the south-east, Coote was doing the same in Ulster. Broghill soon brought Munster to heel. Owen Roe, the only Irish commander with a skill matching that of Cromwell, died in Cavan towards the end of the year. By March of 1650 Kilkenny had surrendered, the Confederation had broken up, Coote's Ulster army had finished its work in the north and had reinforced the southern operations, and Irish Royalist resistance was being conducted by isolated groups of soldiers, acting under no central direction.

Cromwell himself left the country, never to return, in May 1650, and handed over command to Ireton, his son-in-law. Shortly afterwards Ormonde also left, again for France. He took Inchiquin and Preston with him. Desultory fighting, sometimes flaring into sizeable engagements, continued into 1652. By then there was no hope left. The countryside was devastated, and the population reduced by bloodshed, starvation and disease to not much more than half a million.

Irish surrenders were piecemeal, made by individual commanders to their Cromwellian counterparts. They were purely military submissions, and involved no acceptance by the officers who took them of obligations towards the surviving civilian population. As was to be expected of officers trained by Cromwell, the final administrative arrangements were made with a brisk, cold efficiency. Thirty thousand Irish soldiers were allowed to go to the armies of Spain and France. With that potential threat safely out of the way, several thousand ordinary civilians, judged arbitrarily to be guilty, or suspect, or troublesome, were transported to the West Indies to work in conditions of near slavery. A special court was convened in Dublin to try those accused of complicity in the Ulster massacres. It handed out fifty-two death sentences in all. Two of the hanged illustrate the eccentric directions taken by the currents of Irish history. They were Sir Felim O'Neill, a kinsman of the Great Hugh; and Sir Walter Bagenal, a Confederate officer and a kinsman of the

Bagenal defeated by O'Neill at the Yellow Ford.

Cromwell's politics, like those of nearly all his contemporaries, were governed by his religious beliefs. He had overthrown a monarchical system that had taken centuries of painful experience to evolve, and in an associated process he had in England and Scotland also suppressed Anglicanism and Presbyterianism. But of all the deviations from his personal interpretation of what the scriptures taught, the one that he held in most contempt was Catholicism.

God had now placed Cromwell in a conspicuously favourable position. He was a military dictator able to enforce his will through the agency of a superbly trained army of like-minded zealots. The English parliament, stripped of all its inconvenient members, was still available to provide a selective element of constitutional continuity, and could be relied upon to do what it was told, with enthusiasm. An almost depopulated Ireland was ready for distribution among the worthy. By a providential, or divinely arranged, coincidence everything necessary was in the right place at the right time for the early attainment of several complementary objectives.

The Adventurers' Act gave legal validity to the confiscation of former rebels' lands. The army in Ireland was more than capable of supervising the confiscation. The subscribers were ready to move in. As in the Elizabethan wars, arrears of pay to the army could be met in kind by further allocation of land to demobilized soldiers. This would at the same time save the Treasury money and establish throughout the country a corpus of reliable Protestant yeoman farmers, trained to arms and ready to use them. After centuries of indecision and compromise Ireland would at last become what it obviously should be, an extension of England. The strategic worries that had bothered Protestant England since the Reformation would not entirely disappear, but they would be relieved substantially by what would amount to a permanently resident English country-wide garrison. And all these material advantages carried with them a spiritual bonus. Popery would be punished.

The transfer from concept to practice took little time. An early plan for the total confiscation of nine counties was abandoned when it was discovered that the overall acreage was insufficient to meet the applications for land put in by army officers. It was replaced by a more elaborate scheme for the takeover of twenty-six counties,[2] and the introduction of something never tried on a large scale in Ireland before, transplantation. Connacht and County Clare were reserved for those Catholic landowners and their retainers who still remained and who were not positively identified with what had once been patriotism, but was now treason. 'To Hell or Connacht' is often believed to have been a brutally enforced migration of the Catholic peasantry to an infertile and inhospitable province that did not commend itself to the Cromwellians. This is not so. The bulk of the peasantry were left where they were, more or less. They were needed as labourers and servants by the new owners.

The allocation of land in the requisitioned part of the country was eased by a topographical survey conducted by Sir William Petty. The Down Survey (so named not because Petty was based in County Down, but because for the first time ever in Ireland scientifically assembled mapping data were put down on paper) calculated that the Cromwellian settlers took between them eleven million acres. The entire area of the country was estimated at twenty million acres. Of the untaken balance, hundreds of thousands of acres were in the hands of Elizabethan settler families who had either, like Broghill and Coote, distinguished themselves in support of the new regime, or had rapidly accommodated themselves to its success. The exiled Catholics, mostly Old English, held about five million acres, most of them unproductive rock, in the west. Scattered about the country were a few pockets of Catholic land, accidentally overlooked or listed for future disposal. The owners clung on precariously and hoped for better days.

A predictable, but seemingly unpredicted, consequence of paying off soldiers in land was that those soldiers who preferred cash sold the land and went home to England. Since the available market was limited to authorized adventurers, ex-officers with already large holdings, and existing Elizabethan magnates and speculators, the outcome was that many officers in particular were able by shrewd purchase to consolidate their properties into entities much larger than their initial allocations. These New English landlords were the

[2] Not only was Cromwell the first man to govern Ireland under a republican constitution, he was also the first to partition it on the basis of religion into two parcels of twenty-six and six counties.

progenitors of an important and powerful element of the Anglo-Irish gentry.

The Cromwellian settlement was as radical in its urban dispositions as it was in its rural ones. Towns such as Kilkenny, Galway and Waterford, Old English centres of distinctive architecture and ancient traditions, were planted by the New English. The burgesses were expelled, forbidden to live within two miles of any corporate town. All church property became forfeit to the government, and the Church was disestablished. Civic, commercial and religious affairs became, and for generations remained, a near-monopoly of the new dispensation.

The Cromwellians were energetic, fast-moving, and effective. But the reshaping of an entire country is a lengthy process. Much, but not all, had been completed when Cromwell died in England in 1658. The former soldiers among the planters would gladly have taken up arms again to secure the succession of a Lord Protector of similar stamp, but there wasn't one available. The Cromwellian military leaders in England and Scotland concluded that there was no alternative to a restoration of the monarchy. They invited Charles II to return from his French exile. In Ireland Broghill and Coote, agile analysts of self-interest, conformed to the pattern by having Charles proclaimed king in Dublin on 14 May.

It was an opportunist move that carried significant implications for the future. The traditionally royalist elements in Irish society, those who had fought in the convoluted struggles of the 1640s, played no part in the return of the king to his throne. They were unable to, because like the king, they were forcibly excluded from their country. They were owed a debt of gratitude for past services, but the past services had not achieved the result now delivered by reconstructed Cromwellians. If opportunities for the practical expression of gratitude were in any way circumscribed, the king would have to choose his priorities. He began by creating Broghill Earl of Orrery, Coote Earl of Mountrath, and appointing both of them Lord Justices.

CHAPTER SIX

Legislative compromises are guaranteed to make at least some people unhappy, particularly when they are concerned with the distribution of land which, in a small island with no mineral resources and no manufacturing industry, represents power and wealth. The Act of Settlement of 1660 made a great many people very unhappy.

The returned Irish Royalist Protestants, Catholic Old English and Gaelic Irish assumed reasonably enough that the new king would speedily restore to them the property which, by fighting for the monarchy, they had lost to the people who murdered his father. The New English, exalted by God, making frequent references to the Right of Conquest, and satisfied beyond doubt that they had redeemed Ireland from a swamp of popish idolatry, saw no reason to hand back the prizes of their fight for righteousness. The government's solution to the conundrum of how to take a quart from a pint pot, shake it out and pour it all back again, was first to proclaim that all land was at the crown's disposal and then to resort to the application of legalistic formulae, some highly questionable.

Thus the Adventurers' Act passed by the parliament of Charles I was held to be valid, but the endorsement of it by Cromwell's parliament was not. The Catholic Irish who had been under arms between 1641 and 1646 were told that although they had been insistent in pledging their loyalty, and in the latter stages had actually fought for the crown, the technical position remained that they had been rebels.

By these and similar devices, a modified unscrambling was effected. It was of uneven application. Lords Inchiquin and Antrim, sixteen other peers, and a fair number of the larger proprietors got back nearly everything. Some of the Catholic owners deported across the Shannon got partial restitution. Some got none, and stayed in their new possessions in Connacht. Others, even more unlucky, were caught in the comprehensive definition of 'Rebellion' and therefore had nothing at all.

The return of land to Catholics, even on a partial scale, provoked bitter resentment among the New English. The Down Survey had computed that in 1641, before the outbreak of the Rebellion, six and a half million acres or sixty-one per cent of Irish land had been in Catholic hands. More than one and a half million acres had been classified as unprofitable, but unprofitable land was still a symbol of influence and much of it was scenically beautiful and teeming with game. The new king's evident wish to be as fair as possible to both his Catholic and Protestant subjects did not recommend itself to those who believed that pagans who lived by the sword should perish by the sword. The New English were determined that nothing like sixty-one per cent of the land would find its way back to its old owners. They were unable to prevent a considerable amount getting back, but they could hamper and delay and generally frustrate, and they did so.

Ormonde, who had by now been made a duke, once again became Lord Lieutenant in 1662. He was more than a match for the New English. With one important aberration, he saw to it that findings of the recently established Court of Claims were implemented. The court had ruled that the Cromwellian settlers must surrender to Catholics one-third of the lands held by the settlers in May 1659. The aberration was due to Ormonde's personal experience and family antecedents.

The Butlers were the greatest of the Norman-Irish families. For centuries they had given loyal and outstanding service to the crown. During those centuries the constant threat to all that the Butlers stood for had come from the Gaelic Irish. Ormonde now exerted himself to ensure that Norman and Old English families received their entitlements under the Court of Claims ruling, but he was less

98

energetic on behalf of his ancient enemies. For two of them, Lord Antrim and Lord Clancarty, whom he held in special regard, he did what was necessary. For the rest he was half-hearted.

The Protestants were able to compensate for the forced compromise over land ownership by making the Irish parliament entirely their own. The introduction of the Oath of Supremacy, untakeable by any conscientious Catholic, left the legislature, such as it was – its law-making powers were restricted, although it could bring great influence to bear – in the hands of a group mostly of English birth and upbringing, the majority of whom had lived in Ireland for less than fifteen years. Ormonde dealt with them skilfully, and on the whole was successful in keeping an equitable balance between diametrically opposed interests. In one sense he became a protector of the Catholic position. This was helpful, and indeed essential for Catholic survival, but the inability to take part in a forum in which grievances could be aired and matters of significance to them discussed was a handicap which greatly disturbed the Catholic leaders. They were reliant less upon clearly stated and enforceable rights than upon royal patronage, vice-regally applied. Royal policies and attitudes could change because of the need to counter external initiatives that had nothing to do with Ireland. They could also change by whim. It was a worrying and unsatisfactory basis upon which to exist.

Although it was to be a further thirty years before the Anglo-Irish Protestant Ascendancy shifted from a position of powerful influence to one of total domination, the beginning of an outstanding part of their legacy to modern Ireland dates from those Restoration days when Ormonde was the Lord Lieutenant of King Charles II. The credit is largely Ormonde's. During his years of exile in France he had been hugely impressed by the architectural elegance of Paris. Buildings of distinction, he considered, were a visible reflection of a civilized prosperity that derived from peace. If a capital city were to perform its true function effectively, it must make itself the focus of national attention by looking like a capital city. Dublin in the 1660s was a run-down walled town with a nondescript castle, two cathedrals in severe disrepair, some decrepit towers set at intervals on the equally decrepit walls, a jumble of mean houses (some abandoned) within the walls, and a shapeless spread of cabins outside them. There were a few, very few, Elizabethan larger houses near the castle. Trinity College, and not much of it, was a quarter of a mile away. The population was about 9,000.

Ormonde alone could not redesign the city, but he could instigate, encourage, suggest, co-operate and set an example. By the end of the decade an imaginative and energetic city corporation had marked out broad streets, surveyed building sites, encouraged private building of substantial houses and generally provided the outline of much of today's central Dublin. 'Saint Stephen's Greene . . . that now addeth nothing att all to pleasure or profitt', previously unsightly waste land, twenty-seven acres in extent, was kept intact for the public pleasure, planted and surrounded by eighty-nine house lots. There was a surfeit of applications for these houses, and a ballot was held to determine the successful candidates. Their professions throw a useful light on the activities of contemporary Dublin: merchants, aldermen, butchers, tanners, gentlemen, malt-sters, brewers, cutlers, masons, vintners, tallow-chandlers, bakers, smiths and three knights. With the possible, but unlikely, exception of a knight or two, they would all have been Protestants of English origin. The Gaelic Irish had never had any towns of their own and were not much interested in anyone else's, although in this period there is the first record of a tentative settlement of some of them in the revivified Dublin.

It was also an expanding Dublin. From the 9,000 who inhabited it at the time of the Restoration in 1658, it grew to a population of 58,000 by 1681. The spread was to both sides of the River Liffey, which for centuries had been spanned by a single bridge. There were soon four, two of them built amid heated controversy between rival commercial interests. It was a robustly conducted argument that included allegations of intimidation, charges of corrupt conspiracy in the judiciary, and the spreading of malicious rumours about the personal insolvency of the builder. These were so persuasive that the captains of merchant ships owned by the builder set sail with their cargoes in order to safeguard their financial positions. He was finally imprisoned after improper influence had been brought to bear on the government.

The co-ordinators of this spirited opposition to the easing of traffic across the river were pleasingly frank about their motives.

Development on the north side would have an adverse effect on trade on the south side. Besides, they added on a damning note, the man had been administering oaths in a form acceptable to Catholics.

The builder, who completed his bridges despite all these incivilities, was Sir Humphrey Jervis, twice Lord Mayor of Dublin. He was the first in a notable line of what in his day were known as improvers, the precursors of private enterprise property developers.

A personal suggestion of Ormonde's was responsible for the introduction of the riverside quays that still flank the Liffey. Jervis showed Ormonde the plans of a development he intended to build on the north bank. As planned, the houses would back on to the river. Ormonde, doubtless with memories of Paris, suggested that the houses should be turned around and that a paved road should be placed in between their fronts and the river bank. Jervis agreed, and named this innovation Ormonde Quay. It is still there.[1] So is Jervis Street.

Ormonde's most cherished gift to Dublin, although few who make use of it are probably aware of his involvement in it, is the Phoenix Park. It lies to the west of the city. When Ormonde returned to Dublin at the Restoration there was a Vice-Regal Lodge in what was then open country. The lodge was named The Phoenix, and the land had formerly belonged to the Knights Hospitallers, who had had a major house at Kilmainham. Ormonde lived in the lodge for a few years, and while there he looked at plans for a new wing. The amateur architect who drew up the plans was Lord Orrery, formerly Broghill, the parliamentary commander whom Ormonde would doubtless have hanged had he been able to lay hands upon him a few years previously. But Ormonde was now Lord Lieutenant, Orrery was one of the leaders of the Protestant interest in Ireland, bygones had become bygones, and in a versatile community it probably occurred to neither of them that there was anything strange about a leading Anglo-Irish magnate including architecture among his attainments.

Ormonde began to lose interest in the lodge, but he developed a grand design for the land surrounding it. The king accepted, and provided money for, Ormonde's recommendation that the existing

---

[1] In the 1980s the quays along the north side of the Liffey look as if they have suffered prolonged shelling by heavy artillery. This is a false deduction. They are uncared for.

demesne should be expanded by the purchase of adjacent land, an arrangement greatly to the liking of the Chancellor, Sir Maurice Eustace, who owned it and sold at a handsome profit. A further Eustace instalment followed, and at one time the park covered 2,000 acres. It was diminished by about 250 acres when the building of the Royal Hospital at Kilmainham began in 1680.[2] The park now covers about 1,750 acres, which is larger than all the major London parks put together.

After planning the acquisition of land, overseeing its transaction, and taking a major role in designing its layout, Ormonde twice performed a service for which the Irish nation should be grateful. He dissuaded the king from giving it away, first to his illegitimate son, the Duke of Monmouth, and second to his mistress, the Duchess of Cleveland. (The Duchess, incensed by this obstructionism, told Ormonde that she hoped to live to see him hanged. Ormonde replied urbanely that he would be content to live to see her grow old.)

Ormonde's term of office was interrupted from 1670 until 1677, when he was reappointed, and lasted until the death of Charles II in 1685. In his later years he was to comment that if he had not been relieved of his appointment during the 1670s, he would have brought about an accommodation between the various parties in Ireland, which if not acceptable in every detail to all, would at least have been tolerable to most. If anyone could have done it, Ormonde was the man. His family had been pre-eminent in the affairs of Ireland since the first Butler, the 'bottelier' of King John, landed in the twelfth century. In an age when blood-lines generated respect, his lineage gave him immense prestige. His personal qualities amplified it. He was a man of vast experience, who had suffered relatively im-poverished exile as well as enjoying the comforts brought by wealth and position.

The only Protestant in a Catholic family to which he was tied by a deep affection, Ormonde's natural tolerance was strengthened by an intimate knowledge of Catholic attitudes and practices and by an awareness of what intolerance could do to people he loved. He had a high intelligence, enormous common sense, and was morally and physically fearless. He straddled the gulf between the old Norman-

---

[2] The Royal Hospital was refurbished in the early 1980s and is one of the finest Anglo-Irish buildings still extant.

Irish· aristocracy and the new Elizabethan and Cromwellian parvenus. He was not without his prejudices (*vide* his views on the return of lands to the Gaelic Irish), and was on occasion forced to trim his sails with unsavoury consequences, as was to happen during the 'Popish Plot'. But his vision of a peaceful, prosperous, tolerant Ireland went far beyond anything held by his contemporaries, Protestant or Catholic. If only a few of the influential new Protestant Anglo-Irish had absorbed the lesson that he patiently demonstrated to them, the history of the ensuing centuries, with its short-sighted selfishness and the consequent consolidation of hatreds, could have been very different. The lesson was not absorbed.

Cromwell's sweeping ways with religions of which he disapproved were negated at the time of the Restoration by the reinstatement of the Anglican Church as the official faith in both England and Ireland. The ceremonial manifestation of this event in Ireland was the consecration in St Patrick's Cathedral in Dublin on a single day in January 1661 of two archbishops and ten bishops.

This mass clearance of the episcopal promotion block was followed by the imposition, some of it adapted from Cromwellian practice, of legislation designed to ensure that subscribers to the official religion would receive temporal as well as spiritual consolation. The burgesses expelled from the Old English towns remained expelled unless they took the Oath of Allegiance, which presented no difficulty, and the Oath of Supremacy, which did. The corporations, and commerce, thus stayed firmly in Protestant hands.

An amelioration was introduced in the 1670s during the Lord Lieutenancy of Lord Essex. The Oath of Supremacy requirement for house purchase in towns was dropped. Catholics could buy after taking an oath of allegiance. The electorate who selected the mayors and sheriffs was still confined to the aldermen, as had been traditional, and mayors, officers, members of guilds, and so on had in general to take the Oath of Supremacy. But the Viceroy was given discretionary power to permit the admission of Catholics provided that along with the Oath of Allegiance they took another repudiating the papal 'power' to depose monarchs. It was a gesture that was given a conditional welcome by the Catholics, and another example of their dependence upon royal patronage, which could be capricious, instead of upon entrenched legal right. In the event trade and commerce remained effectively a Protestant monopoly.

The ownership of land carried an emotional and social significance that transcended simple economics, but its economics alone were of vital importance to the preservation of the (sharply modified) Catholic position. By 1670 most of the redistribution had been completed. Sir William Petty, still producing his surveys, estimated that of a total of twelve million profitable acres, Cromwellian settlers held four and a half; Elizabethan settlers, together with Norman-Irish and Gaelic Irish converts to Protestantism, held four million; Catholics held three and a half million. Petty's population figures, suspect because no attempt at an accurate census had yet been made in Ireland, but probably roughly accurate, put the total number of Catholics at 800,000 and Protestants at 500,000. The majority of the Protestants were Ulster settlers, now heavily reinforced by further contingents of immigrants from the Scottish Lowlands and from England.

By any reading of the statistics the number of Catholic landowners was badly under-representative of the proportion of Catholics in Ireland. But it should be remembered that the matter at issue was not the allocation of land to independent farmers and smallholders cultivating modest acreages. It was an unashamedly capitalist and patrician age in which on both sides of the religious division proprietors privileged by birth, or in the Cromwellian case by the chance to exploit a favourable situation, owned holdings of thousands of acres that were worked by a dependent peasantry.

Already, in most of the Cromwellian estates, an arbitrary system of land tenure had been introduced that was to bedevil the relationship between Anglo-Irish landlords and their tenants almost until the twentieth century. In Gaelic Irish tradition, land had been shared tribal property. The Gaelic Irish chiefs had in Tudor times unilaterally and wrongly surrendered this right in exchange for English titles, but in practice their descendants administered their lands much as before.

The Old English lords were inheritors of the Norman feudal system, refined and modified down the centuries. It was heavily weighted in favour of the proprietors, but it embodied an intricate code of mutual obligation that ensured that all but the most unscrupulous landowners took a paternalistic interest in the well-being of their employees.

The Cromwellian planters were also inheritors of a feudal philosophy. But in England feudalism had evolved on more sophisticated lines than it had among the Old English in Ireland, and the Cromwellians applied the proprietorial rights of the concept without accepting its responsibilities. The people who worked for them were not the subordinate representatives of the same race whose ancestors had supported *their* ancestors through generations of warlike tribulation and peaceful cultivation. They were alien in origin, custom, speech and religion. They had deservedly been defeated in battle. Unless they were rigorously kept under control their latent potential for troublemaking would soon reassert itself. They could be employed usefully in menial work, but when they were no longer fit for it, or if their performance was unsatisfactory, they had to go. Where they went was their business, not the landlord's. In legal parlance they were tenants at will, the will being that of the landowner. He could evict his tenants and their families, to certain penury and probable starvation, whenever he chose.

An argument which greatly affected Irish interests and which for once had nothing to do with religious differences first came to the surface in 1666. It arose from a measure passed by the English parliament with the innocuous-sounding title of 'The Irish Cattle Bill'. It was far from innocuous. It was the first in a series of self-centred measures to protect English domestic profits, in this instance agricultural, from the ravages of cheaper outside competition: Irish cattle were banned from the English market. Beef, mutton and dairy products, also included in the ban, provided much of the wealth of Ireland. Angry complaints from Protestant cattle breeders, who had most to lose and who regarded this form of protectionism as the gross betrayal of a dedicated group of patriots who were safeguarding England from foreign interference, were indifferently received at Westminster.

A further strain was placed on Protestant Irish tempers, affections and pockets by the extension, in 1670, of the English Navigation Acts. In effect this meant that Irish trade to and from English colonies could only be conducted through England, with the goods carried in English ships. Further Acts, all intended to enhance English wealth at the expense of English overseas possessions, were

105

passed at intervals throughout most of the following century.

In the short term the English undoubtedly became richer. In the longer term the policy was responsible for the loss of the American colonies and for the engenderment among the Anglo-Irish of a bitterness immortalized by Swift, who commented scathingly on a people who 'with the spirit of shopkeepers framed laws for the administration of kingdoms'. Centuries later, the more intractable Irish Protestant Loyalists looked back at these measures and bemoaned the failure of their forebears to interpret them as portents of the treacherous creation of the Irish Free State in 1922.

Catholic uneasiness about their enforced reliance upon royal patronage developed into real alarm when the 'Popish Plot' was unveiled in England in 1678. The plot was the fabrication of an ambitious perjurer, Titus Oates, who combined an urge to acquire fame and money with a total absence of scruple. There was no shortage of credulous believers in his stories, which supplied in elaborate detail evidence of what the believers wanted to believe and what they had suspected all along. Anti-Popish hysteria grew rapidly in London to the point where it could be assuaged only by an official shedding of Popish blood. It was.

The tide of the agitation flowed, unsurprisingly, to Ireland and led to the arrest of the Catholic Primate, Archbishop Oliver Plunkett of Armagh. Archbishop Plunkett was from one of the most distinguished Old English Pale families. He was a kinsman of Lord Fingall and of Lord Dunsany, and by background, temperament and outlook a committed supporter of the crown. He was taken to England, tried on spurious evidence and executed.[3] Over-excitement in official circles in London caused Ormonde to be sent instructions to take further action against Catholics – banish the clergy, disarm the laity – but Titus Oates was exposed as a malicious charlatan, the hysterics abated and Ormonde with much relief was able to resume his policy of 'connived toleration'.

Meanwhile, some threats to the peace came from the Protestants. Discontented settlers who had seen their new possessions reduced in size by the Court of Claims were given to

[3] In the 1970s Oliver Plunkett was canonized.

106

pledging the use of arms to remedy their grievances. Most restricted themselves to words, but one enterprising extremist, Colonel Thomas Blood, devised a plan to kidnap the Lord Lieutenant, capture Dublin Castle and organize a Protestant rising.

These objectives, which were to be achieved simultaneously, could not be met single-handed, but Blood's potential field for recruitment was limited, and some of the recruits he did enlist were too talkative. Ormonde soon became a keen follower at second hand of the progress of Blood's planning conferences. But Blood himself had sources of information inside the castle, and brought forward the timing of his operation by four days. Ormonde got to hear of it and prepared his counter-move, Blood got to hear that Ormonde had got to hear, and the conspiracy was dissolved at speed. Some understrappers among the assault team were captured, but Blood was not with them.

He was riding northwards. In Ulster he persuaded some Presbyterians that he was a Presbyterian, and later some Catholics that he was a Catholic priest. Both groups looked after him hospitably. A move to Scotland landed him in the middle of a minor outbreak of insurgency, to which he lent a hand, before travelling to England, where for a time he earned his keep by rescuing prisoners from the condemned cells of Yorkshire gaols for a fee. Later, he professed himself to be a Quaker and was comfortably maintained by the Society of Friends. During this quiet interlude he turned his thoughts once more to the Duke of Ormonde.

This time Blood decided to assassinate Ormonde in a memorable manner. The most memorable manner that he could think of was a public hanging. Since Qrmonde was now living in London (in between his two periods of office as Lord Lieutenant) the best place to hang him was at Tyburn tree.

The first phase of this scheme went very well. Ormonde, returning in his carriage from a dinner in St James's Street, was waylaid, bundled out of the carriage, tied back-to-back to one of Blood's followers, mounted on a horse and, facing backwards, galloped pillion towards Tyburn. But the preliminaries were noisy, and attracted a certain amount of public attention. Blood failed to notice this. As soon as Ormonde was tied and mounted, Blood rode on ahead to put the rope in place. This took careful work. The victim had still not arrived when the rope was ready, so Blood galloped back to investigate the reason for the delay. He came across a struggle in a roadside gutter. Ormonde had thrown his rider, and the two of them, still roped back-to-back, were conducting a curious trial of strength. Crowds were beginning to close in. Blood cut his losses, tried to shoot Ormonde, missed, and decided that it was time to leave, which he did.

Blood's next project, the stealing of the Crown Jewels from the Tower of London, was partially successful. He made off with the crown and the orb, but was then caught. He talked so persuasively at his trial that the royal pardon that he was aiming at was supplemented by the return to him of his estates in County Clare, the reduction of which had started the whole progression.

In some ways Blood was ahead of his time. His raffish, exuberant, ruthless amorality was more characteristic of the Anglo-Irish bucks of the latter half of the eighteenth century than it was of his own puritanical contemporaries. But a start has to be made somewhere. Blood was a pioneer of sorts.

CHAPTER SEVEN

King Charles II died in February, 1685. He was succeeded by his brother, James II, a Catholic. James was a very autocratic Catholic, lacking in tact and unable to appreciate that the quick achievement of what might seem desirable can sometimes generate disastrous consequences. Whereas his brother Charles had stepped delicately, taking here, giving there, always looking several moves ahead, James looked a short move ahead and then trampled all over the board.

Understandably, as a Catholic his prime preoccupation was with the lifting of the restrictions imposed upon his Catholic subjects in England, Scotland and Ireland. Regardless of how he proceeded, James was bound to meet much grumbling and some actively fierce opposition. But in England and Scotland the number of remaining Catholics was so small, and their loyalty to the crown so manifest, that the problem could have been dealt with relatively unobtrusively, perhaps by starting with an extension of Ormonde's 'condoned tolerance' and progressing carefully to the removal of the obstacles one by one. James had no time for this type of subtlety. He set about dismantling the whole apparatus in the shortest possible time. English Protestant opinion moved steadily from irritation to anger, to outrage and finally to thoughts of whether it would be constitutionally and practically possible to find a replacement king more amenable to the outlook of the great majority of the people. The English Catholics themselves thought that James was moving too far, too fast, too soon.

In Ireland, with its predominantly Catholic population, the situation was radically different. A statesman of the stature of Ormonde might have steered his way through the resentments, prejudices and calls for the protection of privileges, but Ormonde's term of office had lapsed automatically with the death of Charles, and he himself was back in England. His successor, Clarendon, was a Protestant, but he was also the royal brother-in-law and disposed to do what he was told. An appointment that was of greater significance went to Colonel Richard Talbot, who was promoted to Lieutenant General and given command of the army in Ireland. Talbot was from an Old English family who for centuries had owned lands at Malahide, to the north of Dublin. He had soldiered with the French, had been with James during his exile in Cromwellian times, and had represented Irish Catholic interests in London. He was a No-Half-Measures man who knew what he wanted to do and did it. Like many another of his kind he won a metaphorical battle and lost an actual war.

Talbot saw Ireland in simple terms. It was a Catholic kingdom that had fallen upon misfortune. Fortune had now put matters right by providing a Catholic king. Logical corollaries of a Catholic king were a Catholic aristocracy restored to its powers and property, and a Catholic parliament to pass suitable laws for a Catholic people. Protestants might at present own most of the land and conduct nearly all the trade, but these were secondary considerations. They could be dealt with as the occasion arose.

Talbot, now created Earl of Tyrconnel (Red Hugh O'Donnell doubtless turned in his grave: Talbot was on the whole contemptuous of the Gaelic Irish), began with the creation of a Catholic standing army to replace the existing Protestant militia. This force, he explained to the king, would be at the royal disposal to counter any threat to the regime in any of the three kingdoms. The offer was never put to the test, but in the meantime the army's Catholic officers, whose names read like a last roll call of Gaelic Irish, Norman and Old English leadership, trained and deployed their troops, and with the crucial exceptions of Derry and Enniskillen in the north, occupied the major garrison towns.

The king's instructions to Clarendon were explicit. Catholics were to be appointed to the Council, to the judiciary and to the

110

corporations. They were to be made sheriffs of counties. Clarendon, with developing unease, was faithful to his remit. The judiciary was recast so that two-thirds of the judges were Catholics. So were thirty-one of the thirty-two county sheriffs. Constant urgings by Tyrconnel for the introduction of legislation for the repossession of Protestant-held lands by their original Catholic owners finally broke Clarendon's loyalty, and he resigned.

His resignation was also influenced by an external factor. In 1685, King Louis of France revoked the Edict of Nantes, which had guaranteed toleration for French Protestants. Huguenot refugees, many of whom later made a distinctive contribution to Anglo-Ireland, were arriving in England in large numbers. English anti-Catholic feeling was as a result running high.

The king, impervious to English public opinion, replaced Clarendon as Lord Lieutenant by Tyrconnel. The appointment coincided with a royal decision to hasten the emancipation of English Catholics by exercising the king's prerogative and ignoring existing constitutional machinery. Protestant opposition in both England and Ireland hardened.

It became harder still with the 1687 Declaration of Indulgence, which did away with many Catholic disabilities in both England and Ireland, and hard as a rock when the remaining ones were disposed of by a second Declaration in April 1688. This provoked a clerical mutiny by English Anglican bishops, whom James duly brought to trial.

The English decided that what they needed was a king more in sympathy with the national ethos. A suitably qualified candidate was found to be immediately available in the person of William of Orange, a Dutch monarch of French Huguenot extraction who was married to James's daughter Mary, and who was at the time the leading spirit in the League of Augsburg, a continental alliance engaged in a complicated war against King Louis of France. An invitation from the leaders of the Tory and Whig parties was passed discreetly to William. On 5 November 1688, he landed at Torbay in the south of England. There was no English opposition to his arrival. There was some in Scotland, but it was defeated at Killiecrankie. Ireland was left in the curious position of being the only one of the three kingdoms to retain loyalty to a legitimate monarch who had been superseded by a rival selected through an innovatory, if crude, application of the English democratic process.

James himself left for France. Several thousand Irish Protestants left for England. Tyrconnel, ignoring some prudent advice from Keating, the Catholic Chief Justice, about discussing terms from a position of strength with the new *de facto* king, stayed staunchly with the old *de jure* one. In the north, Protestant settlers seized the two unsecured towns of Derry and Enniskillen, in the former case after the Protestant governor had decided to surrender it to the Jacobites but was prevented from doing so by the Apprentice Boys, a display of resolution still commemorated annually by Northern Irish Protestants. Derry was under siege from the middle of April until the end of July. The half-starved garrison's courage and endurance is another evocative memory in the Ulster Protestant folklore.

In March 1689, King James was brought to Ireland by a French naval squadron. With him was French money, ammunition and some French officers. They landed at Kinsale, where Gaelic Irish hopes had floundered with the defeat of O'Neill by Mountjoy more than eighty years before.

James formally accepted Tyrconnel's pledge of the Irish army to his cause, and in May convened in Dublin a meeting of the Irish Estates. It was the last legislative assembly of representatives of the Gaelic Irish and Old English Catholics to meet until the independence of the Irish Free State in 1922. Famous names from past history, many of them destined to be the last of their line, were there. The Earls of Clancarty (MacCarthy), Clanrickard (Burke) and Antrim (MacDonnell); the Viscounts Roche of Fermoy, O'Dempsey of Clanmalier, Magennis of Iveagh, Mountcashel (Justin MacCarthy), Clare (Donal O'Brien); the Barons Plunkett, Fitzmaurice, Fleming, Bermingham and an array of Butlers and Burkes.

Their proceedings were not characterized by moderation. They had suffered much in recent years and they set about the correction of their wrongs with an uninhibited zest that even James found too much. They repealed the Act of Settlement, which had covered the redistribution of land after the Restoration, in a blanket measure that took no account of the rights of later purchasers. They passed an Act of Attainder against 2,400 Protestant landowners, most of whom were by now refugees in England. Under the Act their lands were vested in the crown until the former owners had appeared in

112

person to establish their loyalty. A time limit, incapable of being met by most of the absentees, was attached to this provision. If the time limit were not met the land would be forfeit.

This sort of vengefulness was an understandable and human reaction to past wrongs, and it doubtless brought much emotional satisfaction, but it was irrelevant and harmfully provocative. Irrelevant because it was more suited to victors defining the fruits of victory than to participants in fighting that had hardly started. Harmful because there were still Protestants, some present at the assembly, who were troubled by doubts about transferring their allegiance from one king to another, but who would clearly make their minds up now that they had evidence of what would be in store for them if the Catholics won. There was also the matter of reprisals if the Catholics lost. The losing would not necessarily be determined by events in Ireland. To patriotic orators at the assembly the issue might seem to be the uncomplicated one of fighting it out on Irish soil, but in practice the Irish campaign ahead was a tiny component of a complex struggle between alliances of major European powers who would ruthlessly exploit or abandon Ireland according to their wider interests.

In the North the earlier desultory fighting began to intensify. The Protestant defenders of Derry were relieved on 1 August. A force of locally raised Protestant levies, led by Colonel Wolesley, beat Mount-cashel at Newtown Butler in South Fermanagh, and the Jacobites besieging Enniskillen had to abandon it. Marshal Schomberg, the Williamite commander designated for Ireland, brought ashore an army of 20,000 men at Bangor. The Jacobites withdrew from most of Ulster, took up defensive positions along the River Fane north of Dundalk, and stayed there for the winter, faced by Schomberg. It was an uneventful winter. The weather precluded serious operations.

In the spring of 1690 King Louis completed a transaction unusual in the history of military affairs. His European commitments had left him hard-pressed for men, and he was reluctant to diminish his strength by sending troops to Ireland. The solution eventually agreed upon was that he would send a force of 7,000 professionals to Ireland, to be replaced by 5,000 Irishmen brought back to France in the same transports. Mountcashel commanded this exchange contingent. They saw no further fighting in Ireland, but were embodied *en masse* into the French army, in which they contributed handsomely to the already high reputation of the Irish Brigade.

King William landed at Carrickfergus on 14 June. He joined Schomberg and advanced towards the River Boyne. The Jacobites, now joined by James, fell back slowly to the south bank of the river. The fate of Ireland for the next century and a half, and the fate of the northern part until the present day, was determined at the Boyne. Ireland's position as a junior partner, or puppet, in the international machinations of the great European fight between Louis XIV of France and the League of Augsburg (whose shifting, but relatively constant composition included Holland, many of the German States, Austria, Spain, Denmark and the Vatican) is illustrated by a summary of who did the determining.

The Williamite army was about 35,000 strong. William, a Dutch prince who spoke hesitant English, was the most prominent Augsburg leader. His objective was to tidy up Ireland as quickly as possible and return to his continental responsibilities. He directed his operations in Ireland, and took personal charge of the army when necessary, but its actual commander was the aged Duke of Schomberg, a German who had previously served in the armies of Louis and, later, of the Elector of Brandenburg. Schomberg's son, Meinhard, was the Williamite General of Horse. Another German, the Duke of Würtemberg-Neustadt, commanded a division of 7,000 Danes. William's chief military adviser was Baron Ginkel of Utrecht, and his chief political adviser Hans Willem Bentinck, another Dutchman. The Count of Solms-Braunfels and Count Henry Nassau were also Williamite commanders.

The order of battle was made up of Dutch, Danes, Germans, Swiss, Italians, Poles, Norwegians, Huguenots, English and Irish Protestants. The English were a minority of the force, but they were significant. They fought hard, had a personal interest in the outcome, which if it went wrong would affect England, and some of them afterwards stayed in Ireland and left their mark on future events. Irish Protestants, in no great number, were scattered about the force as volunteers. Their one formed body was the Enniskillen irregular cavalry of Colonel Wolesley, a formidably effective and ferocious group of independently minded rough-riders, who made a major contribution to the success of the Williamites in the battle.

114

Both·they and their commander were the forerunners of a distinguishing strand in the Anglo-Irish tie with England in the years ahead, the provision of soldiers of talent to the British army. The successors to the Enniskilleners became the Inniskilling Dragoons whose service at Waterloo and with the Heavy Brigade at Balaclava went into British military legend. Wolesley's descendant at several generations remove was Sir Garnet Wolesley, one of the most successful, and certainly the most constructively reforming, of the Victorian generals.

On the Jacobite side of the line the national composition was less heterogeneous, but heterogeneous enough. There were about 25,000 men in all, most of them Irish, but including Englishmen loyal to James, some Germans and Dutchmen, a French infantry division 6,000 strong that included two battalions of Swiss and Germans, three further French regiments from the body that had exchanged with Mountcashel, and a regiment of Walloons. The French had no intention of allowing the importance of their contribution to be undervalued. The Count de Lauzun, the French divisional commander, was appointed by Louis XIV as James's military adviser, an intervention unwelcome to Tyrconnel.

The battle lasted for most of the daylight hours of 1 July 1690.[1] The Williamites were superior in numbers, experience, artillery and generalship. They got across the river at several places, out-manoeuvred the Jacobite infantry, many of whom were untrained recruits armed with scythes, withstood a fierce charge by the Irish cavalry in which Schomberg was killed, and by the evening were in full possession of the south bank, some of them skirmishing with the rearguard of the Jacobite retreat towards Dublin.

James was among the first to withdraw. With a small personal staff and an escort of two hundred exhausted Irish cavalrymen he arrived in Dublin at about ten o'clock at night. He had been advised by Lauzun to leave Ireland at once for France. James discussed this recommendation, inconclusively, with the few privy councillors still available in Dublin. On the following day a message from Tyrconnel urged him to take Lauzun's advice. The army was taking up

---

[1] The Gregorian Calendar subsequently adjusted the date to 12 July, upon which it is still celebrated in Northern Ireland with a procession led by fifes and drums, and banners depicting King Billy crossing the Boyne astride a white horse.

positions north of Dublin, which was temporarily secure, but Tyrconnel's intention was to abandon Leinster and to march to the west. Dublin would then fall.

That evening James, accompanied by one of his illegitimate sons (another, the Duke of Berwick, later to be a famous figure in the continental Irish Brigade, was commanding the defences north of Dublin) and escorted by a hundred-strong party of the Horse Guards, rode fast for the south. With intervals for rest he went through Bray, Wicklow town, Enniscorthy and on to Duncannon, which he reached on 3 July. A French privateer picked him up in the evening and on his orders put into Kinsale, where he had landed a year earlier. At Kinsale he wrote his last instructions to Tyrconnel. Tyrconnel was confirmed in his appointments as Viceroy and Commander-in-Chief. He was given discretion to continue the fight or to negotiate terms with William as he thought best. James also sent Tyrconnel the last of his gold coin, a modest sum. On 4 July 1690, King James II embarked on a French frigate that was shepherding a convoy to France, and left Ireland for ever.

James's conduct at the battle, and his removing himself from the scene immediately afterwards, attracted much criticism. Patrick Sarsfield, a resolute and dashing cavalry commander at the Boyne, and later the most prominent Irish leader, remarked after the battle that he only regretted that they were unable to 'change kings and fight it over again'. It was a judgement on James's military skill, and comments about his courage were not long in following. James, during his brief stay in Dublin before he left for Duncannon, embittered by the Irish failure, was reported to have said savagely to Lady Tyrconnel: 'Your countrymen, madam, can run well.' Lady Tyrconnel's response, 'Not so well as your majesty, for I see you have won the race,' was widely enjoyed, but whether the exchange really took place is open to some doubt. But the fact that it went the rounds, and was repeated appreciatively, is symptomatic of a widespread conviction that James tried to use the Irish army to his personal advantage, mishandled it, and ran away.

There is a more prosaic explanation. James, like everyone else at the Boyne with the exception of the Prince of Orange, was being manipulated. Lauzun's insistence that James should leave Ireland immediately owed nothing to his personal concern for James's safety, and everything to the fact that James alive and free was a good card in the hand held by Louis XIV, in his contest with William and the League of Augsburg. A dead or imprisoned James could not provide a focus for Stuart resistance to the new English regime. His heir, his only legitimate son, was an infant. A living James was essential to French plans. He conformed to the wishes of his only powerful backer.

Looked at in strictly military terms, the Boyne was a relatively minor fight, a tactical victory for the Williamites but one that by no means brought the campaign to a conclusive end. There were senior officers on the Jacobite side, including Tyrconnel and Lauzun, who considered that it should not have been fought at all. Far better, went their argument, for a smaller and weaker army to continue to withdraw, destroying crops and livestock as they went, until the Williamites became debilitated by exhaustion, hunger and disease. Dublin was a military irrelevance. Tyrconnel was in favour of abandoning it and leading the Williamites on to the west. Lauzun, with a French disregard for other people's property, recommended razing it to the ground. James overruled both, on the defensible grounds that political objectives are inextricably bound up with military ones, and the loss of Dublin would be widely read as a defeat; furthermore, *pace* Lauzun, he could not authorize the destruction of the largest surviving city in the only part of his realm still under his control.

James's analysis of the psychological importance of Dublin as a political symbol was reinforced by the reaction of his international enemies, or more properly those of Louis, when news of William's victory at the Boyne was passed throughout Europe. What they celebrated was a minor military triumph that they imagined to be more decisive than it was. But their rejoicing made it plain that they regarded the acquisition of the Irish capital as an integral part of the prize. The celebrations in London were considerably muted by an almost simultaneous defeat of the combined English and Dutch fleets off Beachy Head by the French, which rather cancelled matters out, but no such disabilities hamstrung the revels in Austria and Spain. These included the singing of *Te Deums* in Austrian and Spanish cathedrals, a ceremonial Catholic manifestation of thanks-giving that the Irish Protestants among the victors doubtless found as offensive to their convictions as the defeated Irish Catholics found it to theirs. But then both parties had thought that they had been fighting an insular religious civil war with insular religious objectives.

The international guest participation in Ireland continued for some while longer and then began to thin out to meet pressing commitments elsewhere. The Irish army marched to the River Shannon, left in Athlone a garrison under the stalwart leadership of Colonel Richard Grace, and established itself in Limerick. There Tyrconnel separated his civil and military functions by concentrating upon his governmental role and delegating command of the army to Sarsfield, created Earl of Lucan by James. Lauzun was there with his French division and his advice. William, following up, put in an assault on Limerick. It failed, as did every attempt to dislodge Grace from Athlone. William left Ireland shortly afterwards and did not return. Ginkel took over from him. Lauzun, on the orders of Louis, went back to France, taking his division with him. Winter brought an end to serious fighting.

In the late spring of 1691, Marshal St Ruth, a soldier of more effectiveness than Lauzun, was sent by Louis. He brought with him arms, supplies and professional dedication. He raised and trained a new Irish force of 15,000 men. When the campaigning season opened in earnest, Ginkel at last overcame Grace's spirited defenders in Athlone, and forced a passage over the Shannon. St Ruth faced Ginkel at Aughrim. It was a hard-fought battle in which the advantage swung from one side to the other, until St Ruth was killed by a cannon shot. The loss of his inspiration and direction settled the issue. The Irish withdrew in disorder, leaving their dead. Sarsfield rallied split-up remnants and led them to Limerick. Galway and Waterford surrendered to the Williamites, as had Cork and Kinsale, taken the previous year by Colonel John Churchill, later the great Duke of Marlborough. Ginkel followed Sarsfield closely to Limerick and invested it for the second time. Tyrconnel died in August. Sarsfield commanded the defence, held out for a month, saw no prospect and had no news of help from France, and on 3 October 1691, sued for terms.

The terms, embodied in the Treaty of Limerick, were honourable. The subsequent failure to implement important features of them, a defalcation entirely due to the Protestant parliaments of England

and Ireland, was not. The dishonour was the more pointed because of a scrupulous display of integrity by Sarsfield immediately after he had put his name to the treaty. A French fleet sailed up the Shannon estuary with a large French army aboard. With this reinforcement Sarsfield could have overthrown Ginkel. But Sarsfield had given his word, and he kept it. The French ships were used to transport 5,000 of his soldiers to France. A further 2,000 were taken, under truce, on English ships. Another 4,000 followed later, after exercising their right to choose one of three options listed in the military articles of the treaty. About 2,000 picked the second option, of swearing an oath of allegiance to William and going home. About 1,000 picked the third, and enlisted in Ginkel's army.

There were thirteen civil articles in the treaty. Of these, five safeguarded the future status of Irish Catholics, who were to enjoy such privileges 'as they enjoyed under Charles II and as were consistent with the laws of Ireland'. The officers and men 'now in arms under commission of King James', the inhabitants of Limerick or any other garrison in possession of the Irish, and 'all such as are under their protection' in the specified counties of Limerick, Clare, Kerry, Cork, Mayo and, by extended application, Galway, were to keep their former estates and privileges and continue in their professions, provided that they took a simple oath of allegiance to King William and Queen Mary. The clause referring to the oath of allegiance ended with the phrase 'and no other'. Nobody was to be asked to compromise his religious beliefs by taking an oath of supremacy.

Those protected by the treaty retained the right to keep horse and arms sufficient for their defence. And it was reiterated in a further article that the oath to be taken was the oath of allegiance and no other. Ginkel demonstrated his own good intentions by saying to Sarsfield that the king would try to limit the number of attainders that inevitably fell upon the losers in a war of this kind, and would get parliament to enact further measures to secure the Catholic position.

That there were those on Ginkel's staff who did not share his generosity of spirit became evident when the king's copy of the treaty was presented to him for signature. The clause about 'all such as are under their protection' had been left out. William put it back again, in his own handwriting, and signed. There can be no doubt that he, and Ginkel, meant to meet the obligations that they had entered into. Both, however, were Dutch, and unfamiliar with English constitutional practice as it was then developing. Parliament had already demonstrated its power of independent action by contriving the deposing of James and his replacement by William. It now showed its determination to act as it wished by applying its own narrow and vindictive interpretation of the treaty. Had William been an absolute monarch, he would have done much for his Irish Catholic subjects. Instead they were to suffer the most comprehensive subjection in their history because of the operation of the early English democratic system.

The departure for France of Sarsfield and his army, which included among its officers almost the entire hereditary leadership of the Gaelic Irish and of the Old English, left the residual Catholic population almost helpless. They were accustomed to aristocratic direction, and however arbitrary it had been on occasion, it was always applied by families for whom they held a traditional respect, of whose exploits they were proud and whose religion they shared. The people who in the past had defended them and taken up their grievances were now in exile, fighting in foreign armies for foreign causes. The loss to the Catholic community of the concentration of talent, vigour and enterprise in Sarsfield's army was not just the loss of a single group of high quality. It was the cause of a continuing haemorrhage. Soldiers grow old, become invalids. The battle casualties of the Irish Brigade were high. (They included Sarsfield himself, killed at Landen in Holland in 1693.) For generations English governments in Ireland had condoned, sometimes actively encouraged, the enlistment of Irishmen in continental armies. It was a convenient method of exporting potential sources of domestic trouble. For the next hundred years or so, until the leaders of the Irish Brigade found it impossible to conform to the principles of the French Revolution, a steady flow of young and energetic Irishmen went off to the Wild Geese. Their military fame brought Ireland intangible credit. But it was a depletion of a reservoir of ability that could have been put to good use at home.

Another outcome of the Boyne, Aughrim and Limerick was the disappearance from the Irish scene of the Old English community.

The Old English were the original Anglo-Irish. They had kept their distinctive racial identity intact for five centuries. Their law, language, customs and loyalties had been English. Until the strains of trying to reconcile their devotion to the Catholic Church with their allegiance to a succession of Protestant monarchs had forced them to a bitter choice, they had been the instrument of English rule and had consistently fought the Gaelic Irish in the English interest. They had ruled and populated the Pale, which at its most extensive had been not a geographically tiny enclave around Dublin, but an area covering all or some of the present counties of Louth, Meath, Kildare, Dublin, Offaly, Leix and north Wicklow. They had provided the burghers, and kept out the Irish, in the royal charter towns of Kilkenny, Waterford, Cork, Galway and the rest. In the absence of census figures it is impossible to estimate what proportion of the Catholic population they represented in the 1690s, but it would be surprising if it were much less than a third. In the century ahead, in which religious disabilities were shared indiscriminately by all Catholics, the Old English merged in common hardship with the Gaelic Irish. By the time a nostalgic Gaelic nationalism developed in the nineteenth century the two strands of Irish Catholic origins were indistinguishable. If there is a modern Irishman without English blood in his arteries he is a genetic freak. The politician who waxes eloquent about seven hundred years of English oppression may be right, but he is missing what was a central feature of that oppression for five hundred of the seven hundred years. One part of the complainant's ancestry was oppressing the other part.

CHAPTER EIGHT

The decks were now cleared for the unimpeded establishment of an exclusively Protestant Ascendancy in Ireland. Thousands of Protestants returned from their safe havens in England. A parliament was summoned in 1692. There were three hundred members in the Commons and twenty-eight in the Lords, made up of sixteen peers and twelve Anglican bishops. There was no room for conflicting constitutional and religious sentiments. The Irish legislators complied with a preliminary instituted by the Westminster parliament. All members of both houses took an oath of allegiance to the king, made a declaration repudiating the Catholic Mass, transubstantiation and associated papist doctrines, and swore a second oath abjuring the spiritual supremacy of the Pope. Their credentials as a cohesive legislature of a dominant minority thus established, they set about, in a leisurely manner, the rearrangement of the country's affairs. They were in no hurry because speed was unnecessary. The Catholic majority had no voice at all in their discussions, and with its armed men in exile it offered no physical threat.

Aside from an early wrangle with the Westminster parliament about the extent to which Westminster was empowered to interfere in Irish legislation (an argument that was to recur with increasing animosity over the course of the next hundred years), the new Dublin assembly set its sights on two main aims. The first was to consolidate and expand the Protestant ownership of land. The second was to devise means by which the Catholic majority,

122

currently quiescent but potentially dangerous, could be deprived of the resources required to translate endemic discontent into active insurgency. The first aim was met by the formation of a new Court of Claims; the second by the progressive introduction over the next thirty-five years of Penal Laws, part punitive and part restrictive, designed to circumscribe the Catholic capacity for resistance.

The activities of the Court of Claims led to further acrimony with London. The court attainted 4,000 proprietors and declared forfeit 1,100,000 Irish acres. (An Irish acre was just over one and a half times the size of an English acre.) The king kept the promise given on his behalf by Ginkel to Sarsfield, and restored the rights of sixty-five of the larger Catholic owners, thereby reducing the seized area by a quarter. This outraged both the Irish and the English parliaments, who were further upset when William gave grants of huge acreages to two of his Dutch confidants and to his ex-mistress, the Countess of Orkney.

The controversy, and the last large-scale land confiscation in Irish history, was settled in 1700 by the English parliament, which gave its Dutch sovereign another lesson in English constitutional prerogatives. A board set up by a Resumption Bill took over the administration of all confiscated Irish estates, including those of fifty-eight of the sixty-five landowners who had been reinstated by the king, and sold a million acres on the open market. The market was less open than the term usually implies, in that no Catholic was allowed to buy more than two acres. But there was some consolation for some Catholics ('Innocent Papists') in the shape of the return to them of 400,000 acres.

At the beginning of the eighteenth century the Catholic land-holding had diminished to about one-eighth of the total available. In the subsequent four decades it was reduced further. Conversions of proprietors to Protestantism, some doubtlessly from genuine religious conviction, many through a tactical evasion of the disabilities imposed by the Penal Laws, were a significant factor.

The provisions of the Treaty of Limerick had already been broken by the exclusion of Catholics from parliament by means of unacceptable oaths and declarations and by the wholesale sequestration of land. Some of the treaty's articles were honoured, but in the most restrictive sense possible. The few of Sarsfield's soldiers who remained in Ireland, and the civilians listed in the civil articles,

123

were given the minimum privileges to which they were entitled. The 'omitted clause' about 'all such as are under their protection' became a bargaining counter between king and parliament when the treaty came up for ratification by the Dublin assembly. After much haggling the king agreed to take the clause out again if parliament would accept the remainder of the treaty. Parliament did; and the way was clear for it to move ahead with its measures to keep the people thus deprived of protection incapable of organized resistance.

First came a proscription about the carrying of arms. Gentlemen at the time customarily wore a sword for self-defence. Catholics were now forbidden to do so, and were also barred from the ownership of firearms, including those used for wildfowling. Gunsmiths were forbidden to engage Catholic apprentices.

The ban on weapons was supplemented by a restriction upon assembling for offensive, or indeed any other, purposes. No Catholic was permitted to own a horse worth more than five pounds. Education, which might help to perpetuate false beliefs and encourage able children to question their inherited subservience, was attended to by making it an offence for Catholics to run schools in Ireland or to send their children for schooling abroad. And if somehow they overcame these obstacles, by private tuition or learning at home, Catholic children would find themselves unable to take degrees, or to compete for scholarships and fellowships at the only university in Ireland, Trinity College.

A further, codified, instalment in this repressive series came in 1704. Catholics were disqualified from holding the vote, serving in the army, engaging in commerce and practising law. In the matter of land, no Catholic could inherit an estate that had once belonged to a Protestant. Catholics could inherit from other Catholics, but were forbidden to buy land, lend money against mortgages, or take a lease lasting longer than thirty-one years. When a Catholic landowner died, his eldest son was given one year in which to become a Protestant. If he did, he became the owner of the entire estate. If he did not, the estate was split into equal portions between all the sons. In public administration, the need to take the Oath of Supremacy was reinforced, unnecessarily it seems in retrospect, by the formal exclusion of Catholics from offices of state or offices in the corporations. A fifty-pound reward was put on offer for anyone who apprehended a Catholic bishop.

A sinister by-product of all this legislation was the proliferation of paid informers, rewarded by the authorities for furnishing evidence, or allegation, that some land-holder who claimed publicly to be a Protestant was secretly a practising Catholic, or that a disbarred Catholic lawyer had given legal advice illegally, or that someone else had somehow exploited a weakness in the system..

The chief sufferers from this ruthless harassment were, of course, what was left of the Catholic upper and middle classes. The peasantry did not aspire to any of the privileges against which sanctions were being enforced. But they were submerged in a trough of injustices that applied to nearly all of them. Underpaid, appallingly housed, with no legal safeguards against capricious eviction, compelled by the tithe laws to contribute one-tenth of their produce to a church to which they did not belong, sustained by a diet of potatoes and little else, they were probably the most depressed rural class in Europe outside Tsarist Russia.

Looked at three hundred years later, this treatment of a conquered people can only be described as brutish and indefensible. But plenty of contemporary Anglo-Irishmen, who saw themselves as moderate and enlightened, would gladly have offered a robust defence of it. Their case was built upon the recent Catholic record both within Ireland and abroad. There had been the massacres of the Ulster settlers, exaggerated in number possibly, but still massacres in the *genre* of the earlier ones in Munster. Unless the Irish were kept down and unarmed there was no reason to suppose that they would not massacre again. There had been the meeting of the Catholic parliament in Dublin before the Boyne, at which the measures agreed for the disposal of Protestant-held land had been even more extreme than the ones now in force for Catholic-owned land. France, the ally of the Irish Catholics, was currently treating its Huguenots with much more severity than Irish Protestants were treating Irish Catholics. Add all that up, and it seemed apparent to any reasonable person that the only way to deal with the problem was by a policy of repression and of political and professional segregation, strictly enforced.

The parallel is inexact, but there are many resemblances between the society which developed in eighteenth-century Ireland and the *apartheid* regime in twentieth-century South Africa. The rulers felt the same certainties, the same need to take elaborate precautions

125

to guarantee social survival. There was the same phenomenon of two distinct societies living in the same country, communicating with one another only when the master–servant relationship made it necessary, otherwise leading totally separated existences. In one salient respect Ireland was more liberal. Any Catholic who chose to cross the line could do so by becoming a Protestant.

Within its own boundaries there was a flexibility in the Anglo-Irish social organization that distinguished it from the almost immovable structures then prevalent in England and, even more so, in continental Europe. There, power, influence and prestige derived from the hereditary ownership of land and were perpetuated in the hands of a small exclusive aristocratic class by intermarriage. In eighteenth-century Ireland, as elsewhere, land was the key to wealth and power, but few of its owners had much to boast about in the way of ancient lineage. There was a handful of names that had been famous down the centuries and whose present holders had accommodated themselves to the new dispensation. Lord Inchiquin, the descendant of Brian Boru, the current McMorogh Kavanagh, descendant of the kings of Leinster, and a few other representatives of the Gaelic Irish were now Protestant magnates, pledged to loyalty to King William and his successors. So, from the Norman Irish, were the two most distinguished names in Norman-Irish history, the Butlers and the Fitzgeralds. The second Duke of Ormonde had made the change early and had fought as a Williamite officer at the Boyne. The Earls of Kildare had been relatively muted during the commotions of the seventeenth century, but by the beginning of the eighteenth were conforming members of the Anglican Church and loyal subjects of the new monarchy. There were others of Norman-Irish descent who followed their example. But the bulk of the landowning gentry came from families with very tentative roots in Ireland.

It was a little more than a hundred years since the Elizabethan settlers had first put in their appearance. It was not much more than fifty since the arrival of the Cromwellians. The Elizabethan families tended towards a disdain of the Cromwellian latecomers, but in the context of the class prejudices of the times it was an artificial snobbery. The immediate ancestors of both had been adventurers who had helped themselves to what they could get by a combination of the sword and a not always fastidious commercial acumen. The common interests of all the Anglo-Irish lay in their continued monopoly of power in a country in which they numbered a quarter of the population. Since the fraction included the concentration of Protestant settlers in the North, mostly sectarian dissenters of an independent cast of mind and given to a form of trouble-making nearly as pernicious as that of the Catholics, the demographic odds in the South were heavily loaded against the Protestants. Realism dictated that if this minority were to maintain its dominant position it should tap to the full every source of talent available to it.

A result of this thinking was that within the Protestant community there was a high degree of what in modern sociological jargon is called social mobility. The education of a poor boy with brains, determination and a reasonable run of luck, would be encouraged and financed, albeit minimally, by a wealthier patron, landlord or country rector. At Trinity College, modest but adequate sizarships were widely available to cover an ambitious boy's expenses until he had taken his degree. He would then find more patronage helpful, but even without it he was acceptable to the upper reaches of Anglo-Irish society and had access to the employment that it controlled. In the England of the day he would have been sneered at behind his back, or possibly to his face, as a jumped-up *parvenu* with ideas beyond his station. In Ireland he was treated on his merits as a potentially useful contributor to a community which welcomed accretions of initiative and energy.

Many such boys found their way to the professions, politics and commerce. They provided a middle-class stiffening to the new Ascendancy, and in their turn were generous in helping to promote the progress of able boys from other under-endowed families. Some of them, an exceptional few but illustrative of the flexibility of the system, worked their way to the most senior offices in the country.

William Conolly, whose Gaelic surname suggests that he started life as a Catholic, came from a background of which little is recorded except probabilities. He was probably born in Donegal and his father was probably either an innkeeper or a blacksmith. He probably inherited some capital from two old ladies whose interests he had looked after. The certainties begin with his attendance as a member of the Williamite parliament of 1692. He bought land from

127

the Trustees of Forfeited Estates – the 'open market' – became Chief Revenue Commissioner, was the unanimous choice of the House of Commons as Speaker and was a Lord Justice on ten different occasions. He owned land in ten counties. He was a persistent builder of country houses, of which the most durable, Castletown House in County Kildare, still stands as a conspicuous example of Anglo-Irish architectural taste. His income at his prime was about £12,000 a year.

Conolly was unique in the span of his material achievement, but others were not too far behind him. Richard Baldwin, who became Provost of Trinity College, spent his early life as a destitute orphan educated with the help of a charitable fund. Patrick Delaney, who like Conolly sounds as if he came from Catholic stock, was the son of a farmer who subsisted on a few acres. Delaney became Dean of Down, and a prominent figure in the social life of Dublin, a close friend of Swift. Anglo-Irish exclusiveness was not conditioned by prejudices about race or social class. The essential qualification for entry to the club was a professed adherence to the Protestant faith, Anglican branch, without too many questions asked about the fervour with which the faith was practised. The faith itself was enough to establish respectability, synonymous with loyalty.

The administrative machinery at the disposal of the Ascendancy was not as clear-cut or as potent as it wished. It was complicated by a persisting measure, 'Poynings' Law', that dated from the late fifteenth century. At that time the real governors of Ireland had for successive generations been the Fitzgerald Earls of Kildare, confirmed by the monarchy as Lords Deputy. The Kildares had stood on the periphery of the armed dynastic disputes in England between the Yorkists and the Lancastrians, and had prudently hedged their bets until a winner emerged from the confusion. The winner was Henry Tudor, King Henry VII, and he liked neither Kildare's failure to commit himself nor the manner in which he had taken it upon himself to make senior appointments from among the resident Norman Irish and Old English. The offence was compounded by two further aberrations. In the first of these, Kildare had credulously accepted the claim to the throne of a ten-year-old pretender named Lambert Simnel, who was crowned in Dublin as king of England

128

and Ireland. In the second, another youthful claimant, Perkin Warbeck, aged seventeen, was widely acclaimed in Ireland – and in France, Scotland and the Holy Roman Empire – as the true king. Kildare had the sense to treat Warbeck with reserve, but the whole progression was seen by the new king as evidence of Irish unreliability and instability.

He accordingly appointed Sir Edward Poynings as Deputy. Poynings was tough and uncompromising. His instructions were to reduce Ireland to 'whole and perfect obedience', Ireland in this instance being not the unreconciled Gaelic Irish but the likes of Kildare. Kildare himself was locked up in the Tower of London. A set of reforming laws, one of them a ban on the private ownership of artillery, made it clear that the king and nobody else ruled in Ireland. The 'Poynings' Law' which reduced the capacity for initiative of the eighteenth-century Anglo-Irish, until it became obsolete with the Union with Great Britain in 1800, was designed to ensure that an Irish parliament should never act contrary to English interests. Before parliament could be summoned, the king's representative in Ireland had first to submit to the king a list of the legislation that it wanted to pass. If this were found to be acceptable the king and his council, 'after affirming such causes and acts to be good and expedient', issued a licence for parliament to meet.

By the eighteenth century the king's council had effectively become the Westminster parliament. The Irish executive, the Viceroy, the Secretary and the Ministers of State were appointed from London, and were responsible to Westminster. Westminster controlled the army and some of the finance. It was paramount where Irish affairs impinged upon English interests. Only in internal affairs did the Irish parliament have a free hand.

Since Irish affairs frequently impinged upon English interests, and since there were difficulties of definition where the two overlapped, the English ability and willingness to use what in substance was a veto stimulated continuous Irish irritation. The Anglo-Irish, like the American colonists of the same era, found themselves in a classic colonial dilemma. They were emotionally and philosophically attached to the motherland but they were resentful of motherland policies which cost them money.

In North America, after the English finally removed the only serious threat to the English colonies by defeating the French, the colonists were no longer prepared to stand English interference in their internal affairs and revenues, and revolted accordingly. In Ireland, the option was closed. The potential threat was indigenous, from three-quarters of the residents. In any case, geographical ease of access made the ties more intimate. But the feeling began to spread that the link should be preserved through a shared monarch, separately the king of England and the king of Ireland, with Ireland in sole control of its own destinies.

For the Catholic Irish, the eighteenth century was a period in which they were legal nonentities, bereft of elementary rights, punished for their religion, isolated from any say in the development of their own country. For the Anglo-Irish, it was the most constructive and fruitful period of their existence. From 1691 until 1798 there was peace. It was a longer peace than Ireland had ever known. It was accompanied by a growing prosperity, hampered intermittently by English constraints upon trade, but sufficient to produce a surplus that kept the upper levels of society in comfort and encouraged them to begin improving what they found around them. They were elegant improvers.

For the first time ever the houses of country gentlemen could be designed for comfort and appearance, with defensive requirements no longer the overriding consideration. Professional architects were unknown in Ireland during the early part of the century, but to men of imagination and resource their absence was no great handicap. Manuals of practical advice could be sent over from the London bookshops or, later, bought in the Dublin ones. Owners who knew precisely what they wanted prepared sketches, or sought help from more artistically gifted friends and neighbours. In a non-specializing age in which, for example, Royal Navy officers as well as being seamen, navigators and disciplinarians were as often as not botanists, zoologists, rearers of sea-borne livestock and watercolour artists, an Irish landowner was apt to be as versatile as his American colonial cousins. The supervision of the building of a house might be an exceptional call on his talents, but artisans were available, more so in some parts of the country than in others; the materials were to hand; money was adequate; and enthusiasm for the task was consistent and underpinned by a spirit of competitive prestige with

130

other neighbouring landowners similarly engaged.

The results were not of a uniform standard. Few owners could afford the sheer size of Conolly's Castletown or of the Earl of Kildare's Carton. But a remarkable number of the eighteenth-century Big Houses were residences of beauty and graceful proportion. Many of them still stand. Some have suffered the ravages of Victorian modification. Some are ruins, victims of unmeetable maintenance bills or of incineration by vengeful Republicans pointing a lesson in the early 1920s. Of the ones that survive, few are still occupied by the families of the original owners. The incumbents in the 1980s are Catholic religious orders (a nice turn of the wheel) or government departments concerned with agriculture or forestry or in a few cases Arabs with large incomes from Middle Eastern oil and an interest in horses. Hotels and boarding schools are also on the list.

At the same time as the country nobility and squirearchy were putting up their handsome houses, a great and orderly expansion of Dublin was under way. The city that is now the capital of an Irish Republic of which more than ninety per cent of the citizens are Catholic, or were at any rate born to Catholic families, accommodates more than half of the country's people. Dublin's origins and early development were entirely the work of overseas intruders. It was founded and colonized by Norsemen. The Normans turned it into an administrative and military headquarters. The Old English settled and cultivated its hinterland. The Protestant Anglo-Irish of the eighteenth century gave it its unmistakeable architectural elegance and left behind them a superb heritage which, if it does not altogether transcend other memories, certainly earns them an enormous debt of gratitude.

Paradoxically, the reason why so much Anglo-Irish building is still in evidence is that the national impoverishment that followed the departure of rich Anglo-Irishmen to England, after they had been bribed into accepting the Act of Union with Great Britain in 1800, was so great that it was economically unfeasible to knock down what had already been built and replace it with something that would generate a larger cash return. Since the 1960s commercially calculating yahoos have been doing their best to remedy this affront to monetarism. Ugly, angular office blocks, with shiny metallic black or what looks like the colour of dried blood as the favoured

131

colour schemes, have been insinuated into large segments of central Dublin. Graceful old houses have been bought by speculators, partially unroofed, and left to decay to the point where official sanction for their demolition becomes necessary in the interests of public safety, and another horrible utilitarian box can go up in their place. But much of what the Anglo-Irish built so stylishly is still there. A tired traveller could go for a walk around any one of a dozen or so cities in Britain and not know which one he was in. He would have no such difficulty in the unique ambience of Dublin.

Ormonde had begun the process of development at the Restoration of King Charles II but the Williamite War had brought it to a halt. Ormonde's memorials are the Phoenix Park and the Royal Hospital at Kilmainham, built as a home for retired soldiers in the same spirit as, but with more magnificence than, the Chelsea Hospital in London. With the turbulence of centuries now seemingly at an end, and with Ascendancy rule looking as permanent as the peace, the Anglo-Irish devised for themselves a capital that would reflect their status as victors, their confidence in their own future, their wealth and their good taste. The transformation took the best part of a hundred years. It led to a harmonious blend of public buildings of distinction and private houses of elegance, the latter set in broad streets and spacious squares. Its chief designers were four architects – two of them Anglo-Irishmen, one Englishman and one German – who worked independently of each other but in stylistic accord at different times during the century.

The two Anglo-Irishmen, Burgh and Pearce, were the first in the field and were effectively the founding fathers of the Irish architectural profession. Both were of course Protestants, and both were products of a genetic scrambling which was to become almost as common among the Anglo-Irish as it was among the Catholic Irish. Thomas Burgh was one of the many descendants of the Norman de Burgos, the degenerates who had intermarried with the Gaelic Irish and had become Burkes. His father was the Bishop of Ardagh. Edward Lovett Pearce was the grandson of a former Lord Mayor of Dublin. Pearce's mother was a connection of the O'Moores of Leix, which in turn would make him a relative of sorts of Patrick Sarsfield, whose mother was also an O'Moore. For forty years after the accession of King William, Burgh or Pearce had a hand in the design of almost every building of significance in the city, and of some

132

outside it. Pearce's most prominent surviving work, now the Bank of Ireland in College Green, was the home of both houses of the Irish parliament until the Union. A few hundred yards away is the library of Trinity College, Burgh's splendid gift to posterity and one that sadly he did not live to see completed.

In the earlier half of the century the fashionable area to live was north of the River Liffey. Land there was bought in separate parcels by Luke Gardiner, a shrewd and far-sighted banker who subsequently consolidated the parcels and laid out the streets and squares which can be seen today, of which most still have the names given them by Gardiner. Earl Street, Henry Street and Moore Street commemorate Henry Moore, the Earl of Drogheda, from whom Gardiner bought the land they stand on, and Henrietta Street, then the most opulent of all, was named after his daughter.

The existing houses in Drogheda Street all fell into Gardiner's hands, and were levelled to the ground by him. He laid out house lots in their place, widened the street to one hundred and fifty feet by shifting back the house lots on the west side, put in a mall, 'Gardiner's Walk', along the middle, and leased the lots to country gentlemen who in increasing numbers were coming to spend part of the year in Dublin. The street was named Sackville Street and until a few years ago was still referred to as such by conservative-minded members of a diminishing Anglo-Irish community who resented its being renamed after Daniel O'Connell.

Burgh was responsible for the design of many grand new houses on the north side. After his death, continued elegance was assured by the arrival in Dublin of Richard Cassels, a German architect who was first invited to Ireland by Sir Gustavus Hume, to build a family mansion in County Fermanagh beside Lough Erne. Cassels was kept continually busy, mostly with the design of town houses, but partly in the country, as with his modification of the Earl of Kildare's house at Carton. He also designed Lord Powerscourt's house in County Wicklow, which had the loveliest setting of any country house in Ireland. (The house burned down in the 1970s. Its shell, and the lovely setting, remain.)

It was Cassels who provided the plans for Leinster House, the Earl of Kildare's replacement for his previous Dublin establishment, judged inadequate by Kildare's exacting standards. The adequacy of the new establishment may be judged from its later use as the

133

headquarters of the Royal Dublin Society, and its present occupation by both houses of Dail Eireann, the Irish parliament, as well as by the National Library and the National Museum. Leinster House is on the south, then the unfashionable, side of the river. When this was remarked upon to Kildare, he replied with complete and accurate confidence that 'They will follow me wherever I go.'

In the early 1760s work began on the houses in Merrion Square to the rear of Leinster House (although some architectural purists argue that Leinster House is really back to front, which puts Merrion Square in front of it). From that followed, over many years extending into the next century, the complex of fine buildings which takes in Fitzwilliam Square, Baggot Street, Leeson Street, Mount Street and stretches out to Ballsbridge and Donnybrook. For something like one hundred and fifty years this area of roughly three square miles housed the cream of the aristocratic, professional, mercantile, commercial and official classes of Anglo-Ireland. Retired Indian and colonial administrators, army officers, and imperial adventurers returned from their endeavours in distant parts to see out their days among the oligarchy, the bureaucracy, the doctors and lawyers and traders. Most of the names that illuminate the caste lived in this part of Dublin at one time or another. Arthur Wellesley, later Duke of Wellington, spent part of his youth in a house in Merrion Square. So did the young Oscar Wilde, son of Sir William Wilde, an eminent surgeon notoriously deficient in personal hygiene. At a later date and at a maturer personal age William Butler Yeats, poet, had a house in the square, not very far from one previously occupied by a belligerent exotic, Daniel O'Connell, 'The Liberator', champion of Catholic rights and scourge of most that his comfortable neighbours held dear.

Social change, rather than political change, has altered the character of the area. Many of the houses in its outer reaches are still lived in by families. But as in other old cities, high taxes, lower incomes, the unpopularity of domestic service and such matters as the prohibitive cost of heating, have had decisive effects. Offices and flats now predominate.

The last of the great eighteenth-century contributors to the appearance of Dublin was James Gandon, a Londoner born of a Huguenot father and a Welsh mother. He was brought to Ireland in 1781 by John Beresford and Lord Carlow to build a new Customs

House. Its site was the subject of a controversy of much the same origins and intensity as the one about bridges involving Sir Humphrey Jervis a hundred years previously. Entrenched commercial interests stood to lose money unless the Customs House was put up river, where the old one was. Beresford, the Commissioner of Revenue, a powerful man much disliked and mistrusted, wanted it closer to the mouth of the Liffey. Gandon was smuggled in *incognito* to start work on Beresford's chosen site, but since architecture is an art with a large, visible and growing end-product, the secrecy did not survive the preparation of the foundations. There was some harassment from hired mobs, who soon became discouraged, and the work went ahead until its completion as one of the masterpieces of the city framework.

Gandon's other classic, the Four Courts, is also on the north bank of the river but a mile or so farther upstream. The building was badly damaged during the Civil War of 1922, when its garrison of Republican Irregulars was shelled by artillery manned by the soldiers of the Irish Free State army, but it was later restored to its former grandeur. Like the Customs House, it stands today as a tribute to an imported artist of genius.

Burgh, Pearce, Cassels and Gandon were by no means the only designers of buildings in eighteenth-century Dublin. But they were the outstanding ones. Their own work aside, they established the pattern, set the example and influenced their competitors. By the turn of the century Dublin was 'the second city of the Empire', a transplanted replica of contemporary England but with highly individualistic local modifications.

The local modifications were not confined to Anglo-Irish architecture. They ranged right across the political, social and economic spectrum. The Irish destiny was, as the Anglo-Irish saw it, irrevocably linked to that of England, but domestic Irish problems were unique to Ireland and domestic Irish influences moulded, as one generation succeeded another, a distinctive Anglo-Irish character. Part of it was an enormous self-confidence, born of the memory of victory in war, and of pride of achievement, supported by ever-present physical evidence, in peace. There was a conscious feeling of superiority over the vanquished, who were also physically evident, and patently ragged, ignorant and unenterprising. Colonial ruling castes rarely consider the proposition that the defects of the ruled owe at least something to the conditions imposed upon them by their rulers.

In mid-century these conditions were ameliorated when the Viceroy, Lord Chesterfield, lifted the Penal Laws. The immediate reason was tactical, and their lifting partial. Prince Charles Edward Stuart, the grandson of King James II, landed in Scotland in 1745 and raised the Stuart standard once more on British soil. There were fears that he might stimulate a sympathetic rising in Ireland. Chesterfield considered that a placatory gesture towards the Catholics might help to reduce the danger.

There was, in fact, little cause for alarm. Ireland had had enough of the Stuarts at the Boyne and its aftermath, and although most of the peasantry would have joined enthusiastically in support of *any* foreign invasion, preferably French, their objectives would have been social, not dynastic. Anyone who might rid them of their miserable living conditions, their racked rents, their insecurity of tenure and the levying upon them of tithes, could have relied on their support.

To the Catholic upper and middle classes, the easement was a very welcome measure. They could now educate their families openly, practise their religion without fear, enter some of the professions and engage without restriction in trade. Those who met the property qualifications of the franchise could vote. But they could neither sit in parliament nor hold public office. And for those of them with nostalgic dreams of recovering their families' land, there was no comfort.

In spite of these continuing restrictions, the articulate part of the Catholic population showed no sign of disaffection. Their limited objective was to get for themselves and their community as much as they could within the existing system. Irish nationalism, in the sense of united opposition to an external oppressor, was still unheard of and was to remain so until exciting ideas imported from America and France, and developed by thinkers from the oppressors' class, were translated into action in the last two decades of the century.

Protestant self-confidence was not a monopoly of the landed upper classes. It was shared by all in what amounted to a complete and separate Irish Protestant nation with its rich, its poor and its

136

moderately well-off. The Protestant poor were less destitute than the Catholic poor, and their opportunities of moving up the social scale, as Conolly, Baldwin and others did, were enhanced by the fact that commerce was controlled by an increasingly prosperous Protestant middle class. A general feeling of solidarity, analagous to a Free Masonry, held Protestants together. There were, of course, the usual human hates and feuds and disputes within the community, but by and large mutual interests predominated. Protestant employers gave precedence to the employment of Protestant staff, and gave advancement to those who showed promise. Considerations of communal cohesion aside, Protestant workers were looked upon as more reliable and responsible than Catholic ones, and in the main probably were. The Protestant Work Ethic had yet to be defined as such, but its effects were observable. Workers at every level, who had been brought up in a centuries-old tradition of English craftsmanship, manufacture, agriculture and relatively sophisticated urban living, were more likely to possess the attitudes and aptitudes required in an expanding economy than the immediate descendants of generations of cattle-graziers, who in all their history had built no towns, and who until recently had never lived in one.

The badge of loyalty in the South, and to a lesser extent in the North, was membership of the Church of Ireland. But as the century moved on, and the veterans who had actually fought at the Boyne and Aughrim became fewer, and then fell to nothing, old animosities softened and old religious certainties blurred. The fundamental absurdity of penalizing a man, or a whole people, because of their adherence to a differing doctrinal interpretation of Christianity was increasingly recognized. Thus Chesterfield's relaxation of the Penal Laws was thought sound sense by a Protestant generation whose fathers had felt sympathetic to a previous Viceroy's recommendation of compulsory castration for Catholic priests. (The English parliament rejected it.) The new tolerance, however, was a rational identification and cancellation of the irrelevant rather than a serious urge to compromise on essentials. The essentials remained immutable: the continued domination of the island's affairs by the Protestant minority in association with Britain. The precise nature of the association with Britain was the subject of increasingly critical analysis down the years, but its necessity was unquestioned.

The sentiments that underlay this vital bond were encapsulated in a loyal toast, widely popular in the first half of the century. The accepted method of its delivery was for the proposer to stand on his chair, put one foot on the table, and raise his glass to: 'The glorious, pious and immortal memory of the great and good King William; not forgetting Oliver Cromwell, who assisted in redeeming us from popery, slavery, arbitrary power, brass money and wooden shoes. May we never want a Williamite to kick the arse of a Jacobite. And a fart for the Bishop of Cork.' This, followed by a reverential 'Amen' from the company, was the authorized shortened version. More conscientious practitioners added suggestions for the fate of non-subscribers. Part two went: 'And he that won't drink this, whether he be priest, bishop, deacon, bellows-blower, grave-digger or any other of the fraternity of the clergy; may a north wind blow him to the south, and a west wind blow him to the east. May he have a dark night, a lee shore, a rank storm and a leaky vessel to carry him over the River Styx. May the dog Cerberus make a meal of his rump, and Pluto a snuff-box of his skull; and may the devil jump down his throat with a red-hot harrow, with every pin tear out a gut, and blow him with a clean carcass to hell. Amen.'

The brass money from which Oliver Cromwell supposedly helped to redeem the Anglo-Irish is a reference to the debased currency introduced in Ireland during the reign of James II. The wooden shoes were its assumed economic consequences to decent Pro-testants. The flaw in chronology (Cromwell was dead for over twenty years before the advent of brass money) does not detract from the toast's recognition of who was deserving of gratitude. Bishop Browne of Cork, singled out so woundingly, was the author of 'A Discourse of drinking Healths, wherein the great Evil of the Custom is shown'. He wrote it in 1716 to expose the deplorable effect of strong drink combined with emotionally worded formulations upon the holders of already prejudiced opinions. 'The fraternity of the clergy', designated in part two for rather more complicated retribution than the robust insult to the Bishop, were those weak-minded trimmers who shared his views. The author of the wording of the toast is unidentified. Apart from strong views he seems to have had sea-faring experience, a classical education, a familiarity with church organization, and an un-inhibited directness in expressing himself. A Protestant scholar from

Trinity perhaps, on leave from the Royal Navy?

The Protestant population was asymmetrically distributed through the country. In the South, they were at their numerical highest in Dublin, where they made up something like half of the resident total. They were fairly well represented in the rest of Leinster, less so in Munster, except for the city of Cork where there was a large concentration, and least of all in Connacht. Their largest numbers were in Ulster. The margin was small, but in Ulster they probably out-numbered the Catholics.

The Ulster Protestants were a separate case. The nature of the Plantations in the reign of James I had left them in possession of large contiguous blocks of land, scattered with towns that were entirely Protestant. The massacres of 1641 had eaten deep into the collective memory. Catholics were the object of a continuing hate and distrust that were now shared by only a few belligerent extremists in the South. A diluted, but still powerful, measure of both sentiments was felt for the Protestant Ascendancy and its paramount Church of Ireland.

A large proportion of the Protestant Ulstermen, whether of original Plantation stock or from the waves of reinforcement that had continually replenished the Ulster strength, were Presbyterians or members of other Dissenting sects. These people had found themselves conscientiously unable to take the Oath of Supremacy prescribed by the first Williamite parliament in Dublin, and mandatory until well into the eighteenth century. In 1704 the English parliament included in its bundle of no-popery laws a requirement that office-holders must first demonstrate their suitability by taking the Anglican sacrament. This clause summarily disqualified Dissenters as well as Catholics from offices under the crown and in the corporations, as well as from membership of parliament. The Dissenters had to forsake their previous domination of Ulster boroughs, including Belfast. They understandably thought the imposition of these disabilities outrageously ungrateful to a community that had shared in the defence of Derry against the Jacobites and whose volunteers had fought at the Boyne with Wolesley's Enniskilleners.

Some minor concessions were made to the Dissenters in 1719, but they were debarred from public office until 1780. Their frustration was compounded by the peculiarities of their situation. If they tried to right their wrongs by force of arms, which to an innately combative people was a natural solution, they would shatter the Protestant defensive monolith to the inevitable advantage of the equally combative Ulster Catholics. In sixty years up to 1776 a quarter of a million Ulster Dissenters extricated themselves from this unhappy dilemma by emigrating to the American colonies. They were the Scotch-Irish of American history and they played a distinguished role in the War of Independence. Six of the signatories of the Declaration of Independence were Scotch-Irish. Six early United States presidents were of Scotch-Irish origin.

The Presbyterians and other nonconformists who stayed in the North constituted a sub-group within a sub-group. The major Northern landowners, ennobled or otherwise, were almost to a man members of the Church of Ireland and indistinguishable in habit and outlook from the Southern landlords. The way in which they discharged their functions as landlords was modified by two considerations unknown in the South. Most of their tenants were Protestants. And an institution known as Ulster Custom gave Ulster tenants a security not shared by Catholic tenants in the rest of Ireland. Ulster tenants had fixed leases at fixed rents, and could only be evicted after legal proceedings following persistent non-payment of rent. And if a tenant decided to leave his holding and move on elsewhere, the landlord had a legal obligation to compensate the tenant for any improvements that he had made to the property while in occupation. Since the Protestant tenants were on the whole hard-working, competent and frugal, possessing many of the virtues of the rural Lowland Scots, these arrangements were to the mutual advantage of both landlord and tenant. If the Southern Anglo-Irish had had the wit to adapt them to the South, an enormous sum of human misery would have been avoided and the ultimate extinction of the Anglo-Irish as an influence of any significance upon Irish affairs might have been moderated.

About half the Northern Protestants were, like the landlords, members of the Church of Ireland. They were bound defensively to the Dissenters by the potential threat posed to both by the Ulster Catholics. But the Dissenters were more radically minded, less inclined to bless the squire and his relations, less convinced that the

140

current order of things was necessarily the best, and more receptive to ideas from outside about how society could usefully be re-constituted. They were stimulated by the American Revolution in the 1770s, in which so many of their kinsmen were active, and some of them were stimulated further by the heady excitements deriving from the French Revolution in the 1780s. It was from this group that much of the thinking, and part of the planning for the first genuinely Republican movement in Ireland was to come at the end of the century. One of the countless ironies of Irish history is that present-day defenders of the right of a Protestant people living in the truncated Province of Ulster to remain an integral part of a predominantly agnostic United Kingdom, are in a direct line of descent from the begetters of the political philosophy upon which the constitution of the Republic of Ireland is based.

Of the three notable and lasting cultural establishments bequeathed to independent Ireland by the Anglo-Irish, the oldest and biggest is Trinity College, Dublin, which by an arrangement intelligible only to the academic equivalent of constitutional lawyers is also Dublin University: the whole of it. The explanation seems to be that the founders founded a university, started with one college, intended to add others, and never got round to it. Nor did their successors.

The first serious suggestion that Ireland would benefit from a university came in 1547 from Archbishop Browne of Dublin, an Englishman despatched by King Henry VIII to implement the policies of the Reformation. Among the fruits of these policies were the closing and confiscation of an Augustinian monastery and its lands, which lay about half a mile to the east of the city's mediaeval walls. Browne's ideas did not include the use of this site. Nor did another, later, scheme floated by Sir John Perrot, the Lord Deputy. In any case, neither scheme came to anything. But in 1569 proposals were renewed by a letter to London from the Lord Deputy and Council, in which the point was made that a university was needed for the 'reformation of the barbarisme of this rude people'. There was then an interval of procrastination, during which the rude people's 'barbarisme' continued undented, until in 1590 Adam Loftus, the Archbishop of Dublin, Henry Ussher, the Lord Chief Justice, and Luke Challoner, the Prebendary of St Patrick's

141

Cathedral, combined together to devise a definite plan. The Dublin Corporation was induced to provide the derelict Augustinian monastery and its twenty-eight acres. The plan was recommended to Fitzwilliam, the Lord Deputy. Fitzwilliam endorsed it, and Ussher was sent to argue the detailed case with the Privy Council in England.

The central part of the case was that among the advantages of a university would be the planting of 'Religion, Civilitie and True Obedience in the hearts of this people'. These objectives might not commend themselves to a modern undergraduate of Trinity, or of anywhere else, but they convinced the queen. She granted a warrant for the incorporation by charter of 'the College of the Holy and Undivided Trinity near Dublin founded by Queen Elizabeth'. The charter provided for a Provost, three Fellows and three Scholars. The college could confer the degrees of Bachelor, Master and Doctor, could regulate its affairs as its corporation saw fit, and was equipped with a panel of Visitors empowered to settle disputes. 'Education, training and instruction of youths and students' were to be provided so that the youths and students 'might be the better assisted in the study of the liberal arts, and in the cultivation of virtue and religion'.

A supplementary, and less high-minded, motive for the introduction of higher education to Ireland was summarized in a letter written in December 1591, by the queen to Fitzwilliam: '. . . many have usually heretofore used to travel into France, Italy and Spain, to get learning in such foreign universities, whereby they have been infected with Popery and other ill qualities, and so become evil subjects'. From the beginning, the conjunction of moral, doctrinal and political aims clearly required that tuition and discipline should be under the close supervision of ordained senior ministers of the Protestant Church. Archbishop Loftus was the first provost; his successors for over three hundred years, with brief Cromwellian and Jacobite interludes, were Church of Ireland divines.

The first stone of the new college was laid ceremonially by Thomas Smyth, the Lord Mayor of Dublin, on 13 March 1593. The first students were admitted in January 1594. The buildings, none of which still exists, were grouped around a small quadrangle and accommodated the students, the fellows, the provost, a chapel, a hall, kitchens and so on. The whole was surrounded by fields and orchards, and remained so for a hundred years, until the great expansion after the Williamite victory made it no longer 'near Dublin', as its charter has it, but an island of twenty-eight acres in the middle of the city.

Loftus, and most of those who immediately followed him, had been at Cambridge. Cambridge precedents influenced the curriculum and the methods of its teaching. Among subjects taught were grammar, rhetoric, logic, astronomy, arithmetic and geometry. Students were expected to give dissertations and to take part in discussion and debate. Divinity, unsullied by Catholicism or Dissent, took precedence over all else. The study and encouragement of the Irish language was an early and continuing preoccupation, partly because of its usefulness in a country where it was the tongue of the great majority of the inhabitants, partly because the translation of the Bible into Irish and its distribution among the majority was seen as a promising vehicle for their conversion to Protestantism. There were in fact Irish-speaking Catholics among the earliest students, but these were effectively prevented from receiving degrees by a requirement to demonstrate their acceptance of Protestantism at the conferring ceremony of Commencements.

During the first century of its existence, Trinity's influence upon Ireland's affairs was limited. It turned out a number of distinguished and erudite theologians, whose contribution to higher thinking doubtless had its effect on policies with a politico-religious content, but none of the main figures who determined the course of Irish events in the seventeenth century was a product of the university.

It was chronically short of money. Grants from the government were inadequate. Queen Elizabeth endowed it with land confiscated from rebellious Catholics, but the rents from the new tenants were frequently unpaid, and the lands themselves were inaccessible for long periods during the 1641 Rebellion and the Cromwellian and Williamite wars. There were some outside donations, including an interesting one from Mountjoy's army in thanksgiving for his victory over O'Neill at Kinsale. But the academic staff's habit of departing almost *en masse* to England whenever trouble broke out, as it often did in seventeenth-century Ireland, did little for continuity. Neither did two outbreaks in Dublin of the plague.

James II was unimpressed by universities, and in his short time in Dublin he used Trinity College first as a barracks for his troops, and

143

later as a prison for Protestants. A symbolic Mass was celebrated in the chapel, which was then immediately converted into a powder magazine. The troops stole all the college horses, did £2,000 worth of damage, and would have done a lot more but for the firm intervention of Dr Michael Moore, the newly appointed provost, and the only Catholic one in the university's history. Dr Moore and Father McCarthy, the new librarian, stopped the soldiers from burning down the library. Dr Moore also did what he could to improve the conditions under which the Protestant prisoners were held.

Dr Moore's tenure of office was, unhappily, foreshortened as the result of a sermon he preached in Christ Church Cathedral. In this he had some forthright things to say about the Jesuits, of whom he disapproved. This irritated King James, who was fond of Jesuits. Moore was packed off to exile in France. He would certainly have lost his office anyway after the Boyne, but it is ironic that the first Catholic Provost of Trinity should have been sacked by the last Catholic King of Ireland.

In the next century, of uninterrupted peace and Protestant Ascendancy, Trinity became more closely integrated with the dominant apparatus, was more useful to it, produced most of its articulate critics, grew richer, grew in the number and variety of its faculties, grew in its roll of undergraduates and acquired the major part of its elegant architecture. From 1695 onwards it ceased to import its provosts from Cambridge and Oxford. Henceforth all were graduates of the university itself who, with one exception, had previously been fellows.

Of the alumni of Trinity who left their mark on Ireland, in some cases on England, and in a few cases wherever the English language is spoken, three who were at their primes in the eighteenth century attended the university in the closing decades of the seventeenth. The greatest of these, Jonathan Swift, later to be the Dean of St Patrick's, author of *Gulliver's Travels* and the pseudonymous writer of some of the most effectively biting political satire on record, *Drapier's Letters*, was an unsatisfactory undergraduate in constant discord with authority. He was an orphan dependent upon charity, and another example of the way in which the Anglo-Irish looked after their own. His degree was given to him by special grace (i.e. it was unearned), and he left for England in 1689. The patronage of Sir

144

Kilkenny Castle, Kilkenny. It was for centuries
the stronghold of the Butlers, Earls
(later Dukes) of Ormonde.

Russborough House, County Wicklow.
Designed by the German architect,
Richard Cassells

Castletown House, County Kildare. Built for
William Connolly, Speaker of the eighteenth-
century Irish House of Commons

Interior of Carton House, County Kildare. The
country house of the Fitzgeralds, Earls of
Kildare and Dukes of Leinster

Jonathan Swift — savagely satirical
opponent of English economic
exploitation

Edmund Burke — Irish prosperity
inseparable from Empire

Henry Grattan — Irish Parliament,
English King of Ireland

Theobald Wolfe Tone — Republican
separatism by force of arms

Arthur Wellesley, first Duke of
Wellington — Imperial soldier and
statesman

Charles Stewart Parnell — brilliant
leader of the movement for
constitutional Home Rule

Leinster House, the town house of the Kildare
Fitzgeralds, Dukes of Leinster. Now the home
of Dail Eireann, the Irish Parliament

Trinity College

The Customs House, built by James Gandon

The Four Courts, also built by James Gandon

College of Surgeons, St Stephen's Green

Georgian doors in Fitzwilliam Square

Merrion Square/Upper Mount Street

Mansion House

St Patrick's Hall in Dublin Castle

Interior of the National Gallery

Georgian fanlight

Birmingham Tower in Dublin Castle

St Patrick's Cathedral (*left*) and Christ Church Cathedral. Both are of medieval origin. Swift was
Dean of St Patrick's

Commemorations of two Anglo-Irishmen with very different outlooks; the Wellington Monument
in Phoenix Park (*left*), and Wolfe Tone's statue in St Stephen's Green

William Temple gave him both employment and access to high political circles, which he studied with an observant and sardonic eye. He worked and wrote partly in England, partly in Ireland, until he took Holy Orders and became the incumbent of two rural Irish parishes. He was appointed Dean of St Patrick's Cathedral in Dublin in 1713.

As dean he was autocratic, irascible, privately charitable, and appalled at the injustices and inequalities of contemporary society. His weapon of attack upon them was scathing wit. Such works as *A Tale of a Tub, A Modest Proposal* and 'An Argument to prove that the abolition of Christianity in England may, as things now stand, be attended by some inconvenience', were as widely read in England as they were in Ireland. But it was *Drapier's Letters*, six in all, written between April and December 1724 which crystallized Anglo-Irish resentment at English exploitation of their dependence upon England. Drapier's target was a newly introduced Irish coinage, 'Wood's Halfpence'. Through a combination of jobbery, corruption and royal patronage, the contract for the minting of these had been placed with a man named Wood. Their nominal value was forty per cent higher than their intrinsic value, and the forty per cent was shared between Wood and the Duchess of Kendall, the king's mistress. It was obvious to the authorities that Drapier could only be Swift, but there was no evidence to prove it. The halfpence were withdrawn in consequence of the clamour generated by Drapier, and a notable victory for Anglo-Irish nationalism – a political philosophy very different from the currently dormant Irish-Irish nationalism – was scored.

Two other literary contemporaries of Swift's at Trinity were William Congreve and George Farquhar, the playwrights. Like Swift, neither showed precocious signs of promise. Congreve was described as 'very hearty at his victuals and drink, and a shirker of all lectures except the mathematics . . . and those on the Greek poets'. Farquhar, in an early appearance on the boards of the Smock Alley Theatre, added an unfortunate realism to his performance by using a genuine sword instead of its blunted theatrical equivalent, and spiked a fellow member of the cast with it. From then on he wrote plays instead of acting in them. The plays of both have lasted, and are revived on the stage periodically.

George Berkeley, later the Bishop of Cloyne, graduated in 1704, became a Fellow in 1707, was connected with Trinity all his life, and was the foremost philosopher of his generation and of several succeeding it. 'This country may justly boast of its Berkeley, and challenge any university in Europe to produce his superior,' wrote a later provost, accurately if bombastically. Berkeley's *Philosophical Commentaries* and *The Principles of Human Knowledge* remain to the present day required reading in the philosophy schools of the world. He was a humane and compassionate man, ahead of his time in recommending that 'Roman Catholics be admitted to Trinity without obliging them to attend chapel duties, catechisms or Divinity lectures', an innovatory notion not found acceptable until 1793.

Oliver Goldsmith, who got into trouble while at Trinity, and Thomas Moore, who did not, were two further writers who won fame in the eighteenth century. Edmund Burke, whose later impact was more upon British imperial politics than upon Irish domestic ones, but who none the less maintained a keenly sympathetic concern for Irish wrongs all his life, graduated in 1748. His mother was a Catholic and he had many Catholic relatives. He was a tireless campaigner in the Westminster parliament for the abolition of Catholic disabilities and for the repeal of English legislation that hampered Irish trade. But he was entirely opposed to anything approaching independence for Ireland, including the devolution of more power to the existing Irish parliament. He was convinced that peace and prosperity for Ireland, essential to the empire, could only be ensured by giving the Catholics the same rights as Protestants, and by simultaneously tightening English control over the country.

Future politicians, few of whom shared Burke's views and all of whom were in residence at Trinity at one time or another during the eighteenth century, were Henry Grattan, John Philpot Curran, Henry Flood, John Fitzgibbon, later Earl of Clare, Barry Yelverton, later Lord Avonmore, John Foster, later Lord Oriel, and Theobald Wolfe Tone, later to commit suicide in a Dublin prison cell in order to pre-empt a death-sentence passed upon him for treason.

The first systematic study and regulation of modern medicine in Ireland was instituted at Trinity in 1662 by the appointment of Dr John Stearne as Public Professor of Medicine. He was originally the Lecturer in Hebrew and Professor of Laws, and had added medical teaching to his list of interests in the middle 1650s. He founded the

College of Physicians which, after his death and a great deal of argument, agreed with Trinity in 1701 that medical students should be examined by a panel nominated jointly by both colleges. In 1711 the Medical School was equipped with a lecture room, a dissecting room and a laboratory. Ireland, Britain, the British Colonial Empire and the Royal Army Medical Corps have had cause to be grateful to Dr Stearne.

The oldest hospital in Ireland, and the fifth oldest in the British Isles, Dr Steevens's, was endowed in the will of Dr Richard Steevens of the Trinity Medical School and completed in 1733. It still functions. So does Sir Patrick Dun's Hospital, opened in 1808, and named in honour of a Scottish doctor who came to Ireland as physician to the Williamite army, stayed and, as President of the College of Physicians, negotiated the agreement with Trinity about the method of examining medical students.

New faculties added to the university were Feudal and English Law, and Greek in 1761; Hebrew, Mathematics and Modern History, which was separated from Oratory, in 1762; and Music in 1764. The first Professor of Music was Garrett Wesley, Earl of Mornington, father of the future Duke of Wellington. Mornington's enthusiasm for his subject was shared by much of the fashionable Dublin society of the time. He himself was an accomplished violinist, organist and harpsichord player, and in his extramural moments he doubled as bandleader of an organization manned by aristocratic musicians and known as the Fishamble Street Musical Society. It was of high quality. Handel's 'Messiah' was first presented to the world under its auspices. Handel, present in person, was enchanted.

The mission entrusted by the university's charter to the provost and fellows, to assist the 'youths and students' 'in the study of the liberal arts, and in the cultivation of virtue and religion', met, as is common in such establishments, a certain amount of consumer resistance. Dr Narcissus Marsh, who left to Dublin the beautiful and valuably stocked Marsh's Library, became provost in 1678, and shortly afterwards noted in his diary: 'Finding this place very troublesome, partly by reason of the multitude of business . . . and partly by reason of the ill education that the young scholars have before they come to the College, whereby they are both rude and ignorant; I was quickly weary of three hundred and forty young men and boys in this lewd and debauch'd Town; and the more so because I had no time to follow my always dearly beloved studies.'

With the growth of the city, facilities for lewdness and debauch'ry multiplied. One of the lasting charms of Trinity is that it is set at the centre of a national capital. Academic and associated intramural pursuits can be attended to in relative isolation, but a two-minute walk will bring students and staff into immediate contact with a larger world. The other side of the coin is that in Marsh's time, and for long afterwards, students were admitted at an early age (Swift was fourteen at entry, and far from untypical) and the expanding Dublin outside the college walls was studded with ale-houses, brothels and gambling enterprises, as might be expected in a lively city which was also a seaport and the centre for a military garrison.

The college authorities did their best to control the access of the student body to the town. The student body was not very responsive. A pioneer escaper was a man named Weld, who as early as the 1630s was fined £40, an enormous amount of money, for lodging and drinking in the house of an ale-house keeper, Mrs Jones, who managed 'a suspected place for disorder and vice'. Swift himself, fifty years later, was punished for the offence of 'town haunting'. It was a continuing contest of wits, that by the eighteenth century often descended to brawn. A central feature of the contest was a common disposition by the student side of the argument to press their case to extremes. In 1734, for example, an undergraduate who had insulted the junior dean was publicly rebuked. The rebuke was badly received by the insulter's friends. They stoned the junior dean, broke up his rooms, and were joined by non-university passers-by who helped them destroy other parts of the premises. One of these volunteer sympathizers did his best to burn down the college gates. The only response to an offer of a reward, posted by the college board, for information that would help to identify the wreckers was a written threat to the safety of the provost.

Matters were taken further in the course of an incident in 1747. A scholar was arrested for debt and taken by a bailiff to the Marshalsea prison. The arrest, illegal at the time and for a long time afterwards, had been made within Trinity, a sanctuary. A cutting-out party captured the bailiff and doused him under the college pump. A

148

crowd of students, joined again by well-wishing outsiders, then went off to assault the Marshalsea. Two people were killed in the repulse of this attack. Five students were subsequently expelled, and five more admonished, Oliver Goldsmith among them.

Gunplay within the centre of 'Religion, Civilitie and True Obedience' was usually restricted to duelling, which grew in popularity as the century progressed, but non-duelling incidents involving firearms were recorded twice. In January 1789, an undergraduate named Stackpoole wrote a chatty letter to his father which included the unelaborated sentence: 'Last Wednesday a gentleman shot a boy in the Library for throwing snow balls at him.' This brisk episode was ante-dated by a more elaborate incident involving a fellow named Edward Ford, 'an obstinate and ill-judging man'. Ford's precautions against reciprocal bad feeling included the keeping of a loaded gun at his bedside. On a night in 1734 some students threw stones at his window. Ford responded by opening up with his gun. The students withdrew to their rooms to get their own guns, returned, saw Ford still at his window in his nightshirt, and fired. He died of wounds two hours later. The subsequent prosecution caused considerable resentment among the upper classes. They were unable to understand why the sons of gentlemen should be penalized for a display of high spirits. The case ended in an acquittal.

In 1731 a group of thoughtful and practical men, with a shared interest in the improvement of working techniques in all aspects of the Irish economic mosaic, formed the Dublin Society. Their prime concern was agriculture, by far and away the country's leading generator of wealth and employer of people, but they were unrestrictive in their choice of subjects for research and experiment. They were in a sense the heirs of the Philosophical Society, a body that had met during the 1680s but had dissolved because of the dispersion of its members prior to the Williamite war.

There were fourteen founding members of the Dublin Society. All were competent and dedicated, but three in particular guided its early proceedings. These were Thomas Prior, an economist; Samuel Madden, a Church of Ireland country rector; and Arthur Dobbs, the Surveyor-General, a landowner from County Antrim.

They were independent-minded men but all of them had been influenced by two contemporary pamphlets that helped to focus their ideas. One, written eight years previously by Lord Molesworth, was 'Promoting Agriculture and Employing the Poor'. The second, 'A Proposal for the Universal Use of Irish Manufacture', was by Swift. Both papers pointed out that Irish resources were under-used and that there was too much dependence upon imports of materials that could be produced in Ireland with the application of informed effort. Swift himself did not join the society. He despised one of its officials, and the official's father, and that was enough for the querulous Swift to refuse to be associated openly with it.

In its earliest days the society published papers prepared by its members on husbandry, manufactures and 'other useful arts'. Madden, who was rich, introduced the award of premiums, cash prizes, to be paid to the best performers in varied classes of activity specified by the society. Today it seems an obvious enough form of incentive, but nobody had thought of it until Madden introduced it for academic excellence in Trinity. Initially, Madden paid for the premiums himself. Later the government recognized the usefulness of the society and subsidized it handsomely from public funds. Premiums were soon being given for the best crops of wheat, barley and hops; the best breaking of ground; the most potable cider; the greatest number of fruit trees and timber trees to be raised in a nursery; the most effective example of land drainage; and for such non-agricultural activities as drawing, embroidery and sculpture.

Within two years the society's membership had grown to two hundred and forty. The Lord Lieutenant was president, and the Protestant Primate of Armagh, the Head of the Church of Ireland, was vice-president. Among the members were twelve bishops, thirty-four other clergymen, sixteen peers, five judges, and a miscellaneous collection of fellows of Trinity, merchants, retired service officers and country gentlemen. These were not decorative cyphers, anxious to see their names on important-looking lists. They were talented and conscientious contributors, practitioners and exchangers of views.

The scope of the society's researches and advice spread in many directions, all of them of practical value. It opened a model farm and founded the Botanical Gardens. Its members invented, and the society tested, new agricultural implements. There was correspondence with England and continental Europe, notably Holland, about horticultural innovations and the evaluation of soil samples. A drawing school was acquired, and later expanded to take in an architectural division that was supervised by Thomas Ivory, a designer and builder of distinction who had started his professional life as a penniless carpenter in Cork, and was yet another beneficiary of the Anglo-Irish custom of nurturing inherent ability and persistence. The society charged no fees to Ivory's pupils, most of whom were apprentices in the basic arts of stone-masonry and brickwork. They took their knowledge throughout Ireland, and the result was a consistently high standard in eighteenth-century Irish building. The society tapped experience, experimented and disseminated advice about veterinary science, fisheries, bee-keeping and anything else that might promote the national prosperity.

One member, Mr Arbuckle, wrote an appallingly long and appallingly sententious poem about the society's achievements. As poetry it is less than memorable, as a summing-up of what was achieved it is fair.

> Thus if th' endeavours of the good and wise,
> Can aught avail to make a Nation rise,
> Soon shall Hibernia see her broken state,
> Repair'd by Arts and Industry, grow great.

Those are the last four lines. Hibernia's broken state had a few more experiences to go through, none of which was likely to appeal to Mr Arbuckle, but the society continued to prosper and to pursue its responsible and imaginative programmes. When George IV came to the throne in 1820 he indicated that he would be pleased to become the society's patron. The 'indication', or royal command, was seen as the sign of official endorsement that it was intended to be, and the Dublin Society became the Royal Dublin Society. It still is. The RDS is a valued fixture in the life of a country that has been independent since 1921 and a republic since 1948. The royal part of its title goes unquestioned.

When at the time of Independence the new government chose Leinster House as the home of Dail Eireann, the RDS, which had been based at Leinster House since its purchase from the Duke of Leinster in 1815, moved co-operatively and efficiently to its present

151

site at Ballsbridge, an inner suburb. The site covers acres. The best-known annual events held there are the Dublin Horse Show and the Spring Show, both of which attract wide international attendance and generate much profitable trade. The society provides lectures, concerts, reading rooms, and an excellent library. Its present management helps to balance the books, and keeps down the subscriptions of its 13,500 members, by renting the premises for a range of events from circuses to party political conventions. The ghosts of Messrs Prior, Madden and Dobbs should not be displeased.

The youngest, smallest and most exclusive of the three major cultural bodies founded by eighteenth-century Anglo-Ireland dates from 1785. Lord Charlemont, the Commander-in-Chief of the Irish Volunteers, was a scholarly man of wide interests who had travelled extensively in Europe. He felt that there was a need in Ireland for an organization restricted in membership to a small number of distinguished specialists who could pursue their researches, present papers and lodge their findings in a properly serviced institution housed under one roof. He invited a group of like-minded people to his house to discuss the idea. They formed the Irish Academy, the purpose of which was defined as 'to advance the studies of science, polite literature and antiquities'.

Within a few months the value and status of the Academy were recognized by its being granted a royal charter, and by its becoming the 'Royal Irish Academy'. Like the Royal Dublin Society it has retained its prefix beyond the creation of the Republic of Ireland. There are about two hundred and forty members, selected upon the basis of their record of scholarship. The RIA conducted much of the antiquarian research of the nineteenth century. Along with its library of 30,000 volumes there are over 2,500 rare manuscripts in its keeping.

CHAPTER NINE

At the same time as the practical men of the Royal Dublin Society were disseminating useful knowledge, the learned men of the Royal Irish Academy were enthusiastically applying themselves to their researches and the students at Trinity with not so noticeable enthusiasm were applying themselves to theirs, there were others among the Anglo-Irish who were making a name for themselves in a socially less constructive manner. These were people who, operating in the spirit of the late Colonel Blood, showed an individualism that often shaded into eccentricity, and sometimes into outright lunacy.

One individualist has, by definition, little in common with another individualist, let alone the several hundred of them who functioned in eighteenth-century Ireland, and it is impossible to identify hard-and-fast reasons for their being so plentiful at that time. It is, however, possible to list some of the shared characteristics of their background, and some of their shared attitudes. Any competent psychiatrist would have no difficulty in expanding the list.

They were all born in a period of persisting peace. The fighting and the vigilance and the anxieties which had absorbed the energies of their ancestors in the previous century were well behind them. So, for the most part, was the fire and brimstone religious conviction that had inspired their forebears to ferocity in battle, but had at the same time curbed any tendencies towards the 'debauchr'y' deplored by Dr Marsh. In the eighteenth century there was a marked drift towards a rather formless deism, and a spreading lack of interest in theological small print. Protestants were still Protestants and papists were the old enemy, but it was possible to call yourself a Protestant without bothering overmuch about the moral constraints taught by Protestantism. It is notable that the rakes and the bucks and the eccentrics soon faded as a sub-species in the first half of the next century, when the Anglo-Irish knuckled under to the conformist respectability that flowed from Victorian England.

In this easy-going ambience there were plenty of opportunities, for those of the rich who wanted to take them, to do more or less what they pleased. Social rank did not give them total immunity from the requirements of the law, but it did give them a certain latitude where the law's application was concerned, which was not extended to the less privileged. In any case, much of what they chose to do, although surprising, was not illegal.

The isolation and boredom of daily life on remote country estates, surrounded by a sullen people of alien language, religion and custom, could be countered to some extent by hard riding to hounds, or shooting, or fishing, but with an abundant supply of both domestic and agricultural labour available at low wages there were long periods when there was little for a country gentleman to do, unless he was a dedicated silviculturist, or agricultural improver, or had some specialist intellectual interest, which the ones under consideration did not. Add the self-confident arrogance of the conqueror with the conquered all around him, subtract the responsibility towards labourers normally undertaken by equivalent landowners in England, and the conditions are set for the emergence of some strange characters with idiosyncratic habits.

As might be expected, drinking, gambling and women were the basic ingredients, but they were taken to unusual extremes, and led to unusual complications. In addition to them, sometimes in association with them, there was a great deal of duelling, a lot of heiress abducting, some polygamy, extensive bankruptcy, a small incidence of private imprisonment, a larger incidence of public imprisonment, much premature emigration, one apostacy by a Catholic bishop, several suicides, a non-duelling murder or two and a few actual committals for insanity. A pervading factor in the outlook behind all this was summed up, although in a different context, by Sir Boyle Roche, a long-serving member of the Irish

154

House of Commons. 'Why,' Sir Boyle asked the Speaker, 'should we do anything for posterity? What has posterity ever done for us?'[1]

In this part of society, which overlapped without conspicuous discomfort to either side with the steadier, responsible purveyors of constructive action and sophisticated thought, the constants were extravagant hospitality, with or without the resources to pay for it, and a touchy, artificial, sense of honour. For example, Mr Beauchamp Bagenal, of Co. Carlow, who loved entertaining guests, habitually did so with two loaded pistols in front of him on the dining table, so that there should be no unnecessary delay if he had to challenge to a duel anybody who had shown an inadequate appreciation of the claret. 'Rest upon your pistols, my boys,' he counselled his friends, ' occasions will arise in which the use of them is absolutely indispensable.'

The wisdom of this advice would at once have become clear to anyone in Dublin who came within sight of Bryan Maguire. When running short of duelling opponents Maguire selected new ones by emptying muck out of his window on to the head of a promising-looking passer-by, spitting in his face when he stared up, and offering him immediate satisfaction. Mrs Maguire, a good wife, had an important role to play in keeping Maguire in training. She held lighted candles at arm's length while Maguire shot them out.

Others best avoided were Fireball MacNamara and Hairtrigger Dick Martin. Martin, who owned vast estates in Co. Galway, counteracted his readiness to shoot people with whom he disagreed by a deep tenderness for animals of all kinds. Later, when he was a member of the Westminster parliament, he introduced the first legislation to make the ill-treatment of animals an offence. He was effectively the founder of the Royal Society for the Prevention of Cruelty to Animals. By then his nickname had shifted from Hairtrigger to Humanity Dick.

Duelling was governed by sets of rules that at the beginning of the century varied from place to place, but were eventually standardized by the universal adoption of the code formulated in Galway, which in thirty-seven paragraphs covered comprehensively all that a

---

[1] Sir B. Roche's parliamentary offerings also include: 'No man can be in two places at once, barring he was a bird', and: 'If French principles take root in Ireland we will come down to breakfast one morning to find our severed heads on the table staring us in the face.'

duellist should know and do. There was scope for personal preference. One addict always fought stripped to the waist, to avoid infection from pieces of his clothing shot into him. Beauchamp Bagenal's preference was for shooting it out in graveyards. He had been permanently injured in a riding accident, and found it convenient to have a tombstone to lean against. Fighting Fitzgerald practised and perfected a crouch that reduced to the smallest possible size the target that he presented to his opponent. This was regarded as unsporting. Fitzgerald put himself beyond the social pale when it was found after a fight with Hairtrigger Dick Martin in Castlebar that he was wearing bullet-proof plate under his coat. Both men were lightly wounded in this encounter, but Martin rejected with contempt a suggestion of Fitzgerald's that there should be a re-match in Sligo.

Although he had several close competitors, Fighting Fitzgerald was probably the supreme Anglo-Irish example of what can happen when a near-psychopath, with inherited wealth and status, is given the opportunity to exploit his privileges and to exercise local power with complete irresponsibility. Fitzgerald was born in 1748. His father was a connection of the Munster Fitzgeralds, the Desmonds. His mother was the sister of the Earl of Bristol who was also the Bishop of Derry. Fitzgerald was educated at Eton, commissioned in the army, and fought his first duel when he was sixteen. Later, he was wounded in the head when duelling with a brother officer in Galway. (Fitzgerald *père* was told that his son was dying. He demonstrated his distress by running his sword through an offerer of sympathy.) The son survived, resigned from the army, and took to insulting everyone he took a dislike to in Dublin, on off-days making up the number of opponents by jostling strangers in the street. He married a sister of Thomas Conolly of Castletown House, took her on a prolonged honeymoon to France and England, continued to pick off opponents of his choice, ran up £120,000 worth of debts, was left by his wife, who reasonably enough found it all too much for her, and returned, penniless and wifeless, to his father's estate in Co. Mayo.

There Fitzgerald, for a while, actually did some useful work. He drained bog, rehabilitated abandoned land and sowed crops. This interlude by no means sublimated his old interests. He considered most of his neighbours to be socially too inferior for use as duelling material, though good enough to be insulted at whim. He compensated for this by shooting Lord Altamont's dog, a giant Irish wolfhound, a deed that led indirectly to the duel with Hairtrigger Dick Martin, the Animals' Friend. Fitzgerald found attendance at the meets of the local hunt, in the company of people whom it would be demeaning to shoot, so frustrating that he invented a new form of hunting. It took place in the middle of the night, with Fitzgerald himself as the entire field, and his servants illuminating hazardous obstacles with blazing torches.

In 1778 war with France and apprehensions in Dublin Castle about a possible French invasion stimulated the formation of local volunteer units. Fitzgerald founded the Turlough Volunteers, which he soon turned into a private army of uniformed terrorists. They were devoted to their leader, and happy to take it out on people who had incurred his displeasure, but who were not sufficiently well connected for Fitzgerald to settle accounts with personally.

Relations with his father had been deteriorating for some time, largely because the father was as improvident with his money as was the son, and the son disliked the sight of his future inheritance being dissipated in uneconomical living. To correct this tendency, Fitzgerald chained his father to a pet bear, and later gaoled him in a cave in the grounds. These proceedings annoyed Fitzgerald's brother, who swore out a warrant for Fitzgerald's arrest. He was picked up while dispensing justice from the bench in Ballinrobe courthouse, and was tried in Castlebar. There he was found guilty, fined £500 and sentenced to two years' imprisonment. He was taken to the Castlebar gaol, but the Turlough Volunteers soon arrived asking for their Commanding Officer back. After a moderately sized riot, they were given him.

Fitzgerald, on his release, saw as his first priority the need to reach an accord with his father, whereby the old man would rescind his complaint of illegal imprisonment. To underline the importance that he attached to agreement on this point, Fitzgerald rowed his father out to an unoccupied island in Clew Bay, forced him ashore, and threatened to leave him as a castaway unless something satisfactory could be worked out between them. The old man craftily negotiated a payment to himself of £3,000 in exchange for his agreement to abandon the charges, and father and son rowed back to the mainland, where more problems soon arose.

The chief of these was the Dublin government's practical

expression of their dissatisfaction with the activities of the Turlough Volunteers. The government knew whom they were dealing with and took no chances. They sent a company of regular infantry, accompanied by cavalry and artillery, to ensure that the Turlough Volunteers were properly stood down. The Volunteers dispersed before superior force, Fitzgerald's father reneged on the deal that he had concluded in Clew Bay, and Fitzgerald made for Dublin, where he was again arrested and re-tried.

A second conviction brought him a further sentence of imprisonment, once more foreshortened, this time probably through the discreet intervention of his uncle, the combined Earl of Bristol and Bishop of Derry. The bishop certainly used his influence after Fitzgerald was released. He arranged for Fitzgerald to be made a freeman of the City of Derry, an honour that was conferred in a public ceremony with speeches. In his, Fitzgerald said that freedom ran in his blood. A direct ancestor of his had been one of the signatories of Magna Carta.

His return to Mayo was marred by the discovery that a Catholic lawyer named McDonnell had been elected as Colonel of the Mayo Volunteers. Fitzgerald had wanted the job for himself. He found some consolation in shooting as many as he could find of the dogs belonging to the Volunteers who had elected McDonnell, but it was not enough. He consulted a crony of his, a raffish Welsh lawyer named Brecknock, about the best way to get rid of McDonnell. Brecknock's legal advice was that the Turlough Militia, now reconstituted and superficially reformed, but still wistful at heart for the Good Old Days, should mount an operation to arrest McDonnell on spurious charges and then shoot him on the grounds that he had tried to escape. The Turlough Militia did this, and duly killed McDonnell and a friend of his who was sufficiently unlucky to be with him at the time.

The murder, and the excuse for it, were so patently the work of Fitzgerald that he was arrested for a third time, and tried. The elastic tolerance of the law for the likes of Fighting Fitzgerald had been strained beyond its limits. He was found guilty and hanged publicly in Castlebar in June 1786. The Attorney General, who prosecuted in person, was John Fitzgibbon, later the Earl of Clare, Lord Chancellor of Ireland, and principal manipulator of the Union of Great Britain and Ireland in 1800. Fitzgibbon and Fitzgerald had

158

met before. They had fought a duel.

From shortly after the Williamite victory in the 1690s until well into the nineteenth century, duelling in Ireland was considered by the upper reaches of society to be something of a gentlemanly accomplishment. It was not compulsory, but the man who had fought a duel or two, who had 'smelt powder', acquired much the same cachet as one of his present-day successors who has won an international rugby cap or who has been given a place in the Olympic equestrian team. Duelling was, of course, widespread at the time in England and on the continent, but all contemporary accounts suggest that in terms of proportionate numbers of contestants, frequency of participation, and readiness to fight, Ireland was well ahead of all competitors.

Not all Irish duellists brought to duelling the single-minded enthusiasm shown by people like Maguire or Fitzgerald, who in default of genuine provocation engineered their own. But in the professions, particularly in the Law, an insult or what was inter-preted as one was likely to be responded to by a challenge, almost as often as it was among the landed gentry. The standard of marks-manship varied. Deaths were infrequent, but common enough to make a meeting with pistols a real test of physical courage. The Prince Regent, who once asked a contestant in a Galway by-election who he thought the winning candidate would be, was given the terse reply, 'The survivor'.

A Fellow of Trinity, Dr Duigenan, recorded that target practice in the college park was an everyday subject for students, and the sound of the discharge of firearms in college rooms was fairly common. Duels between students were an almost weekly occurrence '. . . some of them have been slain, others maimed'. Casualties among practitioners at the Bar were described by another observer as 'very considerable', including both killed and wounded. There was some Quixotry, with the man who had fired first and missed being spared by the opponent's firing in the air. Beauchamp Bagenal once took this form of charitable reprieve a stage further. He was fighting his nephew, Bagenal Harvey. Harvey fired and missed. Bagenal reproached him noisily for nearly killing his own godfather, and told him to go up to the house and order breakfast, at which his godfather would shortly join him.

There were recognized duellists who gambled, and recognized gamblers who would have nothing to do with duelling, preferring to risk their money rather than their lives. The best known of these pacific gamblers was Buck Whaley, whose transitory fame rested partly upon the scale of his extravagance and partly upon the fact that he ended a failure, always a subject for Irish satisfaction.

He was orphaned in 1769 at the age of three, and inherited an estate in County Wicklow, a superb house in St Stephen's Green, £60,000 in capital and an income of about £7,000 a year (multiply by 100 to approach equivalent 1980s values). He was eighteen before he was allowed to lay his hands upon the money, and thirty-two when he died in poverty. Some of his betting was on cards and dice with fellow bucks in private houses or in Daly's, a fashionable gambling establishment in College Green. Some of it was in France, which he liked, and where he lived for a time until a payment of his for £14,000, lost in one evening, was dishonoured by his Dublin bankers. A fast return to Ireland became necessary.

At dinner one evening in Dublin he accepted a bet of £15,000, subscribed by a syndicate of his gambling friends, against his being able to go to Jerusalem, bring back irrefutable proof that he had been there, and complete the journey within two years. Jerusalem at the time was deep in the Ottoman Empire, a ramshackle structure run by a venal and brutal government, plagued extensively by brigands, and notably ill-disposed towards Christians, of whom a member of the Church of Ireland, even with the habits of Whaley, was one. But the difficulties of the enterprise seem to have been exaggerated by the syndicate's ignorance of the services provided by His Britannic Majesty's diplomatic and consular representatives for British subjects, particularly rich British subjects, journeying abroad. When the time came for Whaley to leave Ireland, cheering crowds, thousands strong, assembled to bid good luck to the intrepid adventurer, rather as if he were making the first attempt to reach the South Pole, or the source of the Blue Nile. The actual itinerary was less taxing. Properly supported by servants, and with a plentiful supply of Madeira, he sailed to Deal and then to Gibraltar. The military garrison in Gibraltar received him hospitably, and the

160

Governor put on a ball in his honour. At the next stop, Smyrna, the Turkish authorities welcomed the ship with a fifty-gun salute, and took Whaley and his companion, Captain Wilson, out hunting. An overland journey to Constantinople ended with a civic reception in the capital, an introduction by the British Ambassador to the Admiral of the Turkish Fleet, an exchange of presents with the admiral, and the provision by him of a *laissez-passer* for admission to Jerusalem. Another sea passage took Whaley and a new companion, Captain Hugh Moore, to Acre, where the production of the *laissez-passer* brought them both under the protection of the Turkish Governor of the Levant, a bloodthirsty autocrat whose protection was clearly worth having. The last leg of the journey was a ride by night, when bandits were less active, after which Whaley and Moore were in Jerusalem. Whaley wrote some descriptive notes about the Holy Places, got the guardian of a convent to write a certificate authenticating his claim to have made the journey, and returned slowly and comfortably home to Ireland.

One might argue that this traveller's tale merely demonstrates that, at the time, a rich young man with the right connections could expect, at the centres which mattered, official hospitality on a lavish scale and official spade-work on a reliable scale. But this niggling approach was not shared by the bucks who put up their stakes, or by the celebrants who greeted Buck Whaley's return home with bonfires. He became known as Jerusalem Whaley. The bucks paid up their £15,000 and after the deduction of travelling expenses Whaley was the richer by £7,000.

He did not keep it for long. The Jerusalem enterprise aside, he was a natural loser. His debts increased and his patrimony decreased. He had a short lift during the controversies which preceded the Union, when his – for practical purposes – hereditary membership of the Irish parliament put him in the position of being able to accept a large bribe to vote in favour of the Union and another one to vote against it. But these were financial drops in the ocean. The estate in Co. Wicklow had to go. So did the house in St Stephen's Green, fifty-odd years later to become the home of the Catholic University of Ireland. He disappeared to the Isle of Man, built a house there with what was left of his money, and died of a chill in a coaching-inn in Knutsford in Cheshire. The Isle of Man house was his last gesture to the trivialities about which the Dublin bucks betted. Whaley had

161

wagered that he could live on Irish soil without being geographically in Ireland. He proved his point, and won his bet, by building his house on a foundation of earth brought in from across the Irish Sea. Buck Whaley really did little harm to anyone, except himself. The methods by which he redistributed his wealth were unconventional, but might repay study by twentieth-century socialist economic theorists. He got rid of his capital. It went initially to other Bucks, but they too were assiduous in getting rid of it. It eventually found its way down to people who put it to productive use, and on its way it generated some entertainment.

Whaley was not the first Anglo-Irishman to visit Turkey. Lord Baltimore was ahead of him by several years. Lord Baltimore's studies of the socio-religious practices of the Ottoman Empire had left him indifferent to most of the theological tenets of Islam, but impressed by one of its physical amenities, women. Polygamy made sense to him. He admired the workmanlike way in which the Turks organized both the initial essentials of acquiring the ladies and the later, more permanent, task of keeping them properly regulated and under control. He adapted the Turkish system to the slightly different circumstances of London, where he owned a large house financed by the rents of his Irish estates. For procurement he took the logical step of employing two London procuresses. Staff for regulation were more difficult to recruit from local resources, so he followed the Turkish example and imported two Nubian eunuchs. His new domestic arrangements kept him contented for most of the year, but he had always enjoyed foreign travel, and he saw no reason to undertake his journeys in lonely celibacy. His arrival with eight women and two black eunuchs attracted some comment in various European capitals, but he dealt shortly with enquiries. A Viennese official who was crass enough to ask which of the accompanying party was Baltimore's wife was told coldly that gentlemen were not in the habit of discussing their marriages with outsiders.

Lord Baltimore used his money to pay for his women. In Ireland, there were repeated attempts by rakes in need of money to use women as a source of it. These attempts went beyond the simple and unscrupulous wooing of heiresses, although that was common enough. Young women of fortune, present or prospective, were kidnapped by 'abduction clubs', who then tried to threaten or cajole them into marriage with one of the club's members. Bogus clergymen

162

were provided to perform the ceremony. It seems probable that some of the girls were frightened into compliance, and were later too embarrassed to admit the origins of their unions. If the abduction clubs had never resulted in marriage it is hardly likely that they would have persisted as long as they did, since the motives were financial rather than sexual, and the penalty on conviction was death. All the available recorded accounts are naturally enough of women who were abducted and who successfully resisted or escaped. One unfortunate girl had to sit through a game of chance in which her future was to be determined by one of twelve men who was luckiest with the fall of the dice. Her resistance was invincible. 'She preserved her castle and her chastity to the last extreme.'

An Anglo-Irishman who tried to preserve his castle at the expense of his chastity was John Butler, who for twenty-three years was the Catholic Bishop of Cork. Not surprisingly, he shared none of the characteristics of Fighting Fitzgerald or Buck Whaley or Lord Baltimore. By all accounts he was an exemplary bishop until he reached the age of seventy. It was then, in 1785, that his nephew died leaving no issue, and the bishop inherited the title of Lord Dunboyne. The bishop was proud of his ancient Norman-Irish lineage. He was the thirteenth successive baron. When he died the title would go to a remote family connection of small account unless he furnished an heir himself, a task that presented difficulties to a man of his calling. He applied for, and was refused, permission to resign from his see and to be absolved from his vows of celibacy. He resigned anyway, selected a young Protestant relation with child-bearing potential, and married her in a Protestant church.

The defection of a Catholic bishop had been unheard of in Ireland since the free and easy days following the Reformation. Catholic opinion, lay and clerical, was appalled. Pope Pius VI was 'seized and overwhelmed' with 'consternation and anguish of mind'. The connubial life of Lord and Lady Dunboyne lasted for thirteen years, but was regrettably unfruitful. He became a Catholic again shortly before his death at the age of eighty-three, and in default of a child to whom he could bequeath his personal estate, he left most of his money to the newly founded St Patrick's College at Maynooth, which trained and ordained the Catholic priesthood. The Butler family tried to frustrate his legacy by reactivating the dormant Penal Laws, still theoretically enforceable. After some involved litigation,

163

during the course of which Lord Dunboyne's confessor was jailed for declining to breach the seal of the confessional, the money was divided up. Maynooth became the richer by a donation of £10,000 from the estate of a prelate whose private life had been perhaps the most unusual in the recent history of the Catholic Church in Ireland.

The list of unconventionalities, amounting in some cases to abnormalities, goes on and on. Some are amusing, some tragic, some boorish, some cruel. Lord Belvedere, persuaded by not altogether convincing evidence that Lady Belvedere had committed adultery with his brother, imprisoned his wife in his country house, after first consulting his father-in-law. Lord Molesworth, the father-in-law, entirely agreed that it should be done. The lady was allowed restricted use of the house and grounds, and was permitted to tell the servants what she wanted of them. They were forbidden to speak in reply. All visits from her children and family were banned. She survived thirty years of silent ostracism. She escaped once, went to her father's house in Dublin, and was sent straight back. Belvedere's death in 1774 released her at last.

It did not release Belvedere's brother, the alleged lover, who had died in the Marshalsea prison. He had been sent there for inability to pay the £20,000 awarded by the courts to Belvedere as the wronged party in a suit for Criminal Conversation. Lady Belvedere maintained to her dying day, and on it, that she was innocent. Belvedere House in Dublin became the nucleus of Belvedere College, the leading Jesuit day school in Ireland.

A prominent figure in the Hellfire Club, which was reticent about its activities but not reticent enough to prevent gossip about Black Masses, diabolism, orgies and similar exotica, was Richard Parsons, the first Earl of Rosse. It was his Puritan ancestor who with Borlase in 1641 had provoked the Old English into allying themselves with the Gaelic Irish of Ulster. There was nothing puritanical about Rosse. His cheerful sinfulness was there for all to see. One of the more scandalized observers was Dean Madden, of St Anne's Church, who made a careful list of Rosse's transgressions and drew on it to compose a letter urging the need for repentance when Rosse was dying. The letter, which began 'My Lord' but carried no other indication of to whom it was addressed, specified a sensational series of offences from fornication and drunkenness to persistent blasphemy. Rosse put it in another envelope and sent it a few doors

164

down the street to the Earl of Kildare, a devout and good-living man, who at once summoned Madden and demanded an explanation for these grossly offensive calumnies. Madden had some difficult convincing to do. Rosse died, presumably laughing.

The Prince of Wales was immoderately entertained by the antics of the three Barry brothers, a high-spending, hard-riding, hard-drinking, self-satisfied, insensitive, self-important, ill-disciplined trio of louts who were the sons of Lord Barrymore. The Barrys were an old Norman-Irish family who had become Protestants in order to hold on to their lands in Co. Cork. There were nearly 80,000 acres of these, worked by a labour-force beset by the usual deprivations of the eighteenth-century Irish peasantry. Their labours paid for the absentee shennanigans of the Barry boys in England, where their father had set himself up in the 1760s. He died when they where young. They too died young. The eldest, who inherited the title, convulsed his brothers and the oafs whom they attracted to themselves, by driving through villages and skilfully breaking windows with his coach whip, or misdirecting waggoners, or pulling up signposts and replanting them so that they misled travellers. In essence, he was a premature soccer hooligan, protected by privilege from official reprisals. His financial resources were infinitely larger than those of his present-day equivalents on the terraces. Barrymore got through £30,000 on nothing worth bothering about in the three years before his death at the age of twenty-four. He was accidentally killed by a loaded shotgun that he had left in his gig at Dover. Before his death he had had to sell most of his property, including a theatre built to London standards in the grounds of his Berkshire house, to meet his gambling debts. The youngest brother, an ordained clergyman who gambled hugely and unsuccessfully, was the next to die, just in time to avoid imprisonment for not paying his creditors. The middle brother kept up the senseless charade for as long as he could, until his creditors too became so much of a threat that he bolted to France, where he died penniless.

The Barrys in themselves were trivial young braggarts. Their achievements, except in a notoriety that they promoted with an adolescent relish, were nil. But they were significant as symptoms, extreme ones, of the complex malaise that in the generations ahead was to destroy the reputation and credibility of the Anglo-Irish in Ireland. They were absentee landlords, whose interest in their estates

165

was confined to the prompt forwarding of collected rents to England, to be squandered on high living.

In 1598, when Hugh O'Neill was still a major force in Ireland and Ulster had yet to be planted by Protestant settlers, a measure granting incomplete but acceptable toleration to Protestants in France was brought into being by the French King Henry IV. This, the Edict of Nantes, prevailed for nearly one hundred years until it was revoked by Louis XIV in 1685. The revocation had effects far beyond the boundaries of France. Two were of bearing upon Ireland.

The first was that the renewed persecution of French Protestants stiffened anti-Catholic feeling in England, which in turn brought down James II and with him what was left of the old Irish Catholic structure. The second was that a flood of Huguenot refugees spread to the Protestant countries of Europe, including England. Some joined the Williamite army which came to Ireland: three hundred officers at the Boyne were Huguenots. A few of these stayed to form the nucleus of a community which grew substantially as families and friends were brought over to join former soldiers who had benefited from the land confiscations, or who took advantage of the commercial opportunities offered by a rapidly growing Dublin, in which trade was a Protestant monopoly. The Williamite nucleus was itself helped by a few earlier Huguenot pioneers, who even before the Revocation of Nantes had read the warning signs correctly and had left France.

Although they were glad to find a sanctuary, the earlier Huguenots in Ireland regarded it as a transient base. 'They looked upon the conquest of this island as the intervention of God and as the preamble to their return to France,' wrote one of their historians. They hoped that the League of Augsburg, or some similarly intentioned successor, would defeat Louis XIV and either restore their old immunities or, better still, give them improved ones. With this hope in view, for the best part of two generations they kept to themselves in a more or less exclusive group. They continued to speak French. Most of them were Calvinists who shared the legal disabilities placed upon Dissenters, but since few had political ambitions in a country that to them was only a temporary haven, and since for language reasons they worshipped in their own exclusive churches, they attracted no unfavourable official attentions.

Their self-regulated insularity did not altogether inhibit them from involving themselves in the life of their temporarily adopted country. In many ways they were as well-equipped a body of immigrants as any country could hope for. They were a compound of experienced entrepreneurs and minor nobility, with skills beyond the range previously known in Ireland, and ample resources of capital. The capital came both from portable valuables, jewellery, gold coins and so on, which they had brought with them from France; and from a curious provision in French law that permitted the sale by exiles of their property in France, and in the case of married couples, the overseas transmission of cash thus realized.

To safeguard the integrity of family wealth, handed down traditionally from father to eldest son by primogeniture, the Irish Huguenots, and presumably their counterparts in the rest of Protestant Europe, practised endogamy.[2] The younger sons were required to be celibate, and whether they were or not, neither they nor their offspring had a finger in the family financial pie, except by benefactions included in wills for reasons of gratitude or affection.

Exclusiveness and endogamy were abandoned by the Huguenots in Ireland when it became evident that the prospects of a return to France in Protestant triumph, or even in tolerated non-conformity with Catholicism, were negligible. They integrated with the Protestant Irish, and their contribution to the country's benefit was distinguished.

They founded the Irish banking system and, after some failed experiments in the South, the Ulster linen industry. The first bank was designed for the convenience of the Huguenots themselves. It was started by David La Touche, who had been an ensign in the Williamite Cailotte Brigade. The bank's usefulness and reliability soon attracted patronage from outside the Huguenot community, and La Touche became prosperous enough to be able to invest in a spread of commercial enterprises judged by him to be potentially profitable. One of these was at Lisnagarvey in County Antrim, a

---

[2] For the anthropologically unenlightened laity, including me before I first read the word, this means that only the eldest sons of any family can marry.

derelict village which had been taken over by Louis Crommelin and seventy-five French weavers and their families. They brought 1,000 looms with them. From these beginnings grew an industry that was to be a major component of the Irish economy. La Touche's bank was run as a private organization[3] by the family for generations, until it eventually became the Bank of Ireland.

Banking and linen apart, the Huguenots were active in ship-building, as goldsmiths and silversmiths, in teaching, and in almost anything that required craftsmanship and disciplined application. By the middle of the eighteenth century they had become completely absorbed into Anglo-Irish society by intermarriage and shared interest. They were later to produce churchmen, architects, writers and soldiers of the same versatile stamp as those from other Anglo-Irish strains. They were responsible and hard-working, and were notably thin on the ground among the bucks and rakes and gamblers. A tribute to one of them, who sounds rather too good to be true, but none the less is representative of the qualities for which the Huguenots were admired, was paid in *Walker's Hibernian Magazine* in 1796: 'While dissipation, debauchery and infidelity to the marriage bed mark the manners of the higher circles of the female fashionable world, a conspicuous exception is to be found in the lady of Peter La Touche, Esq. The lady is eminently distinguished for her unbounded charities, her suavity of manners, her hospitality and all the virtues that the female breast can be susceptible of.' This thumbnail sketch seems unlikely to have made Mrs La Touche many new friends in the higher circles of the female fashionable world, but it is illuminating about them too.

Another outside group, also refugees from Catholic persecution, and also sheltered under the umbrella of Protestant Ireland, were the Palatines. By origin they were Moravians from Bavaria, who in 1709 found their way to the safety of Marlborough's army. Of the total of ten thousand, five thousand were settled in Ireland. They were allotted holdings of eight to ten acres per family in County Limerick on long leases. They were an industrious and close-knit community,

[3] It was the La Touche Bank which bounced Buck Whaley's £14,000 draft, drawn up to settle one night's gambling debt. See page 160.

168

who brought their continental European farming habits with them. When their leases fell in for renewal in the 1760s they were raised from five shillings an acre to thirty shillings an acre. Some paid the increase. Others, still in a cohesive body, took land in County Kerry.

Arthur Young, an English economist who made a tour of Ireland, went to see the Limerick settlement in 1776. The houses, he recorded, were beautifully clean and well equipped. So were the barns. The Palatines sowed wheat, barley, oats and potatoes in rotation. They grew flax. They kept cattle and pigs and poultry. Another visitor at much the same time reported that they still spoke German and kept their own customs but had 'by degrees left off sauerkraut, and feed on potatoes, milk, butter, oaten and wheaten bread, some meat, and fowls of which they rear many'. Whereas 'the labour of the natives is commonly balanced with rent, the Palatines are paid for their work in money'. A husband and wife who toured Ireland in 1844 formed the same favourable impressions – neat houses, fine solid furniture, and an abundance of bacon hanging from the ceilings. The Palatines were still ethnically intact in the 1840s, but after more than 130 years were just beginning to intermarry with the Protestant Irish. The married couple found only one flaw in all this prosperous efficiency. The Catholic Irish peasantry were far more cheerful and kindly, notwithstanding their poverty.

The acceptance into the Anglo-Irish community of these two sizeable bodies of foreigners illustrates neatly several facets of the collective Anglo-Irish make-up. There is generosity towards fellow-Protestants who have suffered for their religion. There is an absence of racial bigotry towards anyone who is not a Catholic (a short-coming that the Irish Catholic could correct by becoming an Irish Protestant). And with regard to the Palatines there is the failure to learn or profit from a practical demonstration of how agriculture could be made to prosper when practised on small-holdings by farmers of skill and dedication.

The Palatines inherited their knowledge and application from a cultural tradition very different from that of the Irish. It would be nonsense to suggest that an eighteenth-century Irish peasant could overnight be turned into a carbon copy of a Germanic cultivator with a Germanic thoroughness in his approach to work. But fifty-year leases, as the Palatines were given, and compensation for improvements, as the Ulster tenants were given, together with a planned programme of advice and encouragement, would have improved the lot of the Southern Irish tenant out of all recognition. It would have diminished agrarian unrest, and helped to bring about a general prosperity which would have left the landlords, as well as everybody else, richer. Instead the tenants were left in their hovels with their fatal reliance on the monocultural potato. When, in the 1840s the potato crop failed in successive years, one and a half million Irish people died of starvation and the diseases associated with it. Another million emigrated. An abiding hatred was born. None of the Palatines died during the Famine. They had plenty of alternatives to the potato.

CHAPTER TEN

In terms of politics, nothing very much happened in Ireland during the first three-quarters of the eighteenth century. Three-quarters of the population were quarantined from political participation. Their deprivations were appalling, but they had no machinery with which to express their resentments, and no leadership to co-ordinate the expression. When the Catholic Irish took to violence, as they not infrequently did, their purpose was not to re-establish Ireland as a nation in which the majority would have a decisive say in the choice of policies. The determination of issues by democratic process was a concept as strange to them as it was to every other mass subordinate labouring community in the Europe of the time.

Traditionally the Catholic Irish had followed hereditary leaders, Gaelic Irish chieftains with English titles, or Norman-Irish aristocrats with Irish habits, or Old English Lords of the Pale with a distinctive style of their own. These had made the decisions, adjudicated in disputes, mustered their followers on the side selected by them whenever they took to arms. The traditional leadership, familiar, understood and, whatever its inadequacies, accepted for centuries, was now gone, its representatives serving in continental armies, or merged with the Protestant Ascendancy, or in the few cases in which Catholic country gentlemen had contrived to retain both their religion and some of their lands, demonstrating their harmlessness to the existing regime by being prominently innocuous.

Without a leadership to steer and articulate there was no

171

cohesion. Travelling poets, story-tellers and musicians kept alive a sad and nostalgic pride in former triumphs and achievements, and in the manner of all folklore magnified bygone virtues and underplayed bygone defects. But the general spirit was of lament for what had been lost rather than of determination to re-establish it.

Such violence as took place was on a small scale, clandestine, and directed at the remedying or avenging of purely local grievances. The Whiteboys, the Steelboys, the Oakboys, operating in small bands independent of one another, sometimes in imitation of one another, first came to be active at about the middle of the century. The causes of their wrath varied, but it was usually inspired by a specific case of injustice which rose above the commonly shared experience of injustice. Landlords, and their agents and employees, who converted their lands to the profitable grazing of livestock and simply evicted tenants to provide more pasturage, were often targets. So were tithe-collectors, over-ardent about the size of their pound of flesh, and tenants who had replaced at a higher rent earlier ones who had been evicted. The bands operated by night. They 'houghed' (hamstrung) cattle, burned farm buildings, destroyed crops and tortured or killed the more accessible of their victims, invariably not the landlord, who was too well-protected. But the quality of landlord protection did not prevent much landlord alarm. Frightened men make poor legislators. The increasingly repressive measures passed in the Dublin parliament were described by Arthur Young, the English touring economist, as 'calculated for the meridian of Barbary'.

The outbreaks were to some extent contained, but were never entirely suppressed. Most of them were carried out with extreme brutality. But in a society in which the chief purpose of the law was to safeguard the rights of property, and where no legal remedy was available to the agrarian dispossessed, or otherwise wronged, the wonder is that there were not many more incidents of the kind.

The legislators had more than rural violence on their minds. To make the parallel with modern South Africa again, much as the white South African looks upon himself and his fellow-whites as South African and the blacks as something different - co-inhabitants, of inferior status - so the Anglo-Irish slowly developed the notion not only that they were Irish, but that they were the Irish nation, full and entire. The idea that a community of immigrants,

172

few of whose families had been in the country for more than a hundred years and many for less, should arrogate to itself the name of the Irish nation, while another Irish nation, the Gaelic component of which had been in Ireland for over two thousand years, was still there and was three times as numerous as the newcomers, has its absurdities. But there was a certain logic behind the thinking. The Gaelic Irish and the others assimilated by them were identifiably a people, with a common language, religion and customs. They were in residence on one island. But they did not meet, and never had met, the definition of a nation as a people organized as a state. They had been unified for the first time as a result of English conquest and occupation. The bulk of them were excluded from many of the privileges of the Protestant Sovereign State because of their Catholicism. They could qualify for membership, as many already had, only by becoming Protestants. In the meantime, the nation consisted of the sum of its citizens who accepted in full the obligations prescribed by the state and who enjoyed its benefits. And since some of its benefits were being progressively eroded by the operation of Poynings' Law and English interference with Irish trade, it was time for this new, 'Irish nation' to stand up and be counted.

In 1718, the fifteenth-century Poynings' Law had been supplemented by a Declaratory Act of the English parliament which empowered it to pass legislation applicable to Ireland. The English parliament was not reticent in the use of this cover to stifle competition with English industry and trade, and to corner for English interests lucrative and exploitable opportunities. Woollen goods, glass and corn, followed cattle and dairy products in being banned for export from Ireland to England. Items that remained acceptable were charged a high import duty on unloading at English ports. Ireland was specifically debarred from charging reciprocal duties on imports from England. The Navigation Acts already forbade Ireland to trade on a direct basis with the American colonies. All trade had to be routed through England.

The Irish nation, Protestant Branch, took cumulative offence. It was suffused with a fresh resentment and inspired by a new line of thought as a consequence of the outbreak of the American War of Independence when the British parliament banned the sale of Irish linen to the American colonies. The American colonists, whose

173

origins, outlook and experience were very similar to those of the Irish colonists, had expressed their exasperation at English rapacity by striking out for independence. The Protestant Irish nation studied this development with interest, modified its lessons to suit its own circumstances, and after a great deal of heart-searching and argument, fell back upon a proposed solution which dated from the previous century. The King of England was also the King of Ireland. That link formalized and established permanently the link between the two countries. The parliament of each should legislate for its own territory alone. A common loyalty and association of interest would remain, but England should no longer have a free hand to control Ireland's affairs to her own advantage.

This concept of nationalism, Anglo-Irish generated, was the root of the Home Rule politics which after Catholic Emancipation came to attract the electoral support of nearly all Catholic Irishmen in the second half of the nineteenth century. It lasted until the middle of the First World War. By then, for sound reasons of self-preservation, the Anglo-Irish had shifted their ground and with a few eccentric exceptions were stoutly against the implementation of the theory that they themselves had invented.

Tortuous reconsiderations and reappraisals supervened. But in the eighteenth century, the war in America, and the fear, to become a reality in 1778, that the French would take sides with the rebellious colonists, prompted a series of connected events that was to leave Ireland a very different country at the turn of the century from that which it had been in 1775. To begin with, four thousand British troops were transferred from Ireland to fight the American colonists. This meant that the country was dangerously undermanned, should the French attempt an invasion.

Invasion nervousness inspired two major responses. The first directly affected the position of the Irish Catholics. The thinking behind it, first formulated in England, later transmitted to the Irish parliament where it was debated intently, was that unless early and substantial concessions were made to the Catholics it must be accepted that if the French landed, most of the Catholics would support them. This assessment was self-evidently correct. It also strengthened the hands of the more liberal-minded members of the House, led by Henry Grattan, who for some time had argued that the remaining Penal Laws were for the most part obnoxious in themselves and in any case no longer served any useful purpose.

The foremost of the surviving disabilities to which Catholics were subjected was to do with the ownership of land. A grudging move had been made in 1771 with the 'Bogland Act' which allowed Catholics to take sixty-one-year leases of up to fifty acres of unprofitable land situated more than a mile from a town. By 1778, fear of Catholic collusion with French invaders, added to a general disposition to do away with what one member, Henry Flood, described as inexpedient as well as inhumane, persuaded the Irish parliament to be far more generous. A motion put forward by Luke Gardiner, of the family who had laid out and developed most of Dublin north of the Liffey, proposed almost total abolition. Provided that Catholics took an oath of loyalty, they should be allowed to buy and sell land exactly as Protestants did.

There was a strong inclination to agree. One of the few who did not was Grattan, whose libertarian temper did not prevent his contributing a far-sighted, and entirely accurate, analysis of what was at stake. Referring to the Catholic numerical superiority he pointed out that '. . . by the natural circulation of property, the lands of this country must be in the possession of the Roman Catholics . . . Under the operation of that (Penal) Law whatever power exists is Protestant. I will not say I would maintain it as a code of behaviour, but I would maintain it as a code to preserve the Protestant authority.' The Protestant parliament took the point. Purchase by Catholics continued to be forbidden. But the next best thing was made immediately available. Catholics were allowed to move into land on 999-year leases, and the inheritance law of Gavelkind, which demanded the splitting up of bequeathed Catholic property among all the sons, was discontinued.

The Catholics responded with declarations of goodwill, loyalty and gratitude. They had further cause for expressions of goodwill and gratitude in 1782, when Luke Gardiner proposed and successfully carried through his second Catholic Relief Bill. The Bill stipulated that, again subject to the swearing of an oath of allegiance, a Catholic could buy and leave by legacy as much land as he could afford. Where land was concerned the Catholics now had the same rights as had Protestants. The Protestants still held nearly all of it, but as Grattan had forecast, numbers, later rather than sooner, would tell. The Anglo-Irish had dug the first sod

175

on the site of the Ascendancy's grave.

In addition the right of Catholics to bear arms was restored, Catholic priests no longer had to register themselves, and a number of other irritants disappeared. Catholics were still denied the vote and the right to hold public office, but those matters too were under serious consideration.

A second consequence of the threat of invasion also led to unexpected developments. The British government offered to replace the troops who had gone from Ireland to serve in America by Hanoverians, at the time still subjects of King George. The Irish parliament declined the Hanoverians and accepted the responsibility of strengthening the defensive manpower of Ireland from Irish resources. There was insufficient public money available to pay for a properly embodied militia and so the Protestant gentry undertook to raise, train and equip a Corps of Volunteers recruited from Protestant tenants and, in the towns and cities, from Protestants of all classes.

The response to a call for recruits was enthusiastic and near-unanimous. Each corps had its own uniform and elected its own officers, a military innovation less democratic than it might sound because the voters tended to vote for their landlords, who had the power to be actively unpleasant to them if they chose, and who in any case had paid for the uniforms. Former regular soldiers provided the training. It soon became evident that although the Volunteers would undoubtedly fight the French if the occasion arose, they saw themselves as having a political function as well as a soldiering one. Their common badge, embossed on belt buckles and woven on standards, was the harp surmounted by the crown. The crown stood for loyalty to the monarchy. The harp stood for an independent Ireland with a parliament not subject to English interference.

The existing Irish parliament had among its members incorruptible and articulate stalwarts like Grattan, Flood and Luke Gardiner, but it was also overloaded with placemen who had been subverted by government bribes, sinecures or honours, and who between them gave the Lord Lieutenant, in his capacity as the *de facto* agent of the English parliament, the power to quash or modify any proposed legislation that he found unwelcome. The Irish parliament thus gave only imperfect expression to the viewpoint of Protestant Ireland.

176

The formation of the Volunteers supplied an alternative, un-inhibited forum, and it was promptly made use of. The Galway Volunteers (Commanding Officer, Colonel Hairtrigger Dick Martin) set the example by taking time off from close-order drill and musketry training to pass a highly unmilitary resolution, in several parts. The first demanded the supersession of Poynings' Law. Succeeding articles called for a blanket cancellation of all English restrictions on Irish trade, and until its implementation the taking of a pledge by all Volunteers to wear only Irish-made woollen, cotton or silken clothing, to eat only Irish-refined sugar, and to drink only Irish-brewed porter. Sanctions were ordained for those who failed to support this form of economic nationalism. A blacklist of back-sliders would be published.

The Galway precedent was widely admired by the Volunteers elsewhere and was soon imitated and improved upon. The govern-ment could manipulate parliament, but it was impossible to ignore the firmly expressed views of eighty thousand armed men who made up the bulk of the country's defensive resources at a time when the French might arrive at any moment. Moreover, the Volunteers numbered among their senior commanders the Duke of Leinster, Lord Charlemont, and similar irreproachable *eminente*. The government gave in, by instalments.

The first instalment was a measure hastily passed by the Westminster parliament. Ireland was permitted the export of glass, wool and woollen products. Direct trade, with minor exceptions, could be resumed with the colonies. But these concessions were not seen in Ireland as sufficient. Grattan stated in parliament that '... no law on earth except the king, Lords and Commons of Ireland is competent to make laws for Ireland', and Yelverton proposed a motion to abolish Poynings' Law. It was defeated by a small majority of placemen, but the government realized that there would have to be further concessions if the Volunteers were to be placated.

The second instalment was delivered after the American colonies had won their independence. The British government had fallen as a result of this defeat, and its successor was better disposed towards Irish claims. It was also influenced by the continuing existence of the Volunteers, who, armed and disciplined, lined the streets of Dublin as Grattan walked to the House to listen to an address by the Duke of Portland, the new Lord Lieutenant. Portland, speaking to instructions, was reasonably conciliatory. Grattan was adamant. The whole nation, he said, was braced for the great act of her own redemption. In January 1783 Protestant Ireland's legislative independence was formally recognized. Portland offered office to Grattan and Lord Charlemont, but they refused. They thought that they could be of more use to their country with the freedom they had in opposition. As matters turned out, they were wrong.

Ireland, declared Grattan, was now a nation. But leaving aside the three-quarters of the inhabitants who were disenfranchised, there were flaws in the instruments of nationhood. The Lord Lieutenant and the Chief Secretary continued to be appointed by the London government. The Lord Lieutenant was answerable to the English Home Secretary, who in turn was answerable to the English Prime Minister. The Lord Lieutenant picked his Irish ministers from Irish privy councillors, but they could not be put out of office by the Irish parliament, and were under no obligation to resign if measures proposed by them were defeated. Bills passed by both houses of the Irish parliament were now sent directly for royal approval, but they might also meet with royal refusal, particularly if, as he often did, the king first asked advice from the English Prime Minister.

These constitutional anomalies at the top were matched by even more serious deficiencies lower down, in the composition of parliament itself, and in the willingness of many of its members to be corrupted. The core of unbribeable members was the thirty-two voters, one from each county, elected by the forty-shilling freeholders, who qualified for the franchise because the annual value of their land was at least forty shillings. The county members were heavily outnumbered by the representatives of the boroughs, a historical legacy, and an unfortunate one. The franchise arrangements varied from borough to borough. In some, all the heads of family had the vote, in others only the borough corporation. In others still the magnate simply appointed his nominee. Many of the boroughs were no longer of any significance, and a few were actually deserted and uninhabited. One hundred and seventy-six borough members were nominated by patrons. If the government wanted to push through some legislation and at the same time give it a look of parliamentary respectability, all they had to do was muster a full turnout of members to whom they had given or promised favours – pensions of various sorts, official jobs with high salaries attached but no work, baronetcies or peerages.

While the machinery for arriving at political decisions cried out for an Augean stable-cleaner, the economy began to flourish as never before. New departures in agriculture, and new industries came into being. Corn, supported by a tariff wall of Irish corn laws, was put into production on a scale never before attempted in Ireland. Its cultivation gave employment to thousands, met the needs of the domestic market, and earned profits from export to England. By 1796 Irish linen exports were worth ninety-eight times what they had been in 1706. Total exports in the same period of ninety years, now that English restrictions had gone, had increased tenfold in value. The government revenue from these increases was used to promote incentives for more growth, to enhance the appearance of Dublin, to pay for such projects as an elaborate national system of canals, and to line the pockets of officials. Anglo-Irish country and town houses were extended, embellished. New ones were built. Country towns began to grow, some of their buildings, both public and private, designed to the Ascendancy standard of elegance. A Catholic mercantile class, unshackled from the Penal Laws, emerged as sharers in the prosperity.

For the fashionable and rich, and for the fashionable not-so-rich or downright poor, it was a period of concentrated social activity. There were balls, masques, dinners, levees and theatre parties, in surroundings which ranged from the magnificent to the plain opulent. A hundred peers had town houses in Dublin, and if some of the peerages derived from services rendered grubbily to the government rather than from the ancient lineage of such as the Duke of Leinster, the peers themselves were hospitable hosts and welcome guests in a tolerant and liberal-minded society. Outnumbering the peers, and often out-rivalling them in the extravagance of their entertainments, were the lawyers, quite a few of whom in due course became peers too. The bucks and the rakes and the gamblers moved easily among them all. The duellists were part of the fabric, not an identifiably separate element within it. Sir Jonah Barrington, one of the chroniclers of the era, and himself representative of it – genial, venal, stylish, high-living, a lawyer and a member of parliament – sums up the distinguishing characteristic of contemporary Irish high

179

society as 'that glow of well-bred, witty and cordial vinous conviviality'.

A young Anglo-Irishman who was certainly witty, cordial, vinous and convivial, but who did not share Barrington's appreciation of the new prosperity and the manner in which its fruits were distributed, was Theobald Wolfe Tone. Tone was the descendant of a Cromwellian settler/soldier. He was born in Co. Kildare, the son of a coach-builder and small farmer. He went to Trinity, was suspended for a time for acting as a second in a duel in which a student was killed, and while suspended was employed as a tutor in Co. Galway by Hairtrigger Dick Martin, who had two younger half-brothers to be educated. While engaged in this task Tone 'became in love to a degree almost inconceivable', as he described it in his diary, with Martin's wife, a highly dangerous thing to be. There is some evidence to suggest that Tone was the father of what was assumed to be Martin's first child to survive, a daughter.[1]

Tone returned to Trinity, qualified at the Bar, married while still young, and began to reflect upon the ostentation and corruption of the society in which he found himself. He was impressed by the objectives and achievements of the recent French Revolution, and interested in their practical adaptation to Irish conditions. He wanted to do away with all privilege, abolish unnatural religious distinctions, unite all Irishmen, reform the parliamentary system so that it would become genuinely representative of all sections of the people, and get rid of English interference once and for all. It was an ambitious programme for a man in his early twenties, but he might have accomplished most of it but for a series of chance happenings, the rogue factor that has recurred so frequently in Irish history.

Tone's first steps in politics were radical, but entirely legal. He became the secretary of the Catholic Committee. This, until recently, had been a moribund and ineffectual organization controlled largely by Catholic peers such as the Earl of Kenmare and Lord Fingall, who disliked making trouble and confined the

[1] Martin was frequently away from home, and for long periods. The daughter was born 'prematurely', eight months after his return from one of these absences. Tone had been in residence for the previous two years. Martin was unsuspicious until years later his wife left him for a man named Petrie. Doubts about the daughter's parentage were raised during the court proceedings. See *Humanity Dick* by Shevawn Lynam (Hamish Hamilton, 1975).

committee's political activities mainly to the production of loyal addresses on suitable occasions. A hardy Dublin merchant named Keogh put a stop to this by manoeuvring out the pacific peers and taking over the reins himself. He employed Tone, and between them they induced the committee to send a deputation to see Pitt, the English Prime Minister. Pitt was tactically sympathetic, and said that if the Irish parliament wished to extend Catholic Emancipation they would find no resistance from England. In the event the Dublin parliament made a few trivial concessions. There was public outrage, a National Convention passed a resolution in Dublin demanding full voting rights, and a further deputation, Tone among it, was sent to London, this time to be received by the king. The king was tactically sympathetic as Pitt had been, but more influential with the Irish executive. His 'wish' that they should consider the circumstances of his Irish subjects was taken as the command that it was. Enough placemen were told which way to vote, and a two-thirds parliamentary majority saw through the Catholic Relief Act of 1793. Catholics could now vote as forty-shilling freeholders in the county seats and for seats in the non-monopolized boroughs. They could become members of corporations, hold minor office, become grand jurors, bear arms, take full degrees at Dublin University without having to avow Protestantism, and they could hold commissions in the army in all ranks below that of general.

Only two major hindrances now remained to Catholics. They could neither become members of parliament nor hold senior offices of state, unless they denied their religion and took the Protestant sacrament, followed by the anti-popish Declaration which had been introduced after the Williamite victory a hundred years before. A motion that would have admitted Catholics to parliament was in fact proposed, but it was defeated by 163 votes to sixty-nine.

That sixty-nine independent-minded and incorruptible members should have voted to allow Catholics into parliament is in itself a remarkable illustration of the way Anglo-Irish attitudes had changed over the previous few decades. The votes against, orchestrated by John Fitzgibbon, the Lord Chancellor, and by John Beresford, the Chief Commissioner for Revenue, both of whose largesse was unbounded on these occasions, illustrate their lack of scruple but also their realism. They genuinely believed in the rightness, as well as the personal profitability, of the Protestant Ascendancy. From their

181

point of view, giving the Catholics the vote was bad enough, but mandatory because of the royal wish. To admit Catholic members to the House and to office would be the first stage in an Ascendancy suicide. Events were to prove this analysis correct but, largely due to the adroitness of these two men, not for a long time to come.

The members of the Catholic Committee expressed their satisfaction at what had been given. They thanked the government in a warmly worded address and thanked Wolfe Tone by presenting him with £15,000 and a gold medal. His satisfaction was not as complete as was theirs. He felt that there was much more work to be done.

While still working for the Catholic Committee, Tone had been the prime mover in the founding of the Society of United Irishmen. The society cut across all religious, social and ethnic divides and aimed at making them a permanent irrelevance in a democratically governed, classless Ireland in which the English would have no say. Tone had no difficulty in finding recruits of a similar turn of mind. The early membership was predominantly Protestant, with a particularly large element of Northern Presbyterians, whose previous enthusiasm for the principles of the American Revolution had been reinforced by their enthusiasm for the French one. But there were plenty of middle-class Catholics. There were Dublin and Belfast merchants and lawyers, landed gentry including Lord Edward Fitzgerald (a son of the Duke of Leinster), several small farmers, and a growing number of the Catholic peasantry or whom the Catholic Relief measures had done little or nothing. There was also an efficient larding of government informers. A government which was adept at bribing parliamentary representatives was equally skilful at penetrating through bribery and blackmail an organization which, although until now it had done nothing treasonable, was close to the edge between permissible criticism and unacceptable action.

It came closer to the edge at the beginning of 1793. In January the French revolutionaries guillotined King Louis XVI, and in February they declared war on England. The previous French war had brought Ireland much incidental benefit. This one did not, although it was yet another example of how internal change in Ireland stemmed more from events outside the country than from political initiatives taken in isolation within it. At first, the domestic Irish auguries seemed to be promising. The Irish Catholic hierarchy was appalled by the excesses in France against the Church and property, and condemned them comprehensively. Pitt sought to supplement the effect on Irish Catholic opinion by engineering complete Emancipation. He appointed Lord Fitzwilliam as Viceroy.

Fitzwilliam, a personal believer in the justice of Emancipation and a personal friend of Grattan, moved more vigorously than was safe at a time when Pitt's overriding concern was to preserve England from revolutionary France, which was demonstrating in continental Europe its abilities both in war and subversion. Pitt wanted a quiet Ireland. To him Catholic Emancipation, to which he felt no particular commitment, was a convenient means of getting it. Fitzwilliam soon concluded that the major obstacles to Emancipation were Beresford and Fitzgibbon. He sacked Beresford, and prepared to sack Fitzgibbon. They complained to Pitt, and convinced him that they could keep Ireland quieter than Grattan and Emancipation could. Pitt sacked Fitzwilliam. His successor, Lord Camden, was briefed to make as few concessions as possible and to keep Ireland in order by the well-tried and reliable method of leaving it to Fitzgibbon's 'Junta' to dispose of unwelcome parliamentary bills by bribery. A Catholic Relief bill proposed by Grattan in 1795, and a Parliamentary Reform bill proposed by Ponsonby in 1797, both went down amidst the waving of greased palms and patriotic clichés about the impropriety of rocking the boat when England was locked in a desperate struggle for survival.

One concession was made to the Catholics, and it was a calculated one. For generations most of the Catholic clergy had been trained in France. The anti-clerical revolutionaries had now made this impossible. Because of the impoverishment and illiteracy engendered among the Irish Catholic peasantry by the Penal Laws, the role of the Catholic priest in rural Ireland was (and to a modified extent still is) a crucial one, going far beyond the performance of the normal liturgical and pastoral functions. His sacred office gave him unquestioned authority. It was strengthened by his bringing spiritual hope and confidence to a people living in conditions of squalor and extreme physical deprivation. He was often the only educated, sometimes the only literate, Catholic within his parish. He was the one person of knowledge and sympathy who could be turned to in time of personal trouble. He gave guidance on many matters other than spiritual. He was immensely respected and immensely

183

influential. He was also at the bottom tier of a tightly disciplined and co-ordinated organization controlled by the Catholic hierarchy. The hierarchy was unlikely to respond to the crude inducements customarily used by Fitzgibbon to influence the course of events, but there was one sweetener that might dispose them to be not unfriendly. The government gave a handsome grant for the foundation of a Catholic seminary at Maynooth. The hierarchy doubtless viewed this benefice as a gift from God, eccentrically routed, and accepted it as they later accepted the legacy from the apostate, fornicating Bishop Butler of Cork. But the government endowment, although welcome, was not needed to sway the hierarchy's views on revolutionary France. They held it in abhorrence.

Tone and the United Irishmen, on the other hand, found the attractions of *liberté, egalité et fraternité* to be progressively more alluring when contrasted with the progressively more cynical opportunism of Fitzgibbon and his associates. A secret oath committing the United Irishmen to the use of force was substituted for the earlier, open one which had been confined to principles. Clandestine negotiations with Republican France were entered upon. The framework of a military organization, directed from Dublin, was set up. Muskets and pikes were distributed. The Northern Presbyterians were to the fore in these activities.

A new, and lasting, element materialized in 1795 and introduced a further complication. A flare-up of the inherited enmity between Catholics and Protestants in the North led to a sizeable sectarian affray in Armagh. 'The Battle of the Diamond' was not much more than a large-scale lethal riot, but one of its outcomes was the formation of a body to protect Protestant interests and to exemplify Protestant solidarity. This was the Orange Order. Its declared aims were to 'maintain the laws and peace of the country and the Protestant Constitution, and to defend the King and his heirs as long as they shall maintain the Protestant ascendancy'. The Orange Order began its campaign to maintain the laws and peace of the country with a series of indiscriminate attacks on Ulster Catholics. Some of the victims fled as destitute refugees to Connacht. Many others were turned into immediate recruits for the United Irishmen. Orange Lodges soon sprang up all over Ulster, Leinster and parts of Munster. Most of the Ulster Presbyterians stayed aloof. They were United Irishmen.

Government coercive legislation reflected the seriousness of the intelligence that Dublin Castle was gleaning from its informers at every level in the United movement. In 1796 the Lord Lieutenant was empowered to proclaim martial law in any district where he though it necessary. The death penalty was imposed for anyone administering an illegal oath; transportation for life was the penalty for taking it. Magistrates were authorized to send suspects for compulsory service at sea with the Royal Navy.[2] Searches for arms were introduced. Later in the year the Habeas Corpus Act was suspended.

In 1793, the Volunteers had been disbanded compulsorily under an Act which limited the bearing of arms to members of government-controlled bodies. To replace the Volunteers, a territorial Militia and then a Yeomanry Force were raised. The Militia was part-Protestant, part Catholic. The Yeomanry was almost entirely Protestant. In 1797, Militia units, along with regular British troops, carried out a prolonged series of arms searches in Ulster which informers' reports, and associated signs of open disaffection, had indicated as the most dangerous of the four provinces. The searches lasted from March to October. General Lake, who commanded the operation, was explicitly ruthless in the framing of his orders. Both the regular troops and the Militia were ill-disciplined and barely under control, and carried out their task with a brutality that exceeded even the prescriptions of Lake. After seven months of floggings, torture, hangings and casual murder, they recovered 50,000 muskets and 70,000 pikes from the homes and farms of, mainly Presbyterian, Ulster United Irishmen.

The size of the arms haul alone was sufficient evidence of the gravity of the threat posed by the Protestant rebels of Ulster to His Majesty's Government. As events were to prove the threat had been heavily reduced, but not entirely eliminated.

Theobald Wolfe Tone had earlier as good as abandoned Ireland and

[2] This aid to the press-gang was not an innovation. Nelson, as a young captain, had to use an Irish-speaking bos'un to transmit orders to his crew. There was a high proportion of Irishmen among the British fleets at the Nile and Trafalgar. Some were volunteers.

the United Irishmen, and had taken his wife and young family to America. But he remained in contact, and followed developments closely. He was too fiercely committed, and too physically brave, to stay away from the coming fight and in 1796 he moved to Paris where his common sense and persuasiveness were invaluable to the United movement. Towards the end of the year the French allocated a 15,000-strong army and forty-three ships for the invasion of Ireland. The force was commanded by General Hoche, and it sailed from Brest in the middle of December 1796. With it was Tone, commissioned as a French colonel, and adequate additional arms for distribution to insurgents after landing.

The ships ran into strong gales almost immediately, and the fleet was split. Some ships, including the one with Hoche in it, never rejoined. Others reached Bantry Bay on 22 December, where the weather was worse than ever. For a whole week they lay off-shore in a continuous gale, interspersed with blizzards of driving snow and dense fog. The ships dragged their anchors. There was a constant danger of collision and of foundering in the shallows. No ships' boats could be put off in the circumstances. The landing attempt was abandoned and the expedition, broken up again by the foul weather when out to sea, returned disconsolately in dribs and drabs to France. The ill-luck of bad weather was blamed for the failure, but it was foreseeable ill-luck. It would not have needed a naval or meteorological thinker of genius to point to the unwisdom of attempting amphibious operations on the south-west coast of Ireland in the middle of December.

Speculative assessments about what would have happened if the French, Tone, and the arms accompanying them had been success-fully landed, proliferated for years afterwards. An over-simplified view was that there would have been a national rising, that the 4,000-odd British regular troops in Ireland would have soon been dealt with, and that an Irish Republic would have come into existence one hundred and fifty years before it actually did. It might have happened. But the reaction of the Catholics in Cork to the prospect of a French presence among them suggests that the preliminaries would have been blood-stained and complex. The Catholic Bishop of Cork and the Catholic Earl of Kenmare may well have regarded the corrupt bigotry of the Dublin Junta as bad, but they thought the concept of being freed from it by French anti-

186

clericals infinitely worse. They rallied the peasantry to the defence of the *status quo*. While the French fleet was riding out the gale off the coast, the peasants were driving their livestock inland to deprive any landed troops of food. Volunteers to the Militia were being hastily armed, trained and deployed. The fact that at this critical time in the country's history the greatest demonstration of practical loyalty to the crown came from the Catholics of Munster, and the most strenuous preparations for severing connection with it came from the Presbyterians of Ulster is not a matter touched upon too often by modern political orators, Republican or Loyalist. It unbalances accepted legend.

The French tried again in June of the following year, 1797. This time they embarked a force of 14,000 troops on ships of a Franco-Dutch fleet assembled at the Texel. The fleet sailed, but was intercepted by the Royal Navy and sunk or dispersed at the Battle of Camperdown. From then onwards, French physical assistance to the United Irishmen was negligible. Napoleon Bonaparte assumed control of France and of French military ambitions. Ireland fell in the scale of French strategic priorities from a likely convert to revolution to a pawn of no intrinsic significance, but which might on occasion be exploited in order to divert English attentions from some profitable French enterprise elsewhere. Napoleon's military genius had recognized the limitations imposed upon his actions by the English command of the sea.[3] He concentrated upon the abundance of targets that he could reach by land. The reliance of the United Irishmen upon effective French aid was as fruitless as had been that of Fitzmaurice, Desmond and Hugh O'Neill upon Spanish aid in the past, and as fruitless as the hopes of the men of 1916 were to be for worthwhile help from Germany.

Despite the satisfying display of reliability by the Munster Catholics at the time of the Bantry Bay episode, and despite the assumed success of the Ulster arms search operation, the government's informers were still delivering a stream of reports about the imminence of an extensive rebellion. The government's response to these warnings seemed calculated more to precipitate a rising than to frustrate it, and indeed there have been suggestions that that was

[3] Napoleon's one major sea-borne initiative, to Egypt, ended in disaster. Nelson destroyed the French fleet at the Nile, and the British beat the French army at Aboukir.

precisely the intention: to drive the government's enemies into the open, and then to smash them. The method used was brute force. Sir Ralph Abercrombie, who took over command of the army at the end of 1797, had a good look at it and described it in a general order as 'in such a state of licentiousness as must render it formidable to everyone but the enemy'. The thought that this humane commander might actually bring to discipline an army whose main asset to the Junta was its uncontrolled ruthlessness was unwelcome in high circles. Abercrombie was superseded by Lake, whose exploits in the North had demonstrated his willingness and ability to do what was required of him.

Connacht and Munster were assessed, accurately as it turned out, as unlikely to be over-troublesome. Leinster was regarded as almost as unstable as Ulster had been. Whether it was or not, much of it rapidly became so when troops, quartered arbitrarily upon villages and requisitioned houses, were given a free hand to flog, torture and hang anybody suspected by junior officers, or even by individual soldiers, to be of rebellious inclination. Some of the victims were undoubtedly United Irishmen, as was proved when under torture they disclosed where their pikes or firearms had been hidden. Many were simply unlucky enough to be in the wrong place at the wrong time or to have provoked reprisal by showing disapproval of some barbarity, or to have encountered Protestant Yeomanry recruited from Orangemen, who regarded all Catholics as rebels and considered that the best way to deal with rebels was to flog the truth out of them and loyalty into them.

The Protestant Yeomanry held the worst reputation for atrocity, but it was by no means a monopoly. A Welsh regiment of Fencibles was particularly notorious, and so was the North Cork Militia, with a high percentage of Irish-speaking Catholics in its ranks. The terror lasted for most of the spring and early summer. The '98 Rebellion started on 24 May.

The United Irishmen's Directory in Dublin had in fact planned the Rebellion to begin on the previous day. They had lost confidence in the prospect of French intervention on Irish soil and had reached the conclusion that the present level of repression was such that the timing must be now or never. The Dublin Castle spy organization

188

was still operating as effectively as ever, and the entire resident membership of the Directory – Tone was still in France – was arrested on the day it was most needed to co-ordinate the Rising. Some were later hanged. Lord Edward Fitzgerald, who fought back spiritedly, was badly wounded and not long afterwards died in prison. Most of the others were imprisoned in conditions of some comfort – they were, after all, Anglo-Irish gentlemen who could afford to pay for decent meals brought in from outside – and were offered their lives in exchange for information. They declined, lived long enough to benefit from an amnesty, and were later sent to comfortable confinement in the Highlands of Scotland, from which they were paroled after a few years.

Without French help, and deprived of its central leadership from the beginning, the Rebellion stood small chance of success. In Ulster, two main bodies of United Irishmen, mostly Presbyterians but with a Catholic element, took to arms. The Antrim body, led by Henry Joy McCracken, put in a fierce assault on Antrim town, fought hard, and was thrown back and dispersed. McCracken was later hanged in Belfast. The Down rebels, Henry Monroe in command, fought two actions at Saintfield and Ballinahinch. The latter was decisive. The rebels broke up and Monroe too was hanged. That was the end of rebellion in Ulster. The confiscation of arms by Lake had been too mercilessly thorough to allow of much further effort. And the increasingly sectarian colouring that events farther south were taking was a disillusionment to Ulster Protestants, who had held staunchly to the United Irishmen's doctrine of mutual religious tolerance.

There was a scattering of outbreaks in north and west Leinster, one of which was put down by a Yeomanry Force led by the Catholic Lord Fingall, but by far the most formidable and prolonged rebel operations were conducted in the south-eastern counties, notably in Wexford. The Rising in these areas was almost entirely a reaction to the excesses of the military. County Wicklow was traditional O'Byrne and O'Toole territory, from which in Tudor times the southern fringes of the Pale had been harassed with persistence, but most of County Wexford was lived in by a conservative Old English conglomerate of mixed Norman, Fleming and Anglo-Saxon blood. These, driven to an alternative between being pitch-capped, flogged and hanged, or fighting it out, chose to fight it out; and caused

189

extreme alarm to the government while they did so. Some Catholic priests defied their bishops' proscription on advancing the spread of French ideas, urged their flocks to die rather than to submit to military terrorism, and unexpectedly showed themselves to be tactically gifted. The Bold Father Murphy of Boolavogue is still commemorated in song, along with the Boys of Wexford and Kelly the Boy from Killanne. But in a stratified society it was still essential to find partially token leadership from established landlords. Several came forward. The commander of the Wexford rebels was Bagenal Harvey of Bargay Castle, the man who after failing to hit his godfather in a duel had been invited to precede him to breakfast.

The Wexford rebels soon dominated most of the county, including Wexford town. Since few of them had engaged in the United Irishmen conspiracy, most had not been issued with arms and had to rely upon pikes run up by local blacksmiths. Inspired by a ferocious resentment, with nothing to lose but their lives, they made up in essence an old-fashioned peasants' revolt, wildly brave, difficult to control, and in some instances undiscriminating and unsophisticated in their violent reactions to earlier outrages by the Orange Yeomanry and their supporters. Just as some of the Orange Yeomanry had automatically equated Catholicism with rebelliousness, so some of the Wexford rebels began to identify Protestantism with oppressive brutality. Although the leadership tried to maintain humane standards, they were universally unenforcible in a volunteer *jacquerie* that had formed haphazardly, had a sketchy organization and held no code of discipline other than to co-operate enthusiastically when orders were given to attack the enemy. There were incidents in which Protestant non-combatants, including women and children, were butchered for no other reason than that they were Protestants. It was reports of these killings which alienated the Presbyterian United Irishmen in the North.

During the first week the rebels beat or drove away a number of small government detachments, but they were themselves repulsed at Newtownbarry when they tried to break through to Wicklow. At Gorey they were successful, which gave them a chance to threaten the southern approaches to Dublin. They did not exploit it. Their most ferocious assault was on New Ross on the River Barrow, a town that dominated the main route to Waterford and Kilkenny. The town was garrisoned by 1,400 government troops supported by

190

artillery. The rebels outnumbered them by about ten to one, but had only their pikes and a small body armed with muskets. A succession of wild pike charges on prepared positions defended by better-armed and better-trained troops was broken up, but the rebels at last fought their way into the town. There confused fighting continued, but rebel inexperience and the lack of control from above exacted their penalty. Cohesion was lost when many of the rebels diverted their attentions to looting and drinking, and the exhausted garrison rallied and forced out the last of the attackers. The rebels lost about 2,000 killed. One of the dead on the government side was Lord Mountjoy. As Luke Gardiner he had introduced and steered through parliament the two Catholic Relief Acts which had brought Catholics the vote and had lifted most of their disabilities. He was a warm and persuasive advocate of total Catholic Emancipation.

On 9 June 1798, Father Michael Murphy (not the Bold Father of Boolavogue) commanded a 19,000-strong rebel force in an assault on the town of Arklow in County Wicklow. The pattern was much the same as at New Ross. Under-armed, fighting with wild courage, they attacked a defence about one-tenth of their strength but in fortified positions and equipped with a full complement of muskets, aided by artillery. Wave after wave of assaults went in and were nearly, but not quite, successful. Father Murphy was killed, and determination dissipated with his death. The rebels withdrew, to join a major concentration on Vinegar Hill, outside Enniscorthy, where many of the survivors of the New Ross fight also assembled.

Reinforcements of government troops, regular, yeomen and militia, arrived in Dublin from England. General Lake marched 13,000 men southwards, reached County Wexford in the latter part of June, and on 21 June attacked the rebel encampment on Vinegar Hill. The rebels were beaten and dispersed. One recorded incident illustrates both the savagery of the battle and the difficulty of assessing the motivation of many participants in this type of civil war. After a small and temporary local success a group of rebels killed some wounded government soldiers whom they had overrun. One of these, from the North Cork Militia, pleaded to be spared on the grounds that he was a Catholic. He was killed. The Wexford rebels were unable to understand the king's soldier. He had spoken in Irish. They were English-speakers of English descent.

The fight at Vinegar Hill was the climax of the rebellion. It persisted afterwards in a few places, but its back was broken. Father John Murphy of Boolavogue led a party into County Kilkenny in the hope of attracting fresh support, but was unsuccessful. He was defeated, captured, and like other leaders of the Wexford rebellion, including Bagenal Harvey, hanged without delay. The heads of three executed country gentlemen were used publicly to point a lesson. They were put on display over the door of the courthouse in Wexford – Bagenal Harvey's, John Colclough's, and that of Thomas Grogan who was an uncle of Colclough and once a member of parliament for Wexford. Harvey had without question served with the rebels, although he had been a moderating influence throughout. There was ambiguity about Grogan and Colclough, but in the heated circumstances of the times suspicion was sufficient to convict. By the beginning of July, the revolt was as good as crushed. A handful of stalwarts joined Michael Dwyer in the Wicklow Mountains, where they lasted in outlawry for years, mounting intermittent guerrilla raids but achieving little except nuisance value.

A new Viceroy, Lord Cornwallis, was appointed in June. He was a soldier, and was also made Commander-in-Chief of the army. He was honourable, humane and sensible, and he at once saw that common justice and stability would best be served by clemency. The Protestant loyalist zealots were still flogging, imprisoning and hanging, thereby generating even greater bitterness. Cornwallis promulgated a general pardon for all rebels apart from the leaders. It led to an almost total submission of those still in the field in Leinster. Michael Dwyer's group in Wicklow was the chief exception.

On 22 August, a little over a month after the amnesty, the French landed in Killala Bay in County Mayo in Connacht. There were only a thousand of them, commanded by General Humbert. They were three months too late. If their arrival had coincided with the start of the Ulster and the Leinster rising in May, they might have inspired and stiffened a third rising in Connacht. But their strategic purpose was diversionary, not inspirational. Napoleon's army was ashore in Egypt and he wanted British attention to focus upon a danger nearer home.

Humbert set up his headquarters, and his headquarters mess, in the house of Dr Stock, the Protestant Bishop of Killala. The bishop was courteously invited to stay in residence, and to eat with Humbert and his officers. He later wrote an interesting account of the experience, of which the closest precedent in the British Isles must have been the billeting of one of the leaders of the Norman Expeditionary Force upon a Saxon bishop in 1066. Humbert was very correct and kept his troops under firm control, but he was disappointed at the small numbers of Connacht Irish who came to join him, and contemptuous of the quality of most of those who did. A handful of the Protestant gentry rallied to him with groups of their tenants in train. John Moore of Moore Hall, an ancestor of George Moore the writer, was proclaimed President of the Republic of Connacht. Many of the Catholic Irish went into hiding until they could see how matters developed.

A week after disembarkation, Humbert, with his mixed force of seasoned Frenchmen and untrained Irishmen, won his first and only victory. He marched his men to Castlebar, where after a short engagement the opposing British force, mainly Irish Yeomanry, took to their heels, discarding a great deal of equipment in their anxiety to leave. 'The Races of Castlebar' were followed by a pause for celebratory dinners and balls, and to allow time for a further component of the expedition, commanded by Hardy, a French officer from an old Irish Brigade family, to catch up. But Hardy was still at sea and did not appear.

Humbert moved eastwards without him, with the aim of crossing the Shannon. But Cornwallis had in the meantime brought a large force from Dublin along the excellent Irish canal system constructed during the thriving 1780s. He caught Humbert at Ballinamuck. Humbert was surrounded and surrendered.

Humbert's French troops were treated as honourable opponents. He and his officers were entertained to dinner by the officers of the garrison in Longford, were taken to Dublin and accommodated in what was later to become the Royal Hibernian Hotel, and were subsequently repatriated to France. Their Irish followers, wearing French uniforms when they were taken, were less fortunate. About five hundred were hanged or shot. Cornwallis was humane, but his humanity was conditioned by the ethos of his times. Rebellion against the crown was a capital offence, and the task of trying the offenders was delegated to courts-martial whose verdicts could be overturned only rarely.

To the Humbert postscript to the '98 Rebellion was shortly added a post-postscript. British warships off the Donegal coast engaged some of the flotilla carrying Hardy's follow-up force. One of the French ships, the *Hoche*, fought back strongly, suffered heavy casualties and damage, and was forced to strike her colours. Her surviving crew was landed on the shore of Lough Swilly, where the officers were treated hospitably. They were taken for refreshment to the house of Sir George Hill. Hill had been at Trinity with Wolfe Tone, and he had no difficulty in recognizing Tone as one of his guests in French uniform. Tone was arrested, hurried off to Dublin under escort and equally hurriedly court-martialled. He made no attempt to defend himself against the charges against him, which as the law stood were unanswerable, but he made one personal request and a short general statement. The request was that since he held a commission in the French army, and was wearing French uniform when he was taken, he should be allowed to die like a soldier and be shot by a firing-squad. He was sentenced to death by hanging. He cut his throat in his cell. Despite medical efforts to mend him sufficiently to be brought to the rope, he died.

If the lasting transformation of a country's entrenched political philosophy is a mark of greatness, Tone must be ranked as one of the greatest Anglo-Irishmen of all. His ideal of a non-sectarian, national egalitarianism was of American and, more strongly, French derivation, but he adapted it, articulated it, and spread it throughout Ireland. From the first arrival, six hundred years before Christ, of the Celtic invaders, the concept that by the natural order of things the only form of social organization was monarchical had gone unquestioned. In the pre-Norman era the inter-tribal fighting was aimed at furthering the purposes of tribal chieftains, not at achieving justice, or improved living conditions, or national unity. The Norman magnates conducted their affairs in the manner of semi-independent absolute rulers, but none of them disputed the ultimate authority of the king, even if they frequently evaded its application.

In the Desmond and O'Neill Wars, the 1641 Rebellion and its aftermath, and the Williamite War, the insurgents either pledged their loyalty to the reigning English monarch or, in the Williamite case, tried to restore the crown to the previous incumbent. The only imaginable substitute for a king, or queen, was another king or

194

queen. For nearly the whole of the eighteenth century, right through the Penal times, Catholic Irish objectives did not include the severance of Ireland from the rule of the British crown. What was sought was an amelioration of Catholic circumstances *under* the British crown.

It was Tone who began to shift the thinking. He was unsuccessful in getting his ideas generally accepted in his own lifetime. The power of the Junta, of British-controlled military strength (the bulk of which was Irish), and of the applied resources of the Catholic Church, which detested his French associates, were too much for him and those who thought like him. But his ideas lingered after his defeat and death. They were elaborated, distorted, and to some extent prostituted by succeeding generations of Republicans. But they were the philosophical root of the constitution of the present Republic of Ireland.

They are also taken to be the philosophical root of the Provisional Wing of the Irish Republican Army and of the Irish National Liberation Army. In his statement at his court martial, made not in an attempt to mitigate his sentence (he knew that it could only be death), Tone had this to say: 'I designed, by fair and open war, to procure the separation of the two countries. For open war I was prepared but if, instead of that, a system of private assassination has taken place, I repeat, whilst I deplore it, that it is not chargeable on me. Atrocities, it seems, have been committed on both sides; I detest them from my heart; and to those who know my character and sentiments, I may safely appeal for the truth of this assertion. With them I need no justification.'

If he were alive today, the holder of those opinions would be unlikely to apply for membership of either the Provisional IRA or the INLA. Both regard Tone as a sort of lay saint, their fount and inspiration. But if in reincarnation, he compromised his principles and attempted to join, he might well have to be rejected by reason of an earlier deviation from doctrinaire patriotism. Before founding the United Irishmen he concentrated his energies on the preparation of the prospectus for a different type of scheme. This was the conquering and colonization of the Sandwich Islands in the Pacific by British troops, with Tone as governor. He submitted a detailed plan to Pitt. Pitt rejected it. Had Pitt approved it, Tone would be dimly remembered by history as a colonial governor, not as the pioneer of Irish Republicanism.

Part of the Proclamation by the Provisional Government of the Irish Republic at Easter 1916 reads: 'In every generation the Irish people have asserted their right to national freedom and sovereignty. Six times during the past three hundred years they have asserted it in arms.'

Was the 1798 Rebellion really an assertion by force of the Irish people's right to national freedom and sovereignty? It certainly had elements that came closer to the description than the Desmond and O'Neill episodes, the 1641 Rising or the support of the Stuart cause against King William. But in '98 too many of the Irish people were in the wrong places on the board to conform accurately to the roles ascribed to them elsewhere in the Proclamation. The Proclamation declares '. . . the right of the people of Ireland to the ownership of Ireland, and to the unfettered control of Irish destinies, to be sovereign and indefeasible. The long usurpation of that right by a foreign people and government has not extinguished the right, nor can it ever be extinguished except by the destruction of the Irish people . . .'

These two passages raise some awkward problems of definition. If the foreign people and government were interpreted as the English in England there would be fewer difficulties, but still some. If the foreigners and their government were the English and Scots *from* England and Scotland, the matter is thrown into immediate confusion. Who, in short, were the 'Irish people' in 1798? Were they the Catholic majority of mixed Gaelic, Norse, Norman and Old English blood? If they were, where did that leave the only natural leaders they had at the time, the Catholic clergy, who with exceptions in Wexford condemned the whole enterprise because of its godless connections with revolutionary France? Where did it leave the majority who followed their Church's lead because it would be unthinkable to do otherwise, or because they thought rebellion to be immoral or pointless, or because life was difficult enough already without a gratuitous multiplication of its sorrows? How did the Ulster Presbyterians fit in to the picture? They were the only large body who voluntarily transformed the theories of the United Irishmen into warlike deeds. Did this entitle them to a share

196

of the right of the people of Ireland to the ownership of Ireland or, since a couple of hundred years previously they had usurped with outstanding efficiency the property of the Ulster Gaelic Irish, should they have been thanked for their contribution to the struggle, and then dispossessed? The Wexford rebels had certainly asserted a great deal, with great gallantry, in arms, but were they asserting their right to national freedom and sovereignty, or were they reacting to murderous provocation and asserting their determination to die fighting in preference to dying supine? What about the luckless Irish-speaking soldier from the North Cork Militia, killed at Vinegar Hill because his patriot captors could not speak what should have been their native language? And – the biggest what-about of all – what about the founders and, until their arrest, directors of the United Irishmen, Anglo-Irish Protestants almost to a man, descendants like Tone of Cromwell's soldiers or of Elizabethan settlers or Ulster planters? Some of them owned quite large parts of Ireland. Were they, as the people of Ireland, entitled to hold on to what they had, or should they, as usurpers, have given it back to somebody else?

The blanket answer to all these questions seems to be that real life, and attitudes to it, were very different in 1798 from the real life and attitudes of 1916. Had the 1798 rebels won, as they might have done if the Wexford Rising had coincided with the Ulster one, or if Munster and Connacht had joined in support of either or both, or if French seamanship and weather-forecasting had been better or if Napoleon had taken a serious interest in Ireland, the United Irishmen might have realized their intentions of governing Ireland by means of a parliament unencumbered by privilege, corruption and religious bigotry. Might, and not would, because a common feature of all revolutions, barring the American one,[4] has been that the eventual outcome is quite different from that which the instigators, who as often as not end up dead, imprisoned or exiled, thought they would achieve. Tone was a humane pragmatist who

[4] The reason for the American exception is that the American revolutionaries were of English and Scots-Irish origin and were obsessive about money, which is what they revolted about. Social issues were not in contention. Slaveowners drafted the Declaration of Independence. In the nineteenth century Catholic Irish emigrants from colonially oppressed Ireland saw no inconsistency in knocking the hell out of the Plains 'Injuns' in the colonial American West.

197

conscientiously recorded his daily experiences and his daily thoughts in a diary that for interest and style rivals Pepys. It is clear from the diary that his ambition was, if he came to power, to destroy the Ascendancy and at least partially redistribute its property. He told a Frenchman who suggested that the peasantry would avenge themselves upon the landlords that: 'I hoped this massacre would not happen, and that I, for one, would do all that lay in my power to prevent it, because I did not like to spill the blood, even of the guilty.' But with too many contenders for too little land, it is hard to see how Tone and his fellow-United Irishmen could have brought about a redistribution without bloodshed. It is harder still to believe that the English would have left him undisturbed to carry out a programme of domestic reform. The English have a record of losing plenty of campaigns, but they have seldom lost a war, the American Revolution again being an exception. Ireland was essential to the English in their war against the French. The English would probably have retaken Ireland amidst a great shedding of blood.

By the time the 1916 Proclamation came to be drafted, some of Tone's aspirations had become realities, other problems had been solved or had altered in nature. Catholic Emancipation had existed since 1829. Successive Land Acts had returned much of the property of Ireland to the people of Ireland. A new, romantic, Gaelic-centred nationalism had developed. It had not existed in any coherent form in the eighteenth century.

CHAPTER ELEVEN

The immediate consequence of the 1798 Rebellion was the abolition of the separate kingdom of Ireland, which had existed, for the most part uneasily, since the reign of Henry VIII in the sixteenth century. It was now incorporated in a single entity embracing the entire British Isles: the United Kingdom of Great Britain and Ireland.

From shortly after the establishment of this unitary state until its dissolution in 1921, the terms Anglo-Irish, Protestant and Unionist were more or less synonymous. There were Catholic Unionists and Protestant Nationalists, but they were rare. The preservation of the Union came to be looked upon by the Anglo-Irish as a semi-sacred trust. 'Disloyalty' was the unspeakable sin. From a slightly later date in the life of the Union it became conversely a semi-sacred objective of Irish Nationalists to break it, and to re-establish an Irish parliament in Dublin. The function postulated for this reborn parliament varied according to the intensity of the views of its advocates, and could be anything from a sort of enlarged county council to the separate legislature of an independent republic. But on the general question there was unanimity among Nationalists of all shades of opinion. The Union was bad, and must go.

During the period of the Union's conception, gestation and birth, many individual Irishmen, and representative groups of Irishmen, looked at its prospect from a different angle from the one they and their heirs were later to adopt.

The idea of a legislative Union between the two countries had been talked about for years as one possible solution to the problem that Ireland repeatedly posed to the safety of Britain. It had been shelved because of the hopes in London that the constitution of 1782, and the removal of Irish grievances over trade, would deflate the Irish potential for causing trouble. Instead there had been rebellion and an enormous diversion of British troops to quell it, and to keep it quelled, at the time of a dangerous war with France. The war continued, and looked as if it would continue for a very long time. Pitt therefore set his mind on Union as soon as it was constitutionally possible. His immediate objective was to do with the war. Ireland could be more tightly controlled from a Westminster parliament in which the Irish members would be in a permanent minority.

Pitt also had in mind a second, longer-term, consideration. The Irish Catholic voters were still too low in number to exercise any significant influence, but the number would in the course of years inevitably grow to the point where the Catholic vote would far exceed the Protestant vote. Catholic Emancipation was inevitable, and a majority of Catholic voters would with equal inevitability elect a majority of Catholic members. After what had been done to the Catholics in Ireland by the Penal Laws and during the suppression of the rebellion, an Irish parliament dominated by Catholics would certainly be a potential, and probably an actual, threat to the security of England. But at Westminster, even if every single Irish member were Catholic, they would all be swamped by the English, Scottish and Welsh vote. The arithmetic of the calculation was so watertight that Pitt was prepared to offer immediate Emancipation as an inducement to Catholics to support the Union.

In Ireland itself Cornwallis, the Viceroy, was instructed to do everything necessary to get the Irish parliament to vote itself out of existence without delay. Castlereagh, who had been appointed Chief Secretary in the early days of the rebellion, and was unusual in that he was an Irishman holding a post normally reserved for Englishmen, entirely shared Pitt's views, including those on early Emancipation. Fitzgibbon, who came from an old Norman-Irish family which had been Catholic until his father's tactical conversion to Protestantism, was now the Earl of Clare and as Lord Chancellor and parliamentary manipulator-in-chief, essential to the success of the undertaking. He was totally committed to the notion of the

Union but adamantly against Catholic Emancipation. In Fitz-gibbon's eyes the advantages of Union were different from those shared by Pitt and Castlereagh. Fitzgibbon saw it as a means of perpetuating the Protestant Ascendancy.

The Catholic hierarchy were in favour of the Union. As they saw it, it would bring the oligarchy at present led by anti-Catholic bigots like Fitzgibbon and Beresford under the control of an English parliamentary majority which was more tolerant in religious affairs than any imaginable Irish parliament was likely to be. Furthermore, the bishops had been told in confidence that although for procedural and presentational reasons it would be inadvisable for the govern-ment to make specific mention of Emancipation in the legislation, they could rest assured that the one would soon follow the other. Among the Protestants, opinion was split. Grattan and his liberal followers bitterly opposed the Union, because it would mean the end of their hopes for an independent Kingdom of Ireland, Protestant to begin with, but as more Catholics came on to the electoral roll, slowly evolving into a nation in which members of both persuasions could work side by side in harmony. Grattan had incongruous allies in the extreme Orangemen. They considered that the Union would hamper them when it became necessary, as in '98, to exercise their right and duty to keep the papists down. English members at Westminster, with no experience of conditions in Ireland, would be likely to apply an inhibiting influence upon old and tested methods of correction.

The legal profession, still predominantly Protestant but with a growing number of Catholics at the Bar including the young Daniel O'Connell, were in the main against, for motives of financial self-interest. Under the existing system their prospects of promotion to highly rewarded jobs in the governmental legal apparatus appeared better than they would in a centralized legal establishment which would cover the entire British Isles. The mercantile community, Protestant and Catholic, also put their balance sheets ahead of their patriotism. They had prospered mightily under the 1782 Consti-tution. Unless they could be convinced that its replacement would be more profitable still, they were inclined to oppose. The Irish Catholic peers, headed by Lord Fingall and the Earl of Kenmare, both of whom had led Catholic troops on the government side during the rebellion, were in favour of Union. They shared in full the

201

views of the hierarchy, and also dreaded the risk posed to property rights should a majority of their co-religionists ever get the upper hand in an Irish parliament.

The matter was put to the parliamentary test on 22 January 1799. Sir Laurence Parsons, a descendant of the land-hungry Puritan who had implacably driven the Old English into rebellion in the 1640s and of the happy old reprobate who had redirected Dean Madden's list of sins to the Earl of Kildare, proposed a motion against the Union. Grattan and his supporters were brilliantly eloquent. Sir John Parnell, the Irish Chancellor of the Exchequer, forsook his previous allegiance in order to support Grattan and Parsons. So did the legal appointee, Fitzgerald, the Prime Serjeant. Parsons's motion was carried by a majority of five, 109 to 104. It was time for the Earl of Clare to readjust the voting pattern.

This he did, with his customary skill and effectiveness. Pitt was set on Union and the resources he provided to achieve it were bottomless. Parnell and Fitzgerald were dismissed. The sum of £1,260,000 was spent upon the purchase of pocket borough votes. The holders of legal and other offices under the crown were promised generous monetary compensation should their jobs go when the Union became a reality. Twenty-eight members of the House of Commons were given peerages, and twenty Irish peers were advanced in rank.

The Junta's familiar tool, shameless bribery, and the familiar Anglo-Irish response to it, shameless acceptance, won the day when the question of Union was debated again on 15 January 1800, the last debate in the beautiful Irish Houses of Parliament in College Green. The rhetoric of the Opposition was colourful and sincere. On the third reading of the Bill on 7 June the Union supporters won the division by 155 votes to 88. With those sixty-seven bought votes the Anglo-Irish sold themselves out. They had a long time yet to go as a caste, but they had demonstrated their chief weaknesses, avarice and corruptibility.

Under the new arrangements Ireland was given one hundred seats in the Westminster House of Commons. Thirty-two representative Irish peers had places in the House of Lords. Holders of the offices of the Lord Lieutenant and the Chief Secretary continued with their staffs in Dublin Castle, still the executive arm of the British government but no longer with an Irish legislature to explain themselves to, or to placate or bribe. The Courts of Law and the legal posts remained much as they had been. The Church of Ireland was still the Church of Ireland, but was formally united with the Church of England. Irish trade with England and the Empire continued unimpeded by tariffs or other interference, and existing incentives to the production of linen and so on were retained.

To the large majority of the people, the Catholic peasantry, these legislative and administrative readjustments meant nothing whatsoever. Most of them were probably unaware that they had taken place. Of those who were aware, few can have much cared. One alien form of governmental organization had been replaced by another, and the change made no discernible difference to a daily life which consisted of living in a crowded hovel on a diet of potatoes, hoping that the landlord and the tithe proctor would not be too extortionate when payment became due, or that some new scheme of land use or caprice of the landlord would not result in summary eviction.

The peasants were also, without either themselves or anybody else giving much attention to it, contributing to a remarkable change in the Irish demographic pattern. They were on the whole a very healthy people. A potato diet is monotonous but exceptionally nutritious. Rural Irish cabins were primitive and squalid, but even in winter they were usually warm, kept so by fires of turf cut from peat bogs which existed almost everywhere. Artificial contraception was unknown to a simple people, and in any case its practice was anathema to the Catholic Church. From the second half of the eighteenth century onwards the rural population began to increase at a rate never before experienced. Official statistics, almost certainly an underestimate, put the rise in numbers between 1779 and 1841 at one hundred and seventy-two per cent. By 1841 a small island with an unbalanced economic and social structure was supporting a population of over eight million people. The outcome was catastrophic.

It became clear, soon after the Union was effected, that some of the things both its supporters and its opponents had thought it would bring were either not happening or were happening in a different manner from the one foreseen. One of these casualties was Catholic Emancipation. Pitt's word to the hierarchy that it would be brought in almost immediately had been given in good faith, but he had not allowed for the malevolent persistence of Fitzgibbon or for the disposition of a king who periodically wobbled into insanity. Fitzgibbon had persuaded King George III that to give his constitutional approval to any parliamentary measure for Emancipation would place him in breach of his coronation oath. Pitt contested this view, but when he did so to the king, the king reacted with such extravagant emotion that Pitt was afraid that if he pressed his case the monarch would once more have to be put under medical restraint. Pitt dropped the matter. The Catholic bishops naturally enough felt that they had been tricked. Clerical influence, very important in Ireland, began to strengthen the opinion already held by many Catholic Irishmen, that the advertised benefits of the Union, like those in the past of the Treaty of Limerick, were a sham contrived by untrustworthy Englishmen. Catholics who had earlier been prepared to give the Union a reasonable trial became disillusioned. Repeal became an objective allied inextricably to Emancipation.

There was disillusionment too for the traders and merchants. This had nothing to do with English trickery and everything to do with English economic advancement. The forecast, reached on the basis of evidence available when it was made, had been that the incorporation of Ireland into a large unified trading area, with no prospect of English restrictions on Irish trade, would give Irish manufacturers and producers access to a large, profitable and permanent market. This situation prevailed for a time. But the growing output of cheap English goods produced at low cost through the agency of the English industrial revolution soon reversed the traffic. Ireland was swamped by imports that were cheaper than the equivalents made locally. Bankruptcies and unemployment followed.

A further souce of commercial discontent was the disappearance from Ireland of a major section of the wealthy class who had previously spent lavishly on building and embellishing their houses, entertaining sumptuously, and equipping themselves with every sort of finery, from carriages to clothes. The Anglo-Irish rich had been accustomed to spend about half the year in their country houses and the other half, when parliament was sitting, in Dublin. Parliament, and the governmental appendages to it that were the founts of power and money, were now in London. So were most of the Anglo-Irish rich.

This change of focus gave rise to a whole range of subsidiary effects, aside from the economic ones. For the whole of the eighteenth century the settlers of style and fashion in Dublin had been, in the broadest sense of the term, aristocratic. When it came to venality or indifference to the hardships of the less fortunate they may have out-paced most of their contemporaries elsewhere, but they were also people with a highly developed taste and with the wealth to indulge it. They built and maintained their splendid houses. They were patrons of the arts, particularly of music and the theatre. They saw to it that great public buildings like the Customs House and the Four Courts and Parliament were designed to standards of excellence. When their numbers thinned out, and London replaced Dublin as the centre for their residences in town, there was no one left with the resources to continue where they had left off. The lawyers and the doctors and merchants who took over their elegant houses had many a man of taste and culture among them, but few had the private wealth of their predecessors. From being a capital city of architectural distinction, Dublin became a rather dull provincial town. The architecture was still there of course, but little or nothing of note was added to it. As the century progressed the city stagnated, and much of it became dilapidated. By the end of the nineteenth century nearly all the old grand houses north of the Liffey had been adapted to use as tenements, some of the most overcrowded and insanitary slums in Europe.

There was another, more subtle, effect of the shift of the site of power to London. The Anglo-Irish who went there began to lose the sense of Irishness which had marked their predecessors. The imperial parliament in which they were now sitting, or around which they had gathered, was preoccupied with a spread of affairs that for obvious reasons extended far beyond the restricted confines of a small island. Ireland seldom came up for discussion. The Anglo-Irish members became aware that they were participants in decisions which affected the future of people not only in Ireland, nor even the British Isles, but all over the world. This doubtless did a lot for the broadening of their minds, but it diminished their concern for, and their effectiveness as representatives of, their own country. Some of them passed more time in England than they did in Ireland. Some passed all their time in England and swelled the list of absentee landlords. In England they were regarded as Irish. In Ireland they came increasingly to be looked upon as English.

The one hundred Irish members of the English House of Commons, and the thirty-two Irish representative peers in the House of Lords, were numerically small but their wealth, power and responsibilities in Ireland itself were enormous. Some of the wealth was illusory, as when the owners of vast acreages of land had fallen into debt through extravagance, or ill luck, or in rare instances had adjusted rents in accordance with the capacity of their tenants to pay, instead of the more usual criteria of what could be squeezed out of them. Their power derived from the landlord's right of eviction and from his *de facto* entitlement to sit on the Bench of Justices in the local magistrate's court, from which he administered laws framed by the likes of himself to protect the rights of property. The responsibility, too seldom met or even recognized, was to the tenants.

An example of the sheer size of some of the Irish estates at the time is the property inherited in 1794 by Hairtrigger Dick Martin, later and more endearingly Humanity Dick, the member at Westminster for County Galway. Martin owned more than one-third of County Galway, together with additional lands in Co. Mayo and Co. Roscommon. One single block alone, in Connemara, covered 200,000 acres, was sixty miles wide, and contained twenty coastal harbours, twenty-five large inland lakes and innumerable smaller lakes and offshore islands. Most of the estate, notably the Connemara section, was unproductive bog and rock. The eastern parts were more suited to agriculture, and from these Martin's income from rents was £3,800 a year. From the loughs, rivers and sea to the west, salmon fisheries and oyster-beds brought him another £10,000 per annum. When Martin came in to this inheritance it was encumbered by mortgages and debts to over £20,000.

The Martins were a Norman-Irish family who had come to Connacht with the de Burgos six hundred years previously, had settled in Galway, and had intermarried with the Gaelic Irish. During the Penal times the then Martin had preserved his estates intact by taking out a certificate of Protestantism, although he continued to be regarded as the leading Catholic in the area by both the Catholics themselves and by the government's local representatives, who held him in deep suspicion. Humanity Dick was the first of the family to have been brought up and educated as a Protestant. His father was thorough about the process and sent him to Harrow and Cambridge. But unlike John Fitzgibbon, the Earl of

Clare, who came from a similar ethnic but financially poorer background, and who after his father's conversion to Protestantism became an embittered opponent of anything to do with Catholicism, Richard Martin was a tolerant and understanding man (except when shooting people in duels). In hard times he commuted his tenants' rents, or cancelled them altogether. He paid pensions to their widows. He never evicted a soul. He held even more legal power than most of his fellow-landlords because part of his inheritance was a manorial court in which he could dispense arbitrary justice as he felt fit. Had he wished, he could have become an intolerable tyrant, and the state would have backed his right as a property-owner to be one. In practice he conducted himself more like the better sort of colonial district officer, an autocratic and genial provider of leadership, help and advice.

With one class of offence, which as matters then stood was not forbidden by any law, Martin was unbending. Anyone he saw ill-treating an animal on his huge estates was arrested, tried and sentenced by the proprietor. He converted a derelict castle on an island into a private prison. Those unable to pay the fines he imposed were escorted by Martin to the shore of Ballinahinch lake, and were personally rowed out by him for a few days' corrective detention. These proceedings were beneficial in that they un-doubtedly reduced the incidence of cruelty to animals in County Galway, and were the preliminary practical steps to the thinking which in 1821 led Martin to introduce to the House of Commons a bill 'to prevent the ill-treatment of horses and other animals'. But in the broader context, the significant point is not that Martin used his personal power to achieve a humanitarian end, but that he held the power at all. His personal choice was for benevolent despotism. Had he instead chosen despotic malevolence there would have been little to control him. It was a situation unique, in the United Kingdom, to Ireland.

Martin had voted for the Union, out of conviction, not for the sake of a bribe of cash or rank. He genuinely believed that the Union would be good for the people of Ireland in whom, rare among his class, he included the peasantry and tenantry of his estates. He was a consistently firm backer of Grattan, now also at Westminster, in his campaign for immediate Catholic Emancipation and after Grattan's death he continued to take an enlightened stance on all Irish issues.

It is a pity that there were not more Anglo-Irish leaders of the liberality of Richard Martin.

From the time of the Union onwards, the collective *persona* of the Anglo-Irish caste began to change. With most of the rank and fashion now as much, or more, interested in England as in Ireland, a sober worthy middle class took over the ordering of affairs in Dublin. It was still a predominantly Protestant city, but the old flamboyance had gone. There was a steadier, more responsible civic-mindedness. Communications with England improved, as steam-powered packet boats, with (usually) reliable timetables, replaced the old sloops which depended upon fair winds and might take anything from a few hours to several days to complete the crossing. The exchange of visits, social and professional, and the exchange of impressions and ideas between Ireland and England increased.

The profits from the industrial revolution were transforming urban England. The new urban poor were on the whole more wretched than the old rural poor, but there was enormous development in municipal building, public health and sanitation, road building, and the building of railways to replace the old stage coaches, which were far slower and could be afforded by relatively few. Dublin was in no need of new municipal buildings – it already had the finest in the United Kingdom – but where English examples were useful to Ireland they were thoroughly studied and applied, by Protestant engineers and technicians. No known city has ever made public heroes of the men who installed the sewage system, or arranged for the street cleaning programme, or designed the railway stations, but without their pioneer contributions life would be considerably less comfortable. Dublin, Cork, Belfast and Limerick have much to be grateful for to these conscientious representatives of the Anglo-Irish professional classes.

The Royal Dublin Society continued its excellent work. The Trinity Medical School, the Royal College of Surgeons, the Royal College of Physicians, and the practical training of medical students in hospitals brought the Irish medical profession to a high peak of reputation throughout the growing British Empire. Catholic doctors qualified in increasing numbers, and by the 1840s some of them were at the head of their profession. But a century of the suppression of Catholic education generated consequences which could not be made to disappear overnight. There was catching up to be done. The Anglo-Irish had been the men in possession. It was they who endowed, designed, built and put into use many of the hospitals still serving Dublin today – the earlier Doctor Steevens's and Sir Patrick Dun's, the later Victorian Adelaide, Meath and Baggot Street.

The innate constructive energy of the Anglo-Irish found a new and congenial outlet in the expanding Indian and Colonial Empire. The first British imperial experience, in North America, had ended in failure. The second, which to some extent overlapped the first, was to end during the mid-twentieth century in, on the whole, honourable disengagement, leaving a legacy of institutions for the provision of law, public administration, education, health, agriculture, conservation, policing and most other aspects of social organization. Many of the legatees squandered their inheritance. Many, such as India and Malaya, preserved, adapted and built upon the best features of it. Colonialism is currently regarded as sinful but, like it or not, it has moulded the attitudes and procedural conduct of half of the present population of the world. The United Nations Charter is based on the principles and ideals of English parliamentary practice. So is the constitution of the Republic of Ireland.[1]

For a great many reasons the younger sons of the Protestant gentry and the Trinity-graduate sons of the Protestant bourgeoisie found government service in British colonial expansionism greatly to their taste. By family background they were colonialists. By nature they were tough and adventurous. Opportunities for respectable, exciting and reasonably well-paid employment were available to them abroad. Opportunities at home were not. Eldest sons inherited; younger sons, although given some financial help, had to make their own way. It was the same in England, but England was rich in mineral resources and was profiting from their exploitation through the new industrial technology. English landed proprietors, whose families had farmed the same land for centuries at a modest

---

[1] This is unusual in that it was written in the English language and then translated into Irish. Both versions are legally binding. But where inconsistencies of interpretation arise, the Irish-language version takes precedence over the English one. The English enthusiasm for 'Irish jokes' is not looked upon kindly in Ireland, but sometimes Ireland leads with its chin.

return, were finding themselves the owners of coalfields, or of the sites of new industrial plants and new industrial towns. By comparison, Irish exploitable mineral resources were meagre to the point of being almost non-existent. Industrial development, almost entirely in the north, did not begin to compare with what was happening in England. The lack was an incentive to emigration, or to temporary exile for a working lifetime.

The emigrants who went permanently chose, usually, the United States and Canada, and later Australia, New Zealand and Southern Africa. In these countries, land was plentiful, the climate was compatible, and the Anglo-Irish (as well as a much larger body of the Catholic Irish) fitted naturally into an English-speaking environment, in which English models of law and administration had been copied or adapted. Most of the temporary exiles went for service in India. Later in the nineteenth century they also went to newly acquired territories in other parts of Asia, in Africa and to remote island outposts such as St Helena or the Falkland Islands. But India saw the majority of them, right up until Indian independence in 1948.

Until the middle of the eighteenth century the control of India had been in contention between the French and the English. The first recorded appearance of Irishmen in the sub-continent is of soldiers of the Irish Brigade in the French army, commanded by Lally de Tollendal, the son of Sir Gerald Lally of Tullanadaly in County Galway. Lally had some initial successes, but in 1761 he was beaten decisively at Wandewash in Madras by a British force led by Sir Eyre Coote. Coote was a Protestant from County Limerick.

British India at this time, and until the Sepoy Mutiny of 1857, was ruled by The Honourable East India Company, a joint stock enterprise based on the City of London. The Company had started by trading in a few Indian ports and then expanded erratically inland, partly for reasons of straightforward commercial expansionism and partly because to survive it had to protect its own assets by annexing and controlling neighbouring territory. For annexation and military control 'John Company' formed its own army, ultimately to become three separate armies – those of Madras, Bombay and Bengal. Most of the troops were native infantry and cavalry, recruited locally and officered by Europeans. There were also some infantry battalions in which all ranks were European. A

210

high proportion of the officers of both the Indian and European units were Anglo-Irish, and a John Company cadetship was a much prized opening for the younger sons of the poorer country gentry and of the Irish professional classes.

After the French Revolution, the Irish Brigade in the French service, which had always been led by monarchist Catholic aristocrats, found itself with few exceptions unable to continue under the new regime. A few years later, when the Catholic Relief Act introduced by Luke Gardiner permitted the carrying of arms by Irish Catholics, these became acceptable to the British army, and many were recruited into the John Company army as well. Between 1825 and 1850, for example, the Bengal army took on 7,620 European recruits. Of these 3,639 were Irishmen, 2,884 were English and 830 were Scottish.

In the late 1850s, the East India Company was dissolved and the government of India became the direct responsibility of the crown. Nine battalions of the Company's army were transferred to the queen's service and six of them were regarded as Irish. A little later British army regiments, previously known only by a number (the 88th Regiment of Foot, and so on), were given territorial designations and their recruiting areas and depots were established in specified regions. The six former John Company battalions were merged into three regiments, of which two were to become the Royal Dublin Fusiliers and the Royal Munster Fusiliers. The Dublins and the Munsters came into the regular British army by a roundabout route, but the pattern thus established of Anglo-Irish officers commanding Catholic Irish soldiers was duplicated in other Irish queen's regiments and in many English and Scottish queen's regiments.

Anglo-Irish officers who followed Eyre Coote's example by distinguishing themselves in India were Ranfurley Knox from Sligo; Abraham Roberts from Waterford, whose son Frederick, 'Bobs Bahadur', was to achieve every military distinction from winning the Victoria Cross while a junior officer to being made Commander-in-Chief in South Africa during the Boer War, ending as a Field-Marshal and an Earl; Carnac, from a family of Dublin Huguenots; and Arthur Wellesley, later the Duke of Wellington, who first made his name as a 'Sepoy General' commanding John Company troops in battle, although he himself was a king's officer.

But the Company did not simply control its huge and growing territories militarily. It provided an elaborate system of orderly administration. Some administrators were appointed as such, but many were recruited by the transfer of able officers from the Company's army. The most outstanding Anglo-Irishmen among these were two brothers from the North of Ireland, John and Henry Lawrence, and John Nicolson, also from the North, a dour, stern, Cromwellian figure of enormous energy who was killed while still in his thirties at the siege of Delhi during the Sepoy Mutiny, and who so impressed the people whom he ruled that they assumed that he must be divine and founded a religion with him as its god.

Not all, of course, reached those heights. The career of William Henry Tone is more typical. He was the brother of Theobald Wolfe Tone.

Commissioned in the Company's army at the age of sixteen he passed his first six years of service with the garrison of St Helena, then Company property. He went on to India, resigned, rejoined, reached the rank of Colonel, resigned again, and hired out his services as a soldier of fortune in the internecine wars in progress at the time between independent Indian rulers. He was killed in an obscure campaign while leading an assault on a fort.

Arthur Wellesley, in terms of military and political achievement within the context of Anglo-Irish orthodoxy, was the most successful member of the caste. As the son of Lord Mornington, the Trinity Professor of Music, Wellesley was born to privileges unknown to the sons of Church of Ireland rectors and minor country gentlemen who served with the East India Company. When still a young man he was given a safe borough seat in the Irish House of Commons as member for Trim, and was made ADC to the Viceroy. By the time of his death he had shown himself to be possibly the most distinguished general in the whole history of the British army. He had won the Peninsular Campaign, had finally defeated Napoleon at Waterloo and had, in an interval between active soldiering, been Chief Secretary for Ireland from 1807 to 1809 (with six months off to fight at Copenhagen and in the Tagus Campaign). After leaving the army he was successively Foreign Secretary, Prime Minister and Leader of the Tory Opposition in the House of Lords. He was politically conservative to the point of being reactionary, but he was a man of tremendous common sense, trenchantly expressed.

212

He was bitingly critical of Irish absentee landlords. When he was Chief Secretary he commented that the absentee position was such that there were few gentlemen left in any of the counties in Ireland 'to whom one could wish to entrust a Commission of the Peace'. His later remarks on the phenomenon included one about Irish landed proprietors who passed their time 'brawling and balling in London' and 'amusing themselves in clubs in London or Cheltenham or Bath or on the Continent'. Whenever they considered the distress in Ireland they expected the government to find a remedy, 'anywhere except in the pockets of the Irish gentleman'. When he was in opposition in 1836 and the Whig government extended the Poor Laws to Ireland, Wellington hoped that the measure would 'induce the gentlemen connected with Ireland, whether resident proprietors or not, to look after their properties and at the same time also to pay some little attention to the state of the population on their estates'. He was an inflexible believer in the rights of property, and opposed the reform of Irish municipalities on the grounds that the election of members of public bodies by ratepayers would give the poorer classes the power to tax the wealthy classes, which would be 'a most monstrous power to confer'. He strongly opposed Catholic Emancipation on principle but was not afraid to change his mind, and those of its other opponents, when he foresaw that the only alternative to granting it would be civil war. He held strongly to the view that inherited wealth and privilege, while right in itself, carried with it a corresponding duty to perform public service 'in any capacity, civil or military, in which I could be useful'.

In a pithy analysis of the economic woes of rural Ireland he identified three salient defects. Absentee landlordism; the repeated subdivision of land leased to tenants until the small plots held by individual lessees were too tiny to be economic; and on many estates, particularly in the west, the absence of cash payment by landlords for labour and its substitution by the free use of a plot of land. Wellington had in fact picked the three most damaging factors that were to contribute to the disaster of the Potato Famine. The remedies that he would have applied, theoretical because he held no direct executive authority for Ireland and was always too taken up with business elsewhere to concentrate upon Irish problems, were 'an enormously heavy' tax on absentee landlords; the imposition by law of a minimum-sized plot below which it could not be sub-let; and the compulsory payment of cash for work done. They were revolutionary ideas for a stanchion of the unfettered rights of property. But his clarity of thought had convinced him that the irresponsibility of many of his own class in Ireland would, unless corrected by drastic means, lead to the destruction of the system that he held in respect.

Had he, at some time after Waterloo, been in charge of exclusively Irish affairs he would not have been liked – which would not have bothered him in the slightest – but he would have been both clear-sighted and efficient. And since his prestige and personal authority was immense he would have been obeyed. He would have done a lot of good and have been criticized for the patrician way in which he did it.

He is commemorated to an unappreciative Irish public by a massive obelisk in the Phoenix Park. The statue of King Billy in College Green, long the focus of pious Loyalist celebration on the anniversary of the Boyne, and of imaginative vandalism by those less pleased with the outcome of the battle, has gone. So has the statue of Queen Victoria which, covered in pigeon droppings, decorated the forecourt of Leinster House, Dail Eireann, until after the Second World War. The statue of General Gough, also in the Phoenix Park, was blown up by people opposed to what he represented. Nelson's Pillar, the memorial to the 'one-eyed adulterer', for generations the Dublin tram terminus for suburban routes, and similar in construction to Nelson's Column in Trafalgar Square in London, was brought down in the 1950s by an efficient demolition job which dropped the pillar along the middle of O'Connell Street. Wellington, alone of the Ascendancy heroes, has been left with his memorial intact. Its survival is a tribute more to the indestructible solidity of its construction that to the regard in which he is held in modern Ireland.

CHAPTER TWELVE

Wellington's defeat of Napoleon at Waterloo in 1815 brought an end to a war with France which, with one short interval of precarious peace, had lasted since 1792. During those twenty-three years agriculture had prospered, in Ireland as well as in England. Much Irish land had been put into grain production, with a consequent rise in rural employment.

The war was followed by an economic slump. Grain prices fell. Landlords changed from corn-growing to the raising of livestock, which offered less employment and led to more evictions, as cabins and potato plots were cleared away to be replaced by pasturage. The evictions, and the fear or threat of more of them, led in turn to an intensification of agrarian violence, on the lines pioneered by the Whiteboys and Steelboys during the previous century, but with an impetus added by memories of the '98 Rebellion. There were murders, beatings, burnings of property, destruction of crops and the houghing of cattle. The government's response was to continue with the coercive machinery which had been brought in before the Rebellion, the suspension of Habeas Corpus and the rest. The military excesses of the Rebellion were not repeated, but a large number of troops remained in Ireland and were called upon repeatedly to maintain order.

Government nervousness had been increased in 1803, when Robert Emmet, a young idealist from a distinguished family of Dublin Protestant lawyers and the brother of Thomas Addis

Emmet, a member of the Directory of the United Irishmen who had been arrested on the first day of the '98,[1] led a badly managed attempt at a fresh rebellion in Dublin. It was a small and ill-co-ordinated affair that was easily put down. Emmet was tried and hanged. He made a moving and eloquent speech from the dock which was circulated widely both in Ireland and in America in tract form. The speech, and the verses written about him by his Trinity friend, Thomas Moore, were an inspiration to generations of Irish revolutionaries. The Emmet episode, the sporadic rural violence and the government's reaction to them made an inauspicious beginning to the life of the Union, which was supposedly going to bring so much good with it. Except for a few short intervals, it was not until 1823 that the government felt able to govern without using a combination of emergency decrees and partial suspension of constitutional rights.

In parliament, those Irish members who continued to work for full Catholic Emancipation were repeatedly rebuffed. The one hundred Irish members, by no means all Emancipators, were a small minority in a House of Commons with an overall membership of 660. Any bill passed by the lower house had still to be considered by the House of Lords. The peers, in particular the Irish ones, tended to regard any loosening of the reins in Ireland as an invitation to the threateners of property to become more active. In the constitutional forum for the discussion and regulation of the nation's affairs Emancipation lay moribund.

One man who thought that he could see a way through the jungle of dishonoured promises, obstructionism and indifference was Daniel O'Connell. O'Connell's father was a Catholic landlord in Kerry. The son was a lawyer, of fine physique and with a resonant, carrying voice which was an asset at mass meetings in a pre-electronic age. He was bilingual in Irish and English, a born organizer, a natural leader, and an ingenious exploiter of any loosely drafted wording in legal enactments. He founded, expanded

[1] He was both the secretary and a member of the executive. With the other leaders he was detained at Fort George in the Scottish Highlands until 1803. On his release he went to Brussels to try to arrange French support for a new rising. He abandoned this after his brother's death, and went to the United States to practise at the Bar. He was Attorney-General of New York from 1812–13.

and controlled the first genuinely populist movement in Irish history.

A relic of 1796 legislation, the Convention Act, banned the formation of organizations consisting of representative delegates. O'Connell's Catholic Association of Ireland, founded in 1823, stepped neatly aside of the prohibition by making no claim that its members represented anyone. They were individuals devoted to winning Emancipation by legal, constitutional means, and they conducted their business by correspondence and by the collection of signatures to petitions. Agents in every parish raised subscriptions of a penny a month, 'the Catholic Rent'. The parish clergy, now of a generation educated at Maynooth and closer to the people than their predecessors trained in France, were enthusiastic supporters. A large and consistent income was soon available, and was used both for propaganda and for contesting in the courts specific cases of injustice against Catholics.

The government passed a Suppression Act to do away with the association. It was effective until O'Connell did some more legalistic side-stepping and brought the association back to life again in an almost identical form, but using a new constitution that met all the requirements of the Suppression Act.

There were by now in the counties about 100,000 Catholic forty-shilling freeholders. The Waterford ones, backed by O'Connell's association, showed their teeth in an election in 1826 when they voted in a Protestant Emancipator named Villiers Stuart, and kept out Lord George Beresford, a leading landlord whose family were the proprietors of most of the county. Freeholders had never before in Ireland voted against their own landlord. He held too strong a power of reprisal. Beresford was greatly put out by this gross display of insubordinate ingratitude.

In 1828 O'Connell demonstrated how one determined man, with a disciplined mass following and an incisive tactical brain, could achieve by constitutional means an end that had been beyond the powers of the gifted advocates of Emancipation in both the old Dublin and the present Westminster parliaments. O'Connell himself stood as a candidate in the Clare election against a local landlord, Vesey Fitzgerald. The Liberator, as O'Connell was to be known, urged the freeholders to defy their landlord and come out for Emancipation. The parish clergy were effective canvassers, and

217

doubtless added to their arguments some reflections upon the likely eternal destinations of those who chose the wrong man. O'Connell won by 2,057 votes to 982 and thereby had the government masterfully hooked.

He could only enter parliament by making the declarations accepting the Protestant faith, which he had no intention of doing. Instead, he grasped that by putting up a candidate at every by-election, using similar tactics to the Clare ones, he could win them all, except for a few constituencies in the North. Parliament would have to be prorogued sooner or later, and there would be a general election. O'Connell's candidates would win most of the Irish seats. And if a majority of the elected Irish representatives were excluded from their own parliament, Westminster would lose whatever moral right it had to rule Ireland. The problem did not end there. The new Prime Minister, the Duke of Wellington, the arch-anti-Emancipator and owner of a rich vein of common sense, foresaw the logical consequences as civil war.

Such a warning from a Prime Minister with the experience and personal authority of the duke was sufficient to induce the House of Lords to accept it at its face value, and the king to follow the advice that he was given. The Emancipation Bill was given the royal assent in 1829. The religious declarations were abolished. The sacramental test for parliament went out with the declarations, and cleared the way for Protestant Dissenters to enter. A simple oath of allegiance replaced the old requirements. The only offices not open to Catholics and Dissenters were those of the Regent, the Lord Chancellor and the Lord Lieutenant of Ireland. The monarch, of course, was Protestant in perpetuity.

It was a famous victory for O'Connell. The government had been out-manoeuvred into belatedly giving what they had undertaken to give voluntarily twenty-nine years previously. They now did their best to destroy whatever credit they might have gained from Irish Catholics for giving it at all. They deprived most of the forty-shilling freeholders of the vote by lifting the franchise limit to ten pounds. They dissolved the Catholic Association. They refused to reform the corporations so that, although Catholics had a legal right to hold office in them, it was in practice almost impossible for them to exercise it. It was this sort of narrow vindictiveness, supported or instigated by most of the Irish peers in the House of Lords and by some of the Irish members of the House of Commons, which ultimately doomed the Union and with it the influence of the Anglo-Irish.

There were two observable elements of opposition to the government in Ireland. The first, and by far the smaller, was represented by the violent men of the agrarian attacks. The second, mass one, O'Connell's, was led by a man who believed in, and had repeatedly stated in public his belief in, the unification of all Irishmen in one nation under the crown – the old Grattan formula. He was a disciplinarian strongly opposed to violence. He had kept, and in the future would keep, his vast following under total control. He had said, and he meant it, that Irish freedom was not worth the shedding of a single drop of blood. Although he himself was a native Irish speaker he regarded lack of English as an obstacle to progress in the modern world and advised monoglot listeners to learn it. He was the 'uncrowned King of Ireland' with astonishing influence, all of it weighted in favour of peaceful and orderly change.

That change was inevitable should have been clear to anyone with half an eye to look at the signs. In the United Kingdom, changes in the franchise qualifications which must sooner or later be introduced to meet English, Scottish and Welsh pressures would apply equally to Ireland. An enlarged Catholic and Nationalist electorate would put in Catholic and Nationalist representatives at Westminster. If these were prevented from delivering by constitutional methods what the electorate wanted, they would be discredited, and the violent men would step in. O'Connell was probably the one man in the course of Irish history with the power over the Irish people to negotiate peacefully a settlement which would have secured for the subjugated majority a place in the scheme of things both temporarily satisfying and capable of the evolutionary improvement which later transformed the political life of Britain. The option was not so much rejected as not considered at all. Property was sacred. Men of property did not do deals with demagogues, even if the demagogue in question was something of a man of property himself. The only way to deal with Ireland in the view of these legislators and proprietors was to repress terrorism and to maintain the *status quo* at all costs. At a lower level the Orange Order, its members spread throughout the country in all classes of Protestant society, and well represented in the magistracy, followed their leaders' *diktat* with a grim assiduity.

In its earlier years Emancipation seemed to have achieved little except the establishment of a principle and the placing of one Catholic MP in the House of Commons. A change of government in 1835 at last brought some improvements. The enduring grievance of the payment of tithes by the Catholic population to support the finances of the Protestant Church was ended in 1837. A Poor Relief Act in 1838 at least acknowledged that there was poverty in Ireland, even if the ameliorations introduced, similar to those in England, were the degrading indignities of the workhouse. The colourful anachronisms of the municipal electoral arrangements went in 1840. Local landlords no longer controlled the appointments of holders of office. The vote was given to those with the appropriate property qualification, Catholics took their places in parliament for the first time since the Boyne, and O'Connell became the first Catholic Lord Mayor of Dublin for two hundred years. A fair-minded and decisive Lord Lieutenant, Mulgrave, assisted by one of the finest administrators ever to have been sent to Ireland, Thomas Drummond, a Scotsman who was Under Secretary, was rigorously impartial in everything from the enforcement of the law to the distribution of jobs at all levels in the government service. Mulgrave and Drummond were dismissive of claims to hyper-loyalty by the Orange Order, 125,000 strong, and for eight years between 1837 and 1845 the order went into abeyance. A letter from Drummond to the Grand Jury of Tipperary illustrates both his attitudes and his forthright style in expressing them. The subject was agrarian crime. Peasant crime, wrote Drummond, arose from peasant wrong. 'Property had its duties as well as its rights.' Such a novel analysis of the defects of the social system caused amazed anger among the gentlemen of Tipperary and among landlords everywhere.

The success of this interlude of benign good government was partly due to the assistance of O'Connell. His constant message was that violence was not only wrong in itself, it was unprofitable. There must be change, but it must be by constitutional means. The narrowness of Orangeism was menacing, but 'the liberal Protestant is an object of great affection and regard from the entire Catholic population'. The message was heeded. Rural crime diminished remarkably. The policing of the country was for the first time put on a regular and systematic basis by the formation by Mulgrave and Drummond of the Royal Irish Constabulary, which covered all areas outside Dublin, and the Dublin Metropolitan Police, which looked after the capital. The RIC were trained and armed for use as a paramilitary force should there be serious trouble, but otherwise they carried out all the usual police functions. They were officered from the same class as the army and the navy, but the constables and sergeants were recruited almost entirely from Catholic countrymen. Competition to join was keen, and standards of physique and intelligence were high for acceptance. Until the Troubles preceding Independence in 1921, and despite their misuse in enforcing evictions in the 1880s and '90s, the RIC were a popular and respected force.

These slowly unfolding political and administrative developments took place against a background, unique in the Western world, of a huge population expansion sustained by a single vulnerable crop. In 1844 a commission chaired by Lord Devon reported thus: 'The potato enabled a large family to live on food produced in great quantities at a trifling cost, and as a result the increase of the people had been gigantic. There had, however, been no corresponding improvement in their material and social condition, but the opposite ... Their sufferings were, in the opinion of the Commission, greater than the people of any other country in Europe had to sustain.'

As a source of nutrition the potato is rivalled by few foodstuffs. It has carbohydrates, protein, mineral salts and vitamin C. With milk it can thoroughly sustain the human body for a natural lifetime. Irish soil and climatic conditions are perfect for its cultivation. It does best in friable soils, is tolerant of the acidity in imperfectly drained bogland, needs a heavy rainfall, and benefits from a high humidity and prevailing westerly winds during the growing season. Ireland has them all. Nutrition and cultivation aside, the potato had great advantages as a crop which could be grown in the conditions of intermittent warfare which prevailed in Ireland for nearly a century and a half after Sir Walter Raleigh introduced the first tubers to Youghal.

Irish potatoes were, and in some places still are, grown in layzbeds, which is a misnomer. The system is to lay the seed potatoes on the surface, previously manured, of the area to be planted, dig a trench around it, and cover the tubers with earth from the trench.

When the foliage breaks through the covering, it is covered with more earth from the trench. The process is repeated until the crop is mature.

In times of trouble only enough potatoes were lifted at any one time to meet immediate needs. The rest stayed securely in the lazybed. Soldiers bent on the destruction of food stocks, a common tactic in the wars of the sixteenth and seventeenth centuries, burned crops and killed or carried off livestock, but would have had to be unusually persistent to locate and destroy the contents of every lazybed. Potato cultivation was a useful counter to scorched-earth policies.

By the middle 1840s, the only warfare for one hundred and fifty years had been the five weeks of the '98 Rebellion and the brief French incursion from Killala, in neither of which had earth been scorched. But the lazybed method of growth had become an inherited custom which was efficient and adaptable. As the pressure for land increased, formerly unused parts of it were opened up. Lazybeds were put in on steep hillsides, and anywhere else where potatoes could be grown. The potato was still a survival food not because of warfare but because for the great majority of the rural people there was nothing else to eat. Grain was widely grown in Ireland, and livestock widely raised, but their consumption was by the rich and their export was to make the rich richer.

Arthur Young, the itinerant English economist, made detailed records in the late eighteenth century of how the country people lived. A typical entry at Gloster in the King's County reads: 'Their food is potatoes and milk for ten months, and potatoes and salt the remaining two; they have, however, a little butter.' He goes on to say that the average consumption of potatoes per person per day was eight pounds. There were usually, then, three children in each family. The men probably ate twelve pounds a day. By the 1840s people were eating more, there were many more children in each family, and there were three times as many people on the same restricted land area as there had been in Young's day.

In 1845, *Phytophthora Infestans*, a fungus that had already done heavy damage to the potato crop in North America, continental Europe and Britain, appeared in Ireland. Its ravages elsewhere had generated an inconvenient and expensive switch to alternative forms of food. For about seven-eighths of the people of Ireland there were no immediate alternatives to switch to.

During the next three years the real evils of the landlord system as practised in Ireland were demonstrated in gruesome, unforgiveable, profusion. There were good landlords who sacrificed their personal fortunes, and in some cases their lives, to help their starving tenants. There were well-meaning landlords who would have done what they could, but who through personal extravagance, and the inherited debts of ancestral extravagance, lacked the resources to do much. There were absentee landlords who adopted the view that the disaster was an act of nature and nothing to do with them, although they were prepared to show their compassion by contributing one penny in the pound from their rental income to a relief fund. There were logically minded, economically orthodox, personally cold-hearted landlords who regarded the inability of a starving tenantry to pay its rents as a God-given opportunity to turn them out, consolidate the property, and at last get on with scientifically planned farming. In the Irish folk memory they have all been lumped together. The Irish Potato Famine of the 1840s was the biggest peacetime calamity in European history since the Black Death, and it was avoidable. It was not avoided because of the irresponsible avarice and arrogance of leading Anglo-Irish land-lords, and because of contemporary English principles of *laissez-faire* economics and devotion to the inalienable rights of property.

There was nothing new to Ireland in having some of the potato crop damaged by disease or frost. There had been four major but not total failures in the previous century. In two successive years in the early 1820s the crop was destroyed almost in its entirety in Connacht and Munster, and Famine Relief Funds in London and Dublin were subscribed to generously. There were partial failures during every year of the 1830s except 1838. Similar, partial, loss was sustained in 1841 and 1844. Each of these events had caused much hardship, much hunger, and some actual starvation. Contingency plans were made for mitigating a moderate disaster after it had occurred, not for identifying and putting right the problems that caused it.

The possession of hindsight is a famously untrustworthy weapon of criticism, but there was no shortage of evidence of the rapidly increasing population pressure upon available land, and of the proven unreliability of the single crop upon which most of the expanding population was dependent. There were also two pieces of

223

evidence that suggested how the problem could be reduced, if not eliminated, in the short term.

The first was the continuing and flourishing presence of the Palatine communities, with their standing demonstrations of how smallholdings, farmed by agriculturally educated smallholders with security of tenure and a vested interest in improving their land and buildings, could be profitable both for themselves and for their landlords. This lesson was supplemented by the example of Ulster, where Ulster custom also provided security of tenure and mixed farming was practised. With the exception of Donegal, Ulster was to be the least affected of the four provinces when the Famine struck. Illiterate cultivators with knowledge of only one implement, the spade, and of one crop, the potato, would clearly have difficulty in learning new methods of diversification, had some form of agricultural instruction programme been established. But they would have learned something; and if landlords had taken steps to provide some elementary advice and encouragement to the people for whom they held responsibility, and if they had been less myopic about leases, hundreds of thousands of lives could have been saved. But the thought seems to have crossed few minds, either in Ireland or in England. When, after thousands of people were already dead, dying or destitute, the Viceroy, Clarendon, suggested to the Treasury in London that instructors should be recruited and deployed by the government, the Chancellor of the Exchequer, Sir Charles Wood, dismissed the idea derisively as one of Clarendon's 'hobbies'.

The second piece of evidence was an illustration of the ease with which a planned programme of emigration could have been set up, to the mutual advantage of over-populated Ireland (8,000,000 people), and under-populated Canada (1,000,000 people). After the Napoleonic Wars cut off Britain from Scandinavian sources of timber, the shortfall was made up from the forests of Canada. At first, since the Canadian market for British exports was so small, most of the timber ships returned to the St Lawrence in ballast. People, if they were prepared to travel rough, were more profitable than ballast. Rough and ready berths were set up between decks, water and fuel were provided by the shipowners, the passengers brought their own food with them, and emigrants could reach Quebec for two or three pounds. Canada got new blood to help to fill the empty spaces, and the income from the fares helped to reduce the cost of transporting the next cargo of timber to Britain. It was one of the few multiple transactions in life that left all parties happy. Most Irish country people of the time felt a tenacious emotional attachment to their native places, despite the poverty and squalor of their daily lives. But in the years before the Famine a voluntary traffic had grown to the point at which it was being exploited by unscrupulous passage-brokers with agents all over Ireland. In 1844 sixty-eight thousand Irish emigrants reached Quebec by this route. Some stayed in Canada. Many made their way to the United States.

It seems obvious (again with the luxury of hindsight), that if government funds, or the private funds of individual or collective landlords, had been provided for a systematic scheme of large-scale emigration, with modest cash inducements to leave, paid or subsidized fares, a small government inspectorate to ensure that the travellers were not abused or exploited, and rudimentary reception arrangements at the other end for initial subsistence and allocation of land, Ireland, Canada and the British taxpayer would have benefited. As matters turned out, three years into the Famine several landlords found it personally cheaper to charter ships to transport their surplus tenantry across the Atlantic than to leave them at home and pay the compulsory Poor Law Rate for their support. But with a few praiseworthy exceptions, what those particular landlords delivered to North America was not a contingent of healthy, ambitious, potential openers-up of new land, but a horde of emaciated human ruins, dressed in rags, and dying by the thousand of typhus, cholera, dysentery and malnutrition. They had travelled in leaking, jam-packed, insanitary, verminous old hulks supplied by profiteers. Their arrival confronted both Canadian and United States ports with a major health threat and some actual epidemics. Most of the emigrants who survived the voyage and quarantine were so debilitated and demoralized that for a generation they provided their new homelands with an insoluble social problem.

The comments of the Duke of Wellington, already quoted, say most of what needs to be said about the Irish landlord system as seen by the most distinguished member of the class that comprised it. The English non-official response to the Famine was sympathetic and generous from the beginning. So was that of the Irish classes, in Ireland and elsewhere, not personally affected by the distress. The first financial contribution to relief was raised in India by the Anglo-

225

Irish officers and the Catholic Irish troops of the queen's and John Company armies. They sent £14,000. In Dublin, the Irish Relief Organization collected £42,000. The General Central Relief Committee, whose President was the Duke of Leinster's eldest son, the Marquess of Kildare, collected £63,000.[2] The Quakers, that Fundamentalist, austere, pacifist, prosperous and tolerant sect, who in the Penal times had sheltered a Catholic Mass centre in a barn in Dublin (Dolphin's Barn is still the name of a large suburb), formed the Central Relief Committee of the Society of Friends. It was to be the most practically effective of all the relief organizations and, when it disengaged itself, the most devastatingly condemnatory of the British government's response to the ghastly four years.

The Quakers set about collecting money in both Ireland and England, organized a widespread pattern of soup-kitchens, and through the agency of resident correspondents all over the country efficiently assembled information about the development of events. Through their association with their fellow-Quakers in the United States they were the first to arrange for an appeal for American voluntary assistance. It was met generously and shiploads of food, two of them carried in vessels of the United States Navy, came to Ireland as a result.

The first signs of potato blight had been detected in Ireland in September 1845. By October it was clear that this was by far the most serious outbreak yet, and one that would require corrective measures well beyond anything that had been undertaken in the past. In early November a delegation went to see the Lord Lieutenant, Lord Heytesbury. The delegates, who included Daniel O'Connell, the Duke of Leinster, and the son of Henry Grattan, were all thoughtful and responsible people. They recommended that

---

[2] In 1984, when film shot by a British television camera team first appalled comfortable Western watchers with the sight of the effects of the Ethiopian famine, the largest *per capita* contribution to relief funds in the EEC came from its poorest member, the Republic of Ireland. It was an Irish rock musician, Bob Geldof, who mustered fellow-musicians to make a top-selling record whose proceeds went to Ethiopia, and who afterwards organized 'Live Aid', an all-day rock concert broadcast to almost every country in the world in the biggest charitable appeal ever made. The Irish have always been handsome donators to charities. Ethiopia struck an atavistic chord.

if a calamity were to be averted, it would be necessary to ban food exports, forbid the use of grain for distilling and brewing, lift all import duties on Indian corn and rice, set up relief organizations in every county to distribute food and employ the hungry for cash wages on public construction works. To pay for all this, a tax of 10% should be levied on the rental income of landlords in residence, and of between 20% and 50% on that of absentee landlords. Irish forests should be put up as security against a loan of one and a half million pounds.

Heytesbury had been given advance notice of these proposals. He read his reply to the deputation. Reports on the damage to the potato crop were still being prepared, he said, and some of the ones completed were inconsistent with others. The proposals would be sent immediately to the government. They would have to be maturely weighed. Most, if adopted, would need new legislation. There was no discussion. Heytesbury bowed the deputation out.

The government did not take the advice offered by a non-partisan group of distinguished and disinterested Irishmen with a deep knowledge of Irish affairs, characteristics and limitations. Instead Peel, the Prime Minister, took two bold initiatives of his own. The first, the repeal of the Corn Laws, the tariff barrier which protected the prosperity of British agriculture and was the central economic plank of his own party's doctrine, was a courageous decision which inevitably split the Tories apart and was soon to put him out of office. The second, made on his own authority without formal approval from his cabinet colleagues, was the purchase from the United States of £100,000 worth of Indian corn, the buying performed by agents of Baring Brothers, the bankers, in separate lots and different places, in order to pre-empt the price rise which would have followed the disclosure that the British government was buying food.

Peel's intended use for the corn was indicative of the philosophy behind the actions of both his and the succeeding government throughout the famine. The corn was not to be distributed to the hungry. To do so would cut across the right of private enterprise to operate without government interference in the natural and healthy interplay of market forces. It was instead to become an integral part of the market forces. It would be stored in Ireland, and if food prices went up too sharply, it would be released in batches to be sold cheaply and thus bring prices down again.

227

This sophisticated concept rested upon an English insular un-awareness of the realities of Irish life. The people who needed to be fed had no experience of buying food and no money to buy it with. In the areas worst affected, the west and the south-west, many who gave their labour in exchange for the use of a patch of land to grow potatoes on, had never in their lives seen money. Even had a philanthropist given them some, it would have done no good. In those places there were no food shops. The people lived entirely on potatoes, grown by themselves. Now there was none. The use of imported corn as an economic regulator had no relevance at all to their situation.

In Dublin an official Relief Commission was set up by the government. Its members included the heads of the Poor Law Commission, the Board of Works, the Coastguard and the Cons-tabulary. Sir Robert Kane, a Catholic, and an agricultural scientist of note, was added shortly afterwards. The main executive member of the commission was Sir Randolph Routh, of the British Army Commissariat, chosen because the commissariat was the body with the greatest experience of feeding large numbers of mouths in complicated circumstances.[3]

By an administrative peculiarity of the day, the commissariat was not a corps of the army, but a civilian department responsible for army supplies directly under the Treasury. Routh thus worked under Sir Charles Trevelyan, the Head of the Treasury, who held the post right through the Famine years and whose influence upon the way matters were handled was supreme. Trevelyan was a highly intelli-gent, enormously hard-working, high-minded Evangelical, utterly confident in the rightness of his decisions. That his qualifications for controlling the governmental effort in a massive Irish emergency were less than total is indicated by his account of himself as 'belonging to the class of Reformed Cornish Celts, who by long habits of inter-course with the Anglo-Saxons have learned at last to be practical men'. Lord Lincoln, the Chief Secretary for Ireland in 1846, held a dissenting view about the last part of this self-portrait. Trevelyan, he considered, 'knew as much about Ireland as his baby, if he has one'.

[3] To have had, within a period of ten years, leading roles in the Irish Potato Famine *and* in the administrative disasters of the Crimean War, gives the commissariat a record for institutional incompetence unique in military, civil or any other history.

The early planning in London was based on the correct assumption, founded on earlier experience of crop failures, that there were several months in hand before starvation set in in earnest. Potatoes lifted early, and those set aside for seed, were stored in clamps. These stocks would keep people alive until the spring of 1846, and would be consumed before the disease penetrated the clamps. In the interval the Relief Commissioners were told to organize local committees of landlords, agents, clerics and other responsible people to collect money to buy food for sale at reduced prices or, in extreme cases of want, for free distribution to the hungry. Landlords were to be encouraged to employ more labour on their estates. The Board of Works were to give further employment by building new roads. Fever hospitals were to be established (fever had always followed famine). The Indian corn, judiciously placed on the market, would regulate food prices. It was a well-thought-out and well-meaning programme that would doubtless have worked admirably had the famine been in Surrey, or Somerset or Yorkshire.

In Ireland it was largely useless. The landlords, who were supposedly the guiding and financial buttresses of the local committees, were in most cases either not interested, not there, or so hamstrung by debt that they could afford neither to contribute to relief funds nor to pay for additional labour on their lands. The Board of Works pointed out that the scope for building new roads was limited by the fact that all the roads worth building had already been built through relief works during previous famines. The only possibilities left were link roads in remote places, which, because they might give advantages to one landlord over another, were specifically excluded as unfair by the Trevelyan theory of market-force economics. The scheme for setting up fever hospitals could work only by requisitioning suitable buildings. Where the Famine was acute there were no buildings at all except the landlord's house and hundreds of makeshift cabins.

English good intentions were thus sabotaged by English misconceptions, and by the ruthless determination of many landlords to exploit the chances inherent in the approaching disaster, or to ignore its foreseeable effects upon human life.

The idea that during a time of general suffering the landlords might collectively and voluntarily relinquish, or be legislatively compelled to suspend, their right to evict was not put up for

229

consideration. It was a matter for individual choice. Good landlords, as before, were kind and understanding. Insensitive ones who invoked their legal right to evict were assisted by the executive arm of the law in the shape of policemen and soldiers to ensure that the proceedings were not blemished by resistance. It was a woman, Mrs Gerrard, a County Galway landowner, who at this time attracted most attention by the manner in which she exercised this privilege. Her tenants had been better off than most. They had paid their rents on time, and had money in hand to pay the rent currently due. They had also drained and brought into cultivation 400 acres of what had previously been unproductive bog. Mrs Gerrard calculated that she would get an improved financial return from the property if she turned it over to livestock grazing. At her instance, the sheriff and a demolition team, guarded by police and a detachment of the 49th Regiment, razed the sixty-one houses of the village of Ballinglass, turned out seventy-six families, and prevented them from taking temporary shelter in ditches and hollows on the estate. They were escorted away, and turned loose.

This action of Mrs Gerrard's was criticized in the House of Lords by Lord Londonderry, one of the largest landowners in the North, who thought it a provocation to violence. Lord Brougham, the authentic voice of property rights and *laissez-faire*, put him right: '. . . tenants must be taught by the strong arm of the law that they have no power to oppose or resist . . . property would be valueless and capital would no longer be invested in cultivation of land if it were not acknowledged that it is the landlord's undoubted, indefeasible and most sacred right to deal with his property as he list . . .' At the same time as Mrs Gerrard was winning her victory for the rights of property, another representative of an Anglo-Irish landlord family, General Gough, leading troops whose European component was made up mostly of Catholic Irishmen, was winning a different type of victory over the Sikhs in the Punjab. His casualties were high. Daniel O'Connell compared the names on Gough's casualty list with those on the list of tenants evicted by Mrs Gerrard. 'A great number' were identical.

In the four famine years the sequence was: 1845, partial famine, with local variations; 1846, total; 1847, partial (blight-free crop but too small because weakened and despairing growers had not planted enough); 1848, total. The only crop affected by the fungus was the

230

potato. Grain crops flourished throughout and grain exports continued. In the three months before February 1846, 62,000 hundredweight of wheat, 701,000 hundredweight of barley and 250,000 hundredweight of oats and oatmeal were sold at a profit in England. In practice, and in conformity with the strange economic workings of the era, about four times as much grain was imported to Ireland as was exported. But the fathers and mothers of starving children who watched convoys of grain being escorted to the ports by armed soldiers could not have been expected to appreciate the finer points of *laissez-faire* economic theory. The survivors remembered what they saw, and related it to other memories of the period.

Some extracts from the reports of commissariat officers in the west and south, and from Quaker observers, give the flavour of the second type of memory. Westport, Co. Mayo: '. . . a strange and fearful sight, like what we read of in beleaguered cities, the streets crowded with gaunt wanderers'. Bundorrogha, Co. Galway: '. . . walking skeletons, the men stamped with the livid mark of hunger, the children crying with pain, the women in some of the cabins too weak to stand . . .' Skibbereen, Co. Cork: 'A woman with a dead child in her arms was begging in the street yesterday . . . the Guard of the Mail told me he saw a man and three dead children lying by the roadside.' Co. Leitrim: 'Two cartloads of orphans, whose parents had died of starvation, were turned away from the workhouse yesterday.' Schull, Co. Kerry (from a report by a naval officer landing Quaker relief supplies, who saw a mass, shallow grave of uncoffined bodies, and unburied bodies gnawed by rats): '. . . two dogs were shot while tearing a body to pieces . . . Never in my life have I seen such wholesale human misery.' Skibbereen, Co. Cork (from a letter from a magistrate to the Duke of Wellington, copied to *The Times*): '. . . the police opened a house . . . which was observed shut for many days, and two frozen corpses were found, lying upon the mud floor, half devoured by rats. A mother, herself in a fever, was seen the same day to drag out the corpse of her child, a girl about twelve, perfectly naked, and leave it half covered with stones. In another house, within 500 yards of the cavalry station at Skibbereen, the dispensary doctor found seven wretches lying unable to move, under the same cloak. One had been dead many hours, but the others were unable to move either themselves or the corpse.' In Skibbereen there were 197 deaths in the workhouse in a period of six weeks, and a hundred bodies had been found on the roads or in cabins.

These are not reports of isolated, unusual, incidents. They are representative samples of what was happening on a huge scale in all the poorer parts of one the poorest countries in Europe. They were all, as it happens, written during the first few months of the four-year ordeal, before the expected outbreak of 'fever', typhus and bacillary dysentery, had further multiplied the death list. There can be no doubt that one of the major reasons for the ultimately enormous total of dead was the bureaucratic rigidity with which Trevelyan controlled Famine Relief operations from the Treasury in London, complicated further by his inability to absorb the fact that the relationship between cause and effect in Ireland was by nature of the country's unique, and appalling, social and economic institutions, very different from its relationship in England. His handling of the introduction of the programme of public works is a case in point.

The idea of employing the hungry on manual work for which they could be paid a small wage to keep them from starving had been tried, not unsuccessfully but usually wastefully, during previous famines. Trevelyan abhorred waste, especially of public money. Instead of delegating responsibility to public works officers on the ground, equipped perhaps with broad guidelines on how they should proceed and a maximum financial limit, Trevelyan worked out an elaborate procedure by which every individual scheme had to be submitted on paper and sent to him for his personal approval. Each scheme was to be initiated by responsible men co-opted on to local committees, channelled through the Office of Works in Dublin, and there costed and commented upon, before being sent to Trevelyan. The notion that in places like Donegal or Erris there might not be a sufficiency of public-spirited, educated, English-type squires, parsons, doctors and yeoman farmers who would automatically and efficiently man the committees did not occur to him. Nor did the thought that the limited Office of Works staff would be better employed in instituting and supervising actual work in the distressed areas than in sifting and redrafting a torrent of semi-literate and unrealistic proposals submitted by committees often composed of self-appointed opportunists with an eye to the main chance.

In the event the weight of paper generated was such that the Office of Works was unable even to look at some of it. When some schemes were at last started, Trevelyan insisted that between the men who were to be taken on a distinction should be made: those destituted by the Famine were eligible, and those who would have been destitute anyway were ineligible. The moral fibre of the second category would have been weakened if they were allowed to benefit from a measure not intended for them. From a desk in Whitehall this lofty concern for other people's self-respect doubtless appeared both good and enforceable. For Board of Works supervisors confronted in Ireland by mobs of half-starved applicants whose families would die unless they were employed, the task of differentiating between acceptable sheep and unacceptable goats was invidious, often impossible, and when it was possible, personally dangerous.

Trevelyan was amazed and irritated by the huge numbers employed on these works, most of whom turned out to be useless. He did not understand that his insistence upon payment for relief food, in areas in which previously there had been little or no money, stimulated desperate men to do anything to get money to feed their families. A consequence of their working on these projects was that they were unable to cultivate their land. When the unaffected potato crop of 1847 matured there was too little of it because too few potatoes had been planted.

In the middle of 1847 Trevelyan, after trying in addition to public works a number of other expedients such as government-subsidized soup kitchens, all conceived with a high-minded sense of responsibility, all administered in a parsimonious, bloodless and bureaucratic spirit of cost-accounting, at last reached a solution that conformed to administrative tidiness and current theories of economics. He persuaded the government to introduce the Irish Poor Law Extension Bill. This shifted financial responsibility for the starving in Ireland from the British taxpayer, who had already paid £8,000,000, to the Irish ratepayers in the affected areas. The thinking behind it was that the Irish landlords had so far done little or nothing for their tenants, and should now be forced to make a major contribution in cash; that ratepayers of all classes must share the burden; that the free issue of government food from soup-kitchens must stop; and that to encourage people to work instead of relying for their subsistence upon government charity, those who sought help must be given it in the most disagreeable conditions i.e. workhouses.

233

Of these objectives, the first, the lifting of the burden from the British Treasury, was achieved. The Irish landlords, and the Irish ratepayers were certainly made to pay more than they ever had before, but the government had failed to take into account the degree to which many of them were in debt. Some of the good landlords, like the son of Humanity Dick Martin, had in fact beggared themselves in helping their hungry tenants. (Martin was later to die of fever, contracted while moving freely among the sick.) Some, unable to satisfy their creditors, had had their estates impounded in the Chancery Courts. Many of the absentees and their agents could not be found. Of the minor ratepayers most were destitute, and at least one was found to be in the workhouse himself.

A clause of the Poor Law made the landlord responsible for the payment of rates for any tenants whose holding was valued at less than £4. Many landlords evaded this obligation by evicting the tenants who were the cause of it. Good landlords, who had suspended rent collections and created unnecessary jobs on their estates, were caught in the ratepaying net along with the bankrupt, the bad and the absentees. They often had to sack their employees in order to pay the rates. When all that could be paid had been paid, there was still not nearly enough to feed the starving in the workhouses.

The workhouses were already overfull with the old, the ill and orphaned children. Under Trevelyan's orders these were turned out to make room for the healthy paupers who must be taught that failure to look after themselves carried a penalty. The evicted were continued on a soup ration, paid from English charitable funds, but since many of them had no home to go back to, their distress was dreadful. From the first beginnings of the Famine, officers in direct contact with the victims were the most sympathetic. Many of those administering the chaos attendant upon the passing of the Poor Law Extension Act warned of its consequences and pleaded for modifications. All were rebuffed or ignored. And then after a hopeful spring of planting, the fungus returned as devastatingly in 1848 as it had in 1846.

In 1848 reactionary governments in Paris, Vienna, Venice, Sicily, Milan and Piedmont were either overthrown or were induced to

234

make constitutional concessions by popular risings. In every case these democratic proceedings had been instigated and orchestrated by members of the national middle-class intelligentsia. The spirit was infectious, and the infection spread to Ireland, where it was warmly received by a group known as the Young Irelanders.

These had originally supported O'Connell and his orderly and constitutional movement for the repeal of the Union, but they soon formed the opinion that he was too orderly and too constitutional, and that the only remedy for Irish wrongs was through armed force. Of their five chief leaders, one, William Smith O'Brien, was a Protestant landlord, a member of parliament, and of the family of Lord Inchiquin; two, Thomas Davis and John Mitchel, were Protestant middle-class graduates of Trinity; and the last two, Charles Gavan Duffy and Thomas Meagher ('of the Sword') were middle-class Catholics. Davis, who died young, was a poet with romantic views about the restoration of Ireland's ancient Gaelic glories. Mitchel was a skilled and vituperative polemicist who hated everything English. All five were spectacularly indiscreet and impractical. Mitchel's paper, the *United Irishman*, published regular advice about the best way to kill English soldiers, and his public speeches urged his audiences to get themselves guns, smash through the Castle of Dublin and tear it down, and similar incitements. He was arrested, tried, sentenced and transported to Australia.

O'Brien continued with his rudimentary preparations for a rising, found almost no support from a people whose major preoccupation was keeping themselves and their families alive in the face of famine, met with almost total opposition from the Catholic clergy, and went ahead on the principle that if he started, others would join. The '1848 Rebellion' another of those in which 'the people of Ireland have asserted their rights to national freedom' by force of arms, was a fiasco. O'Brien's personal courage and integrity were beyond doubt. His oratory was inspiring. Although during a tour of the southern counties he was unable to muster more than a handful of supporters, he was more successful in Tipperary. There, about 6,000 joined him, but not for long. Their admiration of him as a man was not matched by their confidence in him as a revolutionary leader. His instructions to his followers to set up road blocks but not chop down any trees without first getting the landlord's permission, and to equip themselves with rations of oatmeal, bread and hard-boiled eggs, did

235

not appeal to rebels who thought that damaging landlords and their property was what they were there for, and who had been feeding on the government's issue of gruel, and nothing else, for months. The 6,000 dwindled to 500, and the 500 to fifty. By 30 July it was down to thirty-eight, who were engaged by a force of policemen at a farmhouse in Ballingarry. There was a brief, confused, and in some aspects farcical skirmish in which one rebel was killed, two were wounded, and the rest dispersed, to be later arrested. The 1848 Rebellion was over.[4]

As a threat to the Constitution and the continued existence of the Union its effects were nil. It did, however, produce one consequence that was seriously damaging to Ireland. In the eyes of government ministers, most members of parliament, and much of English public opinion led by the press, the 'Rebellion' was seen as an intolerable display of ingratitude. Ireland, through its own mismanagement, and the fecundity and impracticality of its native people, had brought upon itself the calamity of the Famine. At a time of financial stringency in Britain, the British taxpayer, and the British voluntary contributor to charity, had reacted with generosity to help Ireland on to its feet again. The Irish response to these bounties had been not of thankfulness but of sedition, armed resistance, and offensive anti-English propaganda. And not only that. Despite the ghastly precedents of 1845 and 1846, the peasantry had yet again failed to vary their crop, had planted potatoes exclusively, and were now because of their own irresponsibility faced with another year of mass-starvation. This time, Ireland could deal with its self-inflicted difficulties.

Amidst this emotional extravagance, it was useless for those best placed to see the overall picture to point out that there were a few flaws in the analysis. The root of the problem was implanted deep in

---

[4] After being condemned to death, O'Brien and Meagher had their sentences commuted to transportation and were sent to Van Diemen's Land. O'Brien was released because of poor health, and died in Wales in 1864. Mitchel and Meagher both escaped to the United States, where they demonstrated that their idealistic concern for the rights of oppressed peoples was of strictly limited territorial application. Both were upholders of slavery, Mitchel in print (the New York newspaper that he founded was also virulent about Jews), Meagher in the Confederate army during the American Civil War. Gavan Duffy, a lawyer, defended himself with skill and was acquitted. He was later elected to the Westminster parliament, and in frustration at the use by the House of Lords of its veto to kill reforming land legislation, he emigrated to Australia. There he became Prime Minister of Victoria, and Sir Charles Gavan Duffy, KCMG.

the inequality and the inefficiency of the landlord system, still unre-
formed after nearly fifty years of the Union. The British government
had done nothing about it. In many respects Trevelyan's policies,
fully endorsed by Sir Charles Wood, the Chancellor of the Exchequer,
and by Lord John Russell, the Prime Minister, had exacerbated the
problem, not eased it. The insistence that able-bodied peasants
should be genuine paupers before being admitted to workhouses,
enforced by rigorous searches of houses and possessions and the
refusal of admission to anyone who owned anything at all, left them
with absolutely nothing with which to restart their lives, even
without a further famine. Some landlords, like Lord Lucan[5] in Co.
Mayo, who in the winter of 1847 had evicted 10,000 starving people
from one estate near Ballinrobe in order to farm it more rationally,
were of such pitiless cast of mind that they would have disregarded
human obstacles to their plans whatever the circumstances. But the
new rates placed upon already insolvent estates were forcing even
the most responsible landlords to think very carefully about what
they should do. Lord Sligo, for example, had throughout the Famine
period conscientiously looked after the welfare of his tenants, had
twice paid for the maintenance of the inmates of the Westport
workhouse when it ran out of money, had taken a leading part in
charitable work, and had been paid no rents for three successive
years because his tenants had no money with which to pay them. He
had had to borrow extensively to meet the enhanced rates, increased
in order to support paupers who would not have been paupers if
enough of his fellow-landlords had behaved as well as he had. In
1848 his options had been reduced to 'ejecting or being ejected'.

In the matter of yet again replanting potatoes in the knowledge of
their vulnerability, there was evidence of a widespread amalgam of
optimism and fatalism. But in fact there was little else to plant.
Trevelyan had refused a request for funds to buy a variety of seeds.
Wood had jeered at Clarendon's suggestion for the provision of
horticultural instructors. Only the Quakers, as usual, quietly got on
with it and bought and distributed turnip seed. They also planted a
range of vegetables at a model farm established by them at Pontoon
in Co. Mayo, the most badly hit county in Ireland. It says something
for the quality of the government of an integrated part of the United

[5] Lord Lucan was descended from the Elizabethan Binghams (see page 54).

Kingdom, the country at the head of the largest empire the world had ever known, that the lives of a large number of its metropolitan citizens should have been saved as a result of the distribution of a quantity of turnip seed by a charitable organization. As for the sedition and rebelliousness, its physical expression was rather smaller than a single example of modern soccer hooliganism.

As soon as it became widely clear that the problems arising from the failure of the 1848 crop were to be solved by Ireland itself, which meant that they were largely insoluble, a large, new wave of socially and economically significant emigration began. This time it was the relatively successful and prosperous tenants, men who had farmed about thirty acres and who had always paid their rents on time. They left by their thousands. They took their skills and modest capital away from a misgoverned, ruined country in which they would be beggared by having to pay for the consequences of the mis-government. They went for the most part to North America.

After the experiences of the 1846 Irish emigrations, in which of the 100,000 Irish people who embarked for Canada, 17,000 had died of fever at sea, 6,000 had died at the quarantine island in the St Lawrence, 14,000 more had died, before the year was out, in Montreal, Quebec, Toronto and Kingston, and 25,000 had had to be cared for in Canadian hospitals, the Canadian authorities enforced stringent entry rules. So, after a parallel series of disasters, did the United States authorities.

The Irish immigrants of 1848 and 1849 had no difficulty in meeting the qualifications demanded of them. They were healthy, knowledge-able, enterprising, and had all the positive characteristics of pioneers, and none of those of refugees which had marked their prede-cessors. They were an asset to their new countries and a serious loss to their original one. As in the days of the Wild Geese, at the end of the Famine the most vigorous of the Catholic stock of Ireland put their energies into furthering the interests of countries other than Ireland.

The less fortunate, those who were starving but who by selling everything they possessed could scrape together enough money to pay the fare for a short sea journey, also decided in their thousands that the alternative to slow suicide in Ireland in the summer of 1848, made less slow by an inevitable outbreak of cholera, was emigration to Britain. Hordes of hungry, ragged, verminous, feverish, destitute Irish men, women and children had swarmed into Liverpool, Glasgow and Cardiff from the winter of 1846 onwards. The flow had diminished in the better year of 1847, but in 1848 and 1849 it swelled once more. The cities' financial, Poor Law, charitable and health resources were taxed to their limits and beyond. There were extensive fatal epidemics of disease.

The last of the Famine years was 1848. There were subsequent partial failures of the potato crop which brought widespread distress, but none of them approached the devastation of the 1840s. The tally of human life lost during those years was, by the nature of events, imprecisely recorded, but it can be roughly estimated from the census figures. An Irish census was taken every ten years. In 1841 the figure was put at a total population of, in round figures, 8,000,000. This was almost certainly too low. In the more remote, but populous country areas people were inclined to make themselves scarce at the approach of government officials and policemen, who would be assumed to have a more sinister purpose in mind than the counting of heads. But on the basis of a total in 1841 of 8,000,000 the census analysts calculated that the natural rate of increase should have produced by 1851 a total of 9,000,000. The actual 1851 figure was 6,500,000. About 1,000,000 emigrated, many of whom died on the journey or shortly after arrival from the effects of the Famine. About 1,500,000 died in Ireland.

The emigrants to America who prospered, however modestly, sent money to pay for the fares of relatives to join them. In 1851, for example, 220,000 Irish emigrants left for the United States. The process snowballed for the rest of the century. Thousands more crossed to England, Scotland and Wales to work in the cities, on the roads and canals. In a generation or two the Irish who went to England were indistinguishable from the rest of the British, except that they usually retained their Catholicism and had identifiably Irish names (James Callaghan, Dennis Healy, John Lennon, Paul McCartney, Kevin Keegan, etc).[6] The American wing of the migration

---

[6] In some cases of immigrant concentration, notably Liverpool and Glasgow, the process of assimilation was more protracted. The Scotland Road division of Liverpool returned an Irish Nationalist member of parliament to Westminister for years. There were recurrent riots between Irish Catholics and their descendants and Northern Irish Protestant, Orange immigrants. The pattern was reproduced in Glasgow, and stylized by two soccer clubs, Celtic and Rangers, representing Catholics and Protestants. By 1986 the Rangers management still would not engage a Catholic player.

became similarly absorbed into American society, but much of it sustained a bitter hatred of all things British which lasted down the generations and still finds expression in such activities as the raising of funds by NORAID to support extremist violence in Northern Ireland. There are now in the 1980s an estimated 50,000,000 United States citizens of Irish origin. The eminent among them have been legion. Three names will suffice: John F. Kennedy, whose ancestors left from Co. Wexford; Ronald Reagan, whose ancestors were from Co. Tipperary; and Henry Ford of the motor cars, whose grandfather had been a tenant farmer in Co. Cork and whose grandmother died of 'famine fever' shortly after landing in Canada.

Within Ireland, the demographic changes brought about by the Famine, which however horribly arrived at provided an opportunity for improved land administration, were only partially and fortuitously taken advantage of. About a quarter of the population of the two poorest provinces, Connacht and Munster, had disappeared. The subdivision of holdings into impossibly small patches was no longer necessary. Many of the old squalid cabins were abandoned. But no attempt was made by the government for several more decades to eradicate the central obnoxious injustice of the landlord system, the entrenched rights of proprietors to dispossess their tenants whenever they wished with no corresponding obligation to compensate them, or to accept any responsibility for their further wellbeing.

In many cases the plight of tenants became worse in this respect than it had been in the past. About one-third of the old landlords were bankrupted by the Famine. They included those who richly deserved to be, and those, like the Martins in Galway, who had run up unpayable debts to succour the people for whom they felt an affection and a responsibility. An Encumbered Estates Act brought about the sequestration and sale of their lands. The purchasers were unsentimental agricultural businessmen who did their sums, concluded that the abrogation of the Corn Laws by Peel and the resultant flow of imports from North America made grain production unprofitable and, like the deplorable Mrs Gerrard, evicted thousands to raise livestock. Their policy was economically sensible and socially disgusting.

240

The handling of the Famine and its aftermath was the single episode which irrevocably discredited British Rule in Ireland and, by extension, its local agents, the Anglo-Irish. Before it, much that had been done to the Irish by the English had been discreditable. But had the Irish been more efficient, better organized and more successful, they would have done to the English what the English did to them. The Famine was different. A major, *the* major power in the world, which was self-consciously and often rightly disseminating the benefits of systematic government throughout its Empire, had conspicuously failed in a constituent part of its own country to keep one and a half million of its own citizens alive.

Many landlords saw the tragedy through with a humanitarianism that deserves unqualified credit. The Martins were outstanding. From the earliest days, in 1846, the Marquess of Ormonde, Lord Erne, Lord Rossmore, the Duke of Devonshire and others were cutting rents partially, or in some cases entirely until times became better. The Duke of Leinster, of the old family of the Kildare Fitzgeralds, looked after his tenants so well that their number actually increased during the Famine. The Leslies in Co. Monaghan kept a vast cooking-pot permanently over a fire for the benefit of their tenants. In Co. Mayo, Colonel Vaughan Jackson sold many of his family's possessions in order to support the hungry. But these personal initiatives could not excuse an inexcusable system. The last word rests with Captain Arthur Kennedy of the Royal Navy, who in 1848 was a Poor Law Inspector in Co. Clare. Many years afterwards, at the end of a distinguished career during which he had been knighted, he was asked about his recollections of the Famine. 'There were days in that western country,' said Kennedy, 'when I came back from some scene of eviction so maddened by the sights of hunger and misery I had seen in the day's work, that I felt disposed to take the gun from behind my door and shoot the first landlord I met.'

CHAPTER THIRTEEN

For seventy years after the Famine the Anglo-Irish seemed hardly to notice that piece by piece the base upon which their dominance of Ireland was built was disintegrating. They fought various tactical political battles, lost some, saw to it that the power of veto of the House of Lords carried the day on others, and failed to read the strategic portents.

These portents were a consequence of the Union which the Anglo-Irish so stoutly defended. In the second half of the nineteenth century in Britain the first heaves of the surge towards an elective popular democracy were taking place. The old property qualifications for the franchise were being progressively eroded. It would have taken a seer of rare talent to forecast universal adult suffrage, but less foresight was needed to appreciate that universal male adult suffrage was inevitable. When that day came, and indeed considerably before it, the Catholic majority of the Irish people would be represented by parliamentarians arguing for the repeal of the Union.

There were two basic courses of political action open to the Anglo-Irish. The first was to accept the inevitable, make some sort of compromise with Irish Nationalism, influence it from within, moderate its extremists, accept with grace that a minority could not continue to monopolize power indefinitely, and play an honoured and useful role in the domestic parliament of a kingdom of Ireland constituted on the model cherished by Grattan. The second was to dig their heels in stolidly, resist all attempts at change, and give way grudgingly and progressively only when forced to do so by decisions taken at Westminster by British politicians who as often as not were guided by considerations of party advantage.

The Anglo-Irish, through their leaders the Irish peers, chose the second course. Since the Irish peers had staunch allies in the House of Lords among the English peers, who for their own, English, reasons were determined to defend the rights of property to the last stately home, a number of Pyrrhic victories were won by the rejection in the Lords of legislation endorsed by the Commons.

The first bastion to have its status readjusted was the Church of Ireland. The Church of Ireland was an anomaly, an officially established state Church which numbered in its congregation only one in eight of Irish churchgoers. It was disestablished in 1869 by the Gladstone government. It remained rich, and membership continued to be the visible badge of the Anglo-Irish community of all classes. A small proportion of its surplus funds was given to the Presbyterians, and a smaller proportion, £372,000, went to the Catholic Seminary at Maynooth.

Disestablishment was much resented at the time, not least because it was regarded as a betrayal of a clause enshrined in the Act of Union. It was in one sense a warning that in a time of developing egalitarianism in Britain old, privileged institutions could not rely upon venerability for their survival. The lesson was studied, and the wrong conclusions were drawn. To the collective Anglo-Irish mind, Gladstone and the Liberal Party were traitors.

O'Connell had died in Italy during the Famine. His absence, and a general state of national exhaustion, led to a political stagnation which continued into the 1880s. The two outstanding issues were Home Rule and the ownership of land. Both became obscured from time to time by agrarian violence generated by the second. Landlords, particularly the new post-Famine breed of consolidating, ranching landlords, continued to evict tenants with the full backing of the law represented by escorts from the Royal Irish Constabulary. Reprisals grew in frequency. Several landlords were shot. Others lived in a state of near-siege. Such Irish business as was debated in the House of Commons was more to do with Coercion Acts to counter violence than with the fundamental problems. A small, ineffectual group of Irish Home Rule MPs, led by a Protestant lawyer, Isaac Butt, sat in the Commons and conducted a gentlemanly and largely ignored campaign for the devolution of limited powers to a reconstituted parliament in Dublin for the running of purely domestic affairs. The campaign ceased to be either gentlemanly or ignored in the late 1870s when it was taken over, and its tactics redirected, by Charles Stewart Parnell, the most unusual Irish Nationalist leader in history.

Parnell was an Anglo-Irish Protestant country gentleman from Co. Wicklow, a descendant of the Sir John Parnell who had been one of the most outspoken opponents of the Union. Sir John Parnell's opposition had been largely because he thought that the Union would undermine the privileges of his class. Charles Stewart Parnell, although he personally exhibited most of the more arrogant characteristics of that class, set about with vigour to demolish its privileges. He was superficially cold, aloof, self-confident and he was addicted to cricket, none of which attributes would normally endear a politician, and a landlord at that, to an exuberant Irish electorate. They became devoted to him.

As the captain of the County Wicklow Cricket XI Parnell had been noted for the close study which he had made of the rules of the game and for the skill with which he exploited them, precariously on the right side of cheating, to his side's advantage. He applied similar principles to the conduct of Irish Party business in the House of Commons. If the House was unwilling to discuss Irish affairs, other than coercion bills, Parnell saw to it that English legislation was blocked. The actual inventor of the parliamentary filibuster was Joseph Biggar, a Northern member with truculent habits, but it was Parnell who refined and developed the device into a fine art. In 1877 he and Biggar put down notices of opposition against every single government measure from the Army Estimates to legislation for the control of threshing machines, and then monopolized the time available for debate by reading from government publications, talking irrelevancies, and interlarding the whole with references to Ireland. The mother of parliaments was not amused by the paralysis inflicted upon it, but neither the insensitive Biggar nor the icy Parnell was troubled by English disapproval. They had made their point.

Parnell soon had several other points to make. He brought the Irish Party under a firm discipline. In the past, Butt's followers had expected, and had been given, complete latitude to decide independently on how they would vote on any particular issue. Under Parnell the party voted as a block. By 1886, when full manhood suffrage was introduced to both Ireland and England, he had eighty-six Irish members behind him in the House, the landlord system was in disarray, and a clear possibility of Home Rule was in sight. He had achieved all this by keeping the party under tight control, using its voting power as a bargaining counter with which to extract Irish concessions in exchange for support, and by scrutinizing every English measure to see how it could be exploited in the interests of Ireland. His most powerful ally was Gladstone, the leader of the Liberal Party, who was personally committed to reforming Irish affairs, up to and including a form of Home Rule. But Parnell saw nothing sacred in the alliance. Had he thought it opportune to vote with the Conservatives on any issue he would have done so, provided that his vote was rewarded by a compensating benefit to the interests of his own party.

In 1870 Gladstone had brought in a Land Act which gave at least limited security to Irish tenants. A further Land Act, with sharper teeth to it, was passed in 1881. This gave the tenants 'the three Fs', fair rents, fixity of tenure and free sale. It was the first major step in crumbling a discredited system of property administration which had persisted unchanged in its worst features since the Cromwellian settlements of the mid-seventeenth century. The Land League, an association of tenants inspired by Michael Davitt, which by organizing rent strikes and boycotts had applied a sort of primitive agrarian trade-union pressure to the argument, wanted further changes. So did Parnell. The aim shifted from fair treatment of tenants to the changing of their status from tenancy to ownership.

An Act of Parnell's introduced in 1881, and a further Act supplementing it in 1887, ensured a compulsory reduction of rents. Parnell died in 1891, the same year as a Land Purchase Act was implemented, under which landlords could sell out to a Land Commission which in turn sold smallholdings to former tenants on a variant of the hire-purchase system. But in the years before his death Parnell could claim most of the credit for bringing about the state of affairs which made the purchase scheme possible. He had convinced Gladstone and the landlords that to continue under the old dispensation was impossible. The landlords had convinced them-

245

selves that Britain would betray them over the land question as it already had over Church disestablishment. A great many of them cut their losses and sold up. Ireland was on its way to widespread peasant proprietorship.

In 1890 Ireland had seemed also to be on its way to early Home Rule. Parnell was then at the peak of his power. He had emerged unsullied from an incautiously mounted attack on him by *The Times* in London, which in a series of articles published under the heading of 'Parnellism and Crime', had sought to prove on the basis of documents in its possession that he was personally associated with attacks on landlords, and with the 1892 murders in the Phoenix Park of the new Chief Secretary, Lord Frederick Cavendish, and Burke, the Under Secretary. The documents were proved to be forgeries. Gladstone was preparing a Home Rule Bill, to general Anglo-Irish Protestant consternation in the South and to grimmer Protestant preparation for resistance in the North. And then the whole edifice tumbled down.

Parnell had for some years been living, in well-covered seclusion, with Katherine O'Shea, the wife of Captain William O'Shea, a far from admirable opportunist who was a Nationalist member of parliament. O'Shea filed a suit for divorce, citing Parnell. The unbending Parnell could almost certainly have held his political leadership if he had withdrawn discreetly from public life for a few months while the scandalized Victorian English noncomformists who made up the bulk of the Liberal Party's voting strength, and in matters of sex the equally puritanical Irish Catholic hierarchy, became accustomed to the idea and worked their moral disapproval out of their collective systems. He had every intention of marrying Katherine O'Shea[1] when she was free to marry, and indeed looked upon her as his wife.

But evasion and compromise were not in Parnell's nature. He made it clear that he intended to carry on as if the divorce proceedings were of no relevance. It was a grave misjudgement.

---

[1] The name 'Kitty O'Shea' summons visions of a dark-haired Gaelic Irish beauty, with whom Parnell was establishing an inter-racial union as well as one of love. In fact she was the sister of an English VC Field Marshal, Sir Evelyn Wood. Parnell was not the man to let his advanced political views influence his choice of a mate of the right social background for an Anglo-Irish gentleman.

Gladstone said that if Parnell continued in uninterrupted leadership of the Irish Party, he himself would lose the leadership of the Liberal Party. Parnell refused to give an inch. The Irish Party divided in bitter partisan confusion. Gladstone withheld the Home Rule Bill, to the extreme relief of the Anglo-Irish. Parnell married his lover when the period then prescribed by the law permitted him to do so. Shortly after the wedding, he died, aged forty-five.

It was an extraordinary and tragic series of events, whereby one man's deeply-felt love for a woman combined with his personal Anglo-Irish intractability to change the course of Irish history, the history of the Anglo-Irish within Ireland, and the history of the relationship between Britain and Ireland. Hypotheses are often as difficult to resist as they are to prove. One is that if the 'Chief', at heart emotional, in public chilly, had found himself at the head of an elected domestic Irish government of limited powers, he would have extended those powers unscrupulously, but at the same time would have taken care to attract to his administration those Anglo-Irishmen of talent and flexibility who could have reached a working accommodation with the then relatively moderate Nationalist leaders.

Two reminiscent writers, from different ends of the spectrum, who have given first-hand accounts of Irish attitudes, prejudices and practices at the turn of the century are Mrs Nora Robertson in *Crowned Harp*, and C.S. Andrews in *Dublin Made Me*. Much of what each of them records could have been applied with equal validity to prevailing contemporary attitudes in England, before two world wars destroyed the seemingly immovable rigidities of the class structure. Much else of it is peculiar to Ireland.

The old barbarities of the Penal Laws were far beyond living memory. The Famine was a personal experience only of the very old. All male adults had the vote. Irish people had precisely the same political and social rights and disabilities as had English people. Yet both books give a sense of two separate communities, Anglo-Irish Protestant and Catholic native Irish, living alongside one another in the same small island, seeing the same things daily, experiencing the same weather, suffering the same economic vagaries, but in all except the necessary exchanges of commerce as remote from one

247

another as it was possible to be. In England at the same time, dukes and dustmen did not hobnob socially, but they shared a common Englishness. In Ireland there was a common Irishness, but one part of the country looked upon the other as a 'garrison', and the 'garrison' regarded the other part with at best a superior benevolent affection, laced with a standing suspicion that it was superstitious and unreliable.

Mrs Robertson's background was archetypically Anglo-Irish. She was atypical in that writing as 'a Septuagenarian to her Grand-children', she was able to look back on her life with a detached, sardonic, eye and while retaining an immense pride in her heritage as a descendant of an Elizabethan settler, found no difficulty in producing a dispassionate, and at times very funny, analysis of the society in which she grew up. Her father was one of the Parsons family, which has already made several appearances in this book. Her mother came from the Graves family which stemmed from a Cromwellian colonel and down the centuries was impressively representative of Anglo-Irish conventional versatility. They became bishops of the Church of Ireland, admirals in the Royal Navy and Fellows of Trinity College. A medical Graves, a Fellow of the Royal Society, had Graves's Disease named after him. Another Graves wrote *Father O'Flynn*. Robert Graves, poet, died in late 1985. Among their relatives by marriage were Cornelius Grogan, whose head was put on public display above the door of the Wexford courthouse after the 1798 Rebellion, and John Millington Synge, who wrote *The Playboy of the Western World*.

Nora Robertson's father was a regular officer in the Royal Artillery, and was ultimately to become the General Officer Commanding the first entirely Irish division raised by the British army during the First World War. He was stationed variously in India, Jamaica, England and Ireland. She grew up as an army child, living in official quarters in Athlone, Fermoy, Clonmel and Cork, and mixing exclusively with the children of other officers and of Anglo-Irish country families. She was educated at Heathfield in England, accompanied her parents on a posting to India when she was in her late teens, saw her father off to the Boer War, and joined him again in Government House in Cork when he was appointed to the command of the area. There she hunted (with a nervous distaste for horses), accompanied her father on shoots, played good tennis,

248

attended endless dinner parties and balls, was a frequent guest at country house parties, and observantly assembled a mass of sociological material that later she was to put to good and amusing use.

The centre of upper-level Anglo-Irish social life and, increasingly, of Unionist political life, was the Kildare Street Club in Dublin. Its membership was restricted to country gentlemen of standing, senior military officers and senior government officials. Among the country gentlemen there was a higher proportion of noblemen than in England because of the distribution of peerages made in 1800 to secure the passage of the Act of Union. Since they were usually poorer than their English counterparts, Irish peers tended to look for a cash element in their marriages. 'Although breeding was essential it still had to be buttressed by money.' With these factors in mind, and after pointing out that the structure of the Anglo-Irish social hierarchy did not need to be defined but was implicitly recognizable to its members, Mrs Robertson divides them into four 'Rows'.

Row A: Peers who were Lord or Deputy Lieutenants, High Sheriffs or Knights of St Patrick. If married adequately their entrenchment was secure and their sons joined the Guards, the 10th Hussars or the Royal Navy.

Row B: Other peers with smaller seats, ditto baronets, solvent country gentry and young sons of *Row A*. (Sons in Green Jackets, Highland regiments, certain cavalry, gunners and RN.) *Row A* used them for marrying their younger children.

Row C: Less solvent country gentry, who could allow their sons only about £100 a year. These joined the Irish regiments which were cheap; or transferred to the Indian army. They were recognized and respected by *A* and *B* and belonged to the Kildare Street Club.

Row D: Loyal professional people, gentlemen professional farmers, trade, large retail or small wholesale, they could often afford more expensive regiments than *Row C* managed. Such rarely cohabited with *Rows A* and *B* but formed useful cannon-fodder at Protestant bazaars and could, if they were really liked, achieve Kildare Street.

It is notable that in all four of Mrs Robertson's *Rows* it was taken

249

almost for granted that the proper role in life for a young man was as an officer in one of the British armed services. Right up until the Second World War the Anglo-Irish provided, in relation to their numbers, a far higher proportion of British officers, particularly army officers, than the parallel social strata in England, Scotland and Wales. When, on the outbreak of war in 1939, the British Expeditionary Force was sent to France, its Commander was Lord Gort (Gort is a small town in County Galway); its two Corps Commanders were Sir Alan Brooke and Sir John Dill, both Ulstermen; and among the six Divisonal Commanders were General Sir Harold Alexander, from County Tyrone, and General Sir Bernard Montgomery, whose family came from County Donegal. All five became Field Marshals, as did Sir Claude Auchinleck, another Ulsterman from the Indian army.

It was an unusual record for a small section of a minority population. Some past attempts to explain the phenomenon have emphasized the inbred qualities of the fighting stock of a conquering race. Mrs Robertson takes a more prosaic view. She puts it down to lack of money. Younger – and some older – sons in a poor country with few suitable jobs available, who had a fondness for travel and healthy open-air life with plenty of sport could, especially if they were posted abroad and more especially if they were posted to India, almost live on their pay. Sometimes they could even save some of it. In the circumstances of pre-First World War soldiering, the country gentleman, with his experience from boyhood of horsemanship and the handling of guns, was off to a head start.

He might also have been influenced by the widespread presence of the British army in Ireland, a matter of economics, not repression. In the latter half of the nineteenth century, military reforms included the closing of many insanitary old barracks sited in British cities and their replacement by new ones built adjacent to expanses of heathland and moorland suitable for field training. Aldershot is the best-known English example. Ireland held more bog and moor than England and it was cheaper to buy. New barracks were built near country towns, Athlone, Fermoy, Clonmel and the rest, local economies profited from the sale to the military of foodstuffs and animal fodder, and officers' messes extended elaborate hospitality to the neighbouring gentry and their families, who reciprocated. Since in the larger stations the officers often outnumbered the gentry, they exercised a disproportionate social influence, amplified, according to the cheerfully realistic Mrs Robertson, by marriage market calculations. Anglo-Irish accents became increasingly English accents. There was scrimping and saving to send sons to English public schools. After the public schools came usually the Royal Military College at Sandhurst or, for the technical arms, the Royal Military Academy at Woolwich. For those few of the caste who chose to go on to a university, Trinity went out of fashion and Oxford and Cambridge became the magnets. The market-forces element in all this, again to paraphrase Mrs Robertson, was that the indigent Anglo-Irish young man was more likely to meet at these institutions wealthy young Englishmen whose rich sisters could be wooed, or who could be introduced to his own hard-up sisters. It cannot have been organized entirely cynically, but a great many such marriages certainly took place.

One effect of the preoccupation with military life and its attendant hunting, fishing and shooting was that 'some military service in India took the place of a university in Irish county family life'. Grattan, Fitzgibbon, Tone, Yelverton, in fact most of the political leaders around the time of the Union, had been educated at Trinity. The new Unionist and Protestant leaders, the country gentlemen, were educated at Sandhurst and in Indian army cantonments. Several commentators have pointed to the fact that in the libraries of country houses, during the time when there were still plenty of libraries and country houses, the quality of books changed markedly in the second half of the nineteenth century. Before that time the collections were of the classics, history, philosophy, and so on. After that time they were of field sports, and of memoirs of obscure colonial campaigns.

In short, most of the Protestant Unionist leadership in the last years of Southern Irish Unionism were less well-educated than their grandfathers, had rarely heard their political views challenged in reasoned discussion because they associated socially only with people who shared them, and regarded English liberals with much the same puzzled abhorrence as they reserved for Home Rulers. Mrs Robertson was very fond of them as individuals. She had been brought up among them. They were on the whole kind and decent men. But they were 'a collection of rather misguided old soldiers who had never in their lives mixed with educated nationalists . . .';

251

'. . . the natural Anglo-Irish leaders sat in the Kildare Street Club and represented their order'.

Mr C. S. Andrews, author of *Dublin Made Me* and eminent in later life in the direction of state-sponsored commercial enterprises in the Republic of Ireland, was born in 1901, a decade or so after Mrs Robertson. His classification system is applied to a different set of subjects, Dublin Catholics, and he begins on a forthright note, which puts his observations in context. He writes:

> From childhood, I was aware that there were two separate and immiscible kinds of citizens: the Catholics, of whom I was one, and the Protestants, who were as remote and different from us as if they had been blacks and we whites. We were not acquainted with Protestants but we knew that they were there – a hostile element in the community, vaguely menacing to us . . .

The Protestants viewed by Mr Andrews were not the grandees dealt with in Mrs Robertson's assessment. These ones were 'small-time employees of the great Dublin commercial firms, together with solicitors' clerks and the like . . . They were . . . very respectable . . . their children never mixed with the village children.' Their other offences, in the Andrews indictment, were travelling inside trams instead of on top, reading the *Irish Times*, which was then a committedly Unionist newspaper, and wearing gloves while escorting their families to church in a formed body, instead of following the Catholic practice of letting everyone go to worship independently.

The Protestants thus attended to, Mr Andrews, from the point of view of a second-class citizen of the lower middle classes, has a go at Edwardian Catholic society. Its gradations as listed by him can conveniently be adapted to the *Row* formula used by Mrs Robertson.

Row A: The Catholic upper middle class. Medical specialists, fashionable dentists, barristers, solicitors, wholesale tea and wine merchants, owners of large drapery stores and a very few owners or directors of large business firms. Their accents were indistinguishable from those of the Dublin Protestants. They lived cheek by jowl with their Protestant counterparts in the fashionable

252

squares and in the more exclusive suburbs. They played golf, tennis, hockey, cricket, rugby, tennis and croquet. They sent their sons to Ampleforth, Stonyhurst, Downside and other English Catholic public schools, or sometimes to Clongowes, an expensive Jesuit school run on similar lines in Co. Kildare. The sons often went on to Trinity, despite the Catholic hierarchy's ban on attendance at a Protestant educational institution. 'An invitation to a garden party at the Vice-Regal Lodge or to a reception at Dublin Castle was the realization of their social ambitions.' They were 'the Castle Catholics', a term that in the estimation of Mr Andrews and of those who thought like him, was synonymous with the as-yet-to-be invented 'Quislings'.

Row B: The Catholic middle middle class. General medical practitioners, less successful solicitors, grocers, publicans, butchers, tobacconists who did not live over their shops, civil servants, journalists, coal merchants and bank managers. Their politics were Nationalist. They sent their children to fee-paying day-schools run by religious orders. They had fewer servants than *Row A*, but usually ran to three. They played rugby, cricket and tennis, but not golf or croquet. They held musical evenings as their principal form of entertainment. They were obsessed with respectability. Their ambitions were to be made Justices of the Peace, which would entitle them to put JP after their names. Their longer-term ambitions were to get their own souls into heaven and to leave enough money for their children to be able to become Castle Catholics.

Row C: The Catholic lower middle class. Shopkeepers and publicans who lived over their shops, clerks, shop assistants, lower-grade civil servants and skilled tradesmen. They took no holidays and seldom entertained. Their children played soccer and cricket on vacant lots, regarded golf, tennis and croquet as effeminate, and rugby as the preserve of the Protestants and Castle Catholics. Gaelic games, hurling and football, were thought by them to be fit only for country yokels. The children were educated by the Christian Brothers or the Dominican nuns, who charged very low fees. *Row C*'s collective ambitions were to own their own houses before they died, and for their children to acquire sufficient education to get good jobs and ultimately rise to the middle middle class.

Row D: The Catholic have-nots. The unemployed, dockers, coal-heavers, domestic servants, messenger boys, etc. They sent their children to the national schools for as short a time as possible. Many came out illiterate. Their housing was the worst in Western Europe. They were politically uninterested. Their earthly ambitions were minimal. They accepted their privations as God's will, and were confident that their fortitude in accepting them would be rewarded in the life to come. They were the main source of recruitment to the Royal Dublin Fusiliers.

In comparing the two lists it is easy to take Mr Andrews's point about the differences between blacks and whites even though, as he himself confirms, there was considerable social mixing between Mrs Robertson's *Row D* and the *Row A* allocated to Mr Andrews. But the social contact rarely led to marriages across the religious divide. Catholic bishops allowed mixed marriages only in special circumstances, when they granted a dispensation. One of the invariable conditions was that all children of the union must be brought up as Catholics. It was very seldom indeed that an Irish Catholic bishop was defied. Protestant parents brought great pressure upon their marriageable children, not excluding threats to disinherit them, if they showed signs of falling in love with Catholics. There were many sad instances of the breaking of hearts, and one natural, peaceable method of bridging the gap between the two communities was closed. It still is.

The unexpressed assumption by the dwellers in Mrs Robertson's *Rows*, that with minor adjustments there was no reason to suppose they would not continue indefinitely as they were, looks less myopic when considered in the light of Mr Andrews's *Rows*. The general aim of the Catholic *Row A* was to gain friendly recognition and acceptance by the king's representative in Ireland. *Rows B* and *C* wanted little more than promotion in the league table, which would logically bring them closer to the Castle, although after Home Rule the Lord Lieutenant would represent the king in a country with its own domestic parliament. The depressed and politically apathetic *Row D* wanted nothing much, except an eternal heavenly reward. All the elements for a continuing and long-term stability seemed to be comfortably in place. Sixteen years into the century a large crack was forcibly inserted into the structure. Five years after that the structure had entirely disappeared and was replaced by another one.

CHAPTER FOURTEEN

In 1858 a secret political society, the Irish Republican Brotherhood, was formed in Dublin. As its title suggests, its aim was the total separation of Ireland from the English crown and government, and the establishment of an Irish Republic. Its choice of method was force.

The ideas of the IRB appealed widely to Irish emigrants in the United States, who provided finance and, when the American Civil War was over, thousands of militarily experienced volunteers to the 'Fenians' who had pledged to come back to Ireland to fight for independence. As was by now traditional, the Fenians at an early stage in their development were penetrated by an English spy, named Le Caron, who soon rose to a fairly senior position in the organization and passed high-grade information about its intentions to those whose job it was to frustrate them.[1] An armed Fenian raid over the Canadian border was unsurprisingly unsuccessful, as was a small rising in Ireland in 1867. There were sporadic dynamitings in England, and a rescue attempt on a prison van in Manchester in 1868, in the course of which a warder was killed. Three Fenians were hanged for this killing and became the 'Manchester Martyrs'.

[1] Le Caron finally broke his cover to give evidence openly to the commission appointed to enquire into *The Times*'s articles about Parnellism and Crime. This exposure left him unemployable in his old trade, and a vacancy in the councils of the Fenians. He retired, wrote and published a book about it all and, rather surprisingly, died in his bed.

Overtly, the Fenians had little success. Covertly they maintained an intact, efficient directorate, and were active in propaganda, particularly in North America. The more romantic side of their political objectives, the restoration of an Ireland that would draw its inspiration from the Gaelic past, was paradoxically given a great boost by the simultaneous, frequently concerted, literary activities of a gifted group of Protestant Anglo-Irish poets, playwrights and scholars, financed to a large extent by the wealthy, misogynist, Catholic Anglo-Irish landlord of an estate in Galway.

In the early 1890s, the Irish literary renaissance came into flower. William Butler Yeats, Lady Gregory (the widow of a former Governor of Ceylon and a Galway landowner), George Russell (who wrote as 'AE'), Standish O'Grady and John Millington Synge, between them found an irresistibly attractive subject for their work in the ancient Irish heroes of legend, or in the speech patterns and cadences of a rural people who, now more English-speaking than Irish-speaking, possessed a richness of vocabulary and metaphor which owed much to inherited renderings of Irish thought into English expression. Douglas Hyde, the son of a country Church of Ireland rector, had as a boy become fluent in Irish, and in 1893 he founded the Gaelic League. Its aim was to revive the Irish language, which, discouraged by Daniel O'Connell, many parish priests, and parents who wanted their children to be linguistically fitted for emigration to America or to Britain, was in danger of disappearing altogether.

With the exception of Edward Martyn, the Galway landlord who was a talented playwright himself, and who contributed lavishly to both the Gaelic League and to the funding of the precursor of the Abbey Theatre in Dublin, none of these writers felt a commitment to political separatism.[2] But the sudden rise in public interest in a Gaelic culture which for centuries had been passed on orally in

[2] Martyn saw no inconsistency in combining the honorary presidency of the initial version of Sinn Fein with membership of the Kildare Street Club. Many other members did. All of them did when he took to writing letters to the press, some on club paper, protesting about a planned visit to Ireland by King Edward VII, in one of which he described the Ascendancy as a 'grotesque minority'. He was expelled, sued the club, and won his case. A friend who assumed that he would not go back to a club that did not want him was told: 'Of course I will. It's the only place in Dublin where I can get caviare.' Once back, he caused more occasional annoyance by kneeling down to say the rosary in the morning room.

peasant households, its written texts disregarded except by specialist scholars, generated a new and powerful spirit of pride in the Gaelic past. Compulsory primary education had added greatly to the number of people who could read. The Gaelic Athletic Association, founded in 1884, had added a popular sporting element to Gaelic nationalism, underlined by the association's strictly enforced rule that its members must play only the games of Gaelic football and hurling. Any member caught playing the 'foreign games' of rugby, soccer, hockey and so on, was expelled, and membership was barred to those in the crown forces, including the Royal Irish Constabulary. Much of the feeling behind this revival of enthusiasm for all things Gaelic was spontaneous. Some was initiated, or helped along, by the skilful, clandestine work of the Irish Republican Brotherhood. Added weight was given to it by the government's handling of a complex situation which in early 1914 was beginning to develop from the imminent passing of a Home Rule Bill in the Westminster parliament.

Home Rule, seemingly so near in the late 1880s, had been put back by the pious furore attendant upon the O'Shea divorce. Liberal Party adherence to the principle remained, but so did the power of the House of Lords, dominated by obstinate Conservative peers, English and Irish, to throw out any legislation to which they objected. They objected to quite a lot of things besides Home Rule. But they overreached themselves in 1909 when they discarded the budget introduced by Lloyd George, the Liberal Chancellor of the Exchequer.

Asquith, the Prime Minister, with the backing of the Irish Party led by John Redmond, and by means of a threat to drench the House of Lords with an infusion of newly created amenable peers if there were any more intransigence from the Upper Chamber, put through the Parliament Act in 1911. This reduced the veto of the Lords from a total rejection to a limited power to delay. Any bill approved by the Commons, but refused by the Lords, would become law after two years. A Home Rule Bill, giving Ireland a limited autonomy, but one that could be built upon, was passed at Westminster in 1912. The House of Lords used their authority to delay. There was no constitutional hindrance to its coming into effect in 1914. Several other hindrances at once presented themselves.

In north-east Ulster, the Protestant fortress, there was

conspicuously fervid resistance to the notion that a Protestant minority should be under the control of a Dublin government which would have a permanently Catholic majority in its legislature. The Northern Protestants had, and still have, a long folk memory and a shrewd and practical capacity for isolating from the political verbiage what they were, and are, or think they are, up against. The memories included the 1641 massacres and, for the Presbyterians, the betrayal in the 1798 Rebellion of the brotherly standards set by Wolfe Tone and the United Irishmen in the form of the religiously inspired slaughters of Protestants in County Wexford by Catholic rebels. To the Orange Order, Catholics were simply what they always had been, treacherous and disloyal.

In the eyes of the Northern Protestants, the moderate, reasonable, stance of the Irish Party in the South, still overwhelmingly elected at all tests of popular opinion, had to be assessed in the context of resurgent Gaelicism. This was growing in shrillness. It ignored the Norse, Norman and Old English constituents in its ethnic make-up, which it probably knew as little about as the Northern Protestants knew or cared about it. Its opposition to all things English and Protestant caused grave alarm in Ulster, expressed in precautionary action. Two hundred thousand Protestant Ulstermen, following the lead of a brilliant Dublin Protestant lawyer of Italian descent, Sir Edward Carson, signed a Solemn Covenant to reject Home Rule at all costs. One of the costs that they were prepared to pay was armed resistance.

A consignment of small arms was landed at Larne, and distributed. Protestant volunteers began to drill and train openly throughout the province. Slogans such as 'Home Rule is Rome Rule' and 'Ulster will fight and Ulster will be right', crystallized the outlook and determination of Protestant, Loyalist Ulster, which was firmly supported by Bonar Law, the leader of the Conservative opposition in the House of Commons. Emotion ran high. Few people indulging in it gave much reflection to the proposition that for the leader of His Majesty's Loyal Opposition, with solid party backing, to give enthusiastic support to a large group of His Majesty's loyal subjects who had made plain their intention of shooting anyone who tried to enforce a constitutionally enacted measure of His Majesty's Government, was, to put it at its lowest, strange.

There was reciprocal arming in the South, where a Nationalist Volunteer Force was formed. A cargo of rifles and ammunition was smuggled into Howth in a yacht owned by Erskine Childers, a Protestant clerk to the House of Commons, and the son of a former cabinet minister. There was some military interference with the distribution of these weapons, and several deaths ensued during a scuffle on Bachelor's Walk in Dublin. A lesson was drawn. Northern Loyalists, it seemed, could land illegal weapons while the authorities turned a blind eye. Southern Nationalists, doing the same thing, were fired at and killed.

A further lesson was drawn after an incident misnamed 'The Mutiny at the Curragh'. The Asquith government decided that the position in the North had by the spring of 1914 become so threatening that extra troops should be sent there to preserve order. A powerful Unionist group of serving officers in the War Office, manipulated by General Sir Henry Wilson, a landowner from County Cavan, pointed out forcefully to the government that given the high Anglo-Irish content among army officers, this move could in some circumstances oblige officers to use armed force against their own people. To preserve them from this intolerable conflict of loyalties, would it not be sensible, and in the interests of the morale and efficiency of the army, if officers domiciled in Ulster were to be told in confidence that they could quietly and temporarily make themselves scarce if their units were to be posted to their home province? The exemption would apply only to officers who were Ulstermen. Any other officer who objected to service in the North must resign his commission.

This reasonable provision was badly implemented by the Commander-in-Chief in Ireland, General Sir Arthur Paget. Instead of having word passed discreetly to those eligible, Paget summoned a mass meeting of the officers of a cavalry brigade stationed at the Curragh Camp which had been ear-marked for service in the North. To these, Paget put the wrong question. He did not describe the role of the army in the North as to preserve order. He described it as the forcible coercion of Ulster Loyalists into acceptance of Home Rule. Any officer reluctant to carry out this duty would have to resign. Brigadier General Hubert Gough, his brother John, and fifty-six other officers out of a total of seventy said, put like that, they would prefer dismissal. The Goughs, and most of the others, were Anglo-

259

Irishmen. They were disciplined soldiers who took their duty to the army seriously. If the case had been properly presented to them, they would have reacted differently. In the War Office, Henry Wilson, whose concept of military discipline became elastic when it impinged on Unionist politics, was delighted at the embarrassment caused by the Curragh incident to the Asquith government. In Nationalist circles in the South of Ireland it was interpreted as yet another example of the untrustworthiness of British governments and their public servants.

The position of Redmond, the leader of the Irish Party, was considerably weakened by these examples of muscular Protestant resistance to Home Rule, all of which were applauded by Southern as well as Northern Unionists. He advised his supporters to join the National Volunteers, until now largely a monopoly of Nationalists committed to the use of force. The exclusion of Ulster from any implementation of Home Rule would clearly undermine the Irish Party's standing with the electorate, who would regard partition as a clear signal that the British government was incapable of delivering its promises, made constitutionally by parliament. The result would be a growth in numbers of those favouring force. If it came to force, the Ulster Unionists, grouped cohesively, would be capable of looking after themselves. The dispersed Southern Unionists could only survive if protected by a massive and continuing involvement of the British army. Few Southern Unionists drew the conclusion that political evolution had moved so far that no British government could undertake an indefinite commitment of that sort. Civil war seemed to be a real possibility. And then the Germans invaded Belgium and the First World War began.

Redmond put the Irish Party unambiguously behind the British war effort. He accepted a postponement of Home Rule until the war was over. He sponsored a recruiting drive for the British army that was an immediate success. The Sinn Fein element in the Volunteers, led by Epion MacNeill and Patrick Pearse, stayed scornfully aloof, but Redmond's old followers joined in their thousands. So did the Ulster Volunteers. Some 250,000 Irishmen, from North and South, Catholic and Protestant, in addition to the large number of Irish regular soldiers already serving, enlisted in the army as volunteers in the First World War. Over 50,000 were killed. But it was those who stayed at home who made a lasting impact on Ireland.

The Easter Rising of 1916, led by Patrick Pearse, the son of an immigrant English father and an Irish mother, was doomed militarily from the start, as Pearse and its other leaders knew it to be. It was, in essence, a deliberately and bravely instigated blood sacrifice, designed to focus the country's attention upon the necessity of fighting for its freedom, instead of trying to negotiate it with a nation which at the Treaty of Limerick, at the time of the Union, and recently over Home Rule, had consistently reneged on its promises. The morality and efficacy of blood sacrifices are open to argument. There was at the time little public sympathy for the 1916 Rising. People with relatives fighting in France, Flanders and Mesopotamia saw it as a stab in the back. Others saw it as a fore-ordained failure. In size it was minuscule when compared to the contemporary fighting elsewhere in the world. The total number of killed, rebel and civilian combined, was 318. (There were 50,000 British casualties on the first day of the Battle of the Somme, two months later.) Rebel prisoners were hissed and spat at by hostile crowds.

It was within the legal rules of the day for rebels to be executed in time of war. The leaders were court-martialled. Fifteen, including Pearse, were sentenced to death. They were shot at intervals spaced over ten days. The executions, legally capable of justification, were psychologically and politically disastrous for the future of British rule in Ireland. A general revulsion was followed by a drastic fall-off in recruitment to the army. A threat to impose conscription united resistance further. At the first post-war general election in December 1918, Irish Party candidates were defeated by Sinn Fein opponents in three-quarters of the Southern Irish constituencies.

Next came two and a half years of sporadic guerrilla warfare, accompanied by sporadic atrocities by both sides. The introduction by the British government of the Auxiliaries and the Black and Tans, temporary policemen with a free hand to make Ireland 'a hell for rebels to live in', further outraged Irish opinion (and a great deal of British opinion, including that of the Church of England). It was realized in Britain that Ireland was no longer governable at an acceptable cost in money and manpower. There was first a truce and then a treaty. The Irish Free State, less six of the nine counties of the

261

province of Ulster, came into being as a dominion with full powers of self-government on 6 December 1921. A civil war broke out shortly afterwards between supporters of the treaty and opponents who wanted a republic and nothing less. It dragged on for another year, during which much bitterness was engendered and much loss of life, dislocation and damage to property was incurred.

The collective existence of the Anglo-Irish as a caste holding political influence in Ireland came to an end with the formalities of the handing over of power by the British government to the government of the Irish Free State. In the six counties of Northern Ireland, Ascendancy rule lasted with the almost automatic election of prime ministers from patrician families until a businessman, Mr Brian Faulkner, succeeded Captain Chichester Clarke in 1971. Looking back on it all from a well-detached distance, it is fairly easy to identify the major steps on the downhill path of the once omnipotent oligarchy.

The summit was Grattan's parliament of 1782. In some ways it was a false crest, but from 1782 to the Union in 1800 the Anglo-Irish in most matters controlled Ireland. The sell-out of the Union was a long drop down. Catholic Emancipation and the progressive extentions of the franchise were longer drops still. Once male adult suffrage was introduced by Westminster, Home Rule in one form or another was inevitable. It was the failure, not so much to compromise with the inevitability as to identify it, that led to the downfall. The choice was clearly between an Ireland run by Redmond and an Ireland run by, from the Anglo-Irish point of view, something less pleasant. The Irish Unionists consistently did their best to block and hinder Redmond, and by so doing provided an endless supply of ammunition for their own destruction. Had they come to realistic terms with him in a loosely shaped constructive alliance, working together for the country's good, it is at least arguable that popular support for physical force would have been minimal, change would have been evolutionary, the link with the crown would have been preserved, and history would have been different. Historical ifs, if absorbing, are irrelevancies.

There was, not unnaturally, a considerable exodus of Anglo-Irish families of all classes after the establishment of the Irish Free State.

A rough guide, with some margin of error, is the membership returns for the Church of Ireland from before the 1914–18 War. In 1911 there were 250,000 people on the rolls of the Church in the twenty-six counties. By 1926 there was a decline of 34% to 146,000. By 1985 the number was down to 100,000 of whom 40,000 were in Dublin.

Not all of the decline was brought about by emigration. The Catholic bishops' hold is less firm than it was, but it is still fairly firm. Children of mixed marriages must to this day be brought up as Catholics. Nor was all the emigration due to a reluctance to live in a country governed in accordance with the social principles of the Catholic Church, or by ministers until recently regarded as unscrupulous gunmen. Some certainly went because they found the prospect of one or the other, or both, abhorrent, and some went because their record in the Troubles, or the Anglo-Irish War, or the Black and Tan War, or whatever nomenclature was chosen, was such that they might be in physical danger if they stayed. But a great many left for simple economic reasons. The pickings were richer in Britain than in a small island bereft of natural resources. In the 1920s and 1930s, thirty per cent of the population of the Irish Free State, liberated at last from British oppression, emigrated to Britain.

The ones who chose to stay found remarkably little difference of substance in their daily lives. The symbols of flag and national anthem were different. There were very few instances of reprisal or ostracism for past slights or wrongs. The rich still lived in the Big Houses, hunted, shot, fished, farmed, were stewards of the Jockey Club, judges at the Dublin Horse Show, employers of large domestic and agricultural staffs and lavish entertainers of guests. The doctors doctored, the solicitors solicited, the judges judged, the businessmen still controlled most of Ireland's trade and commerce. Sons continued to go into the British armed services, and were unmolested when they came home on leave. Trinity continued to be a largely Protestant university, not because the board who managed its affairs wanted to keep Catholics out, but because the Catholic hierarchy wouldn't let them in. Christchurch and St Patrick's Cathedrals in Dublin, confiscated by the reformed Church from the Catholic Church in the reign of Henry VIII, continued as Church of Ireland property, with the symbols of the old regime, the king's and regimental colours of now disbanded Irish regiments, on public display, as they are to this day. Former soldiers of the British army, now members of the British Legion, most of them Catholics who liked the idea of an independent Ireland but who preserved affections for the old days, marched wearing poppies to the War Memorial at Islandbridge every Armistice Day to lay wreaths and take part in a commemorative service. That was regarded by some as a provocation, and there were occasional scuffles, particularly in pubs after the parade had dispersed. But none of it was at all serious.

The Anglo-Irish, in sum, were still there, an unassimilated distinctive entity, rarely but sometimes active in national or local politics, some still socially aloof, more of them acquiring Catholic friends but still haunted by the spectre of mixed marriages and Catholic grandchildren. Irish neutrality in the Second World War caused resentment in some, but since there was nothing that they could do about it, and since the Irish interpretation of neutrality permitted such un-neutral acts as the enlistment of Irish citizens in the British forces, they had small cause to complain. Of the 38,554 Irishmen and 4,695 women from the Irish Free State who enlisted, most were probably Catholics, but a great many from Protestant families volunteered as a matter of course.

The 1948 announcement in Ottawa that Ireland was to become a Republic ruffled a few more feathers, but again in practice it made little difference to daily life. Regardless of the change, Anglo-Irish products of Trinity, Sandhurst and Woolwich came back on retirement from the Indian Civil Service, the Indian professional services and their colonial counterparts, or from the British and Indian armies. They settled in Co. Wicklow, Co. Galway or West Cork. Brendan Behan's definition of an Anglo-Irishman as a Protestant on a horse dates from this period.

The numbers began to thin out noticeably in the 1960s. The old were dying off. India had been independent since 1947. The Colonial Empire was in the process of dismantlement. Britain had ceased to be a World Power. The British armed forces were being cut to the bone. The traditional outlets for overseas employment had disappeared or had been whittled down to almost nothing. A brief economic boom in Ireland brought a new prosperity to many, but it raised prices, hitherto low and reasonably stable, to a point uncomfortable for retired officers on fixed pensions or to the inheritors of leaking and under-maintained country houses.

264

There really was no longer much point in *being* an Anglo-Irishman. To the new generation, with no recollection of Ascendancy privileges, it became increasingly obvious that the real choice was between becoming an unhyphenated Irishman, or going away and becoming British, or North American, or Australasian. Of those who have to earn their livings, probably many more have gone than have stayed. The stayers, more often than not, are those who can rely upon a place in a family business, or a partnership, or who inherit a farm. Of the peers analysed so graphically in Mrs Robertson's *Rows* a handful still hold on to at least some of their estates, doing what they can to survive taxation and the modern equivalent of death duties. Lord Altamount is an imaginative operator in the Stately Homes business in Sligo. Lord Inchiquin at Dromoland Castle in Co. Clare entices rich Americans to come and 'live like a lord' as highly paying guests for long weekends, and doubtless lets them look at his family tree which places him thirty-second in direct line of descent from the High King, Brian Boru, who beat the Danes at Clontarf in 1014. Lord Mount Charles is unusual in that he is active in party politics, hopes to stand for election to the Dail, and runs open-air rock concerts at Slane Castle.

But most of the peers no longer live in Ireland. A survey of the heirs of the Knights of St Patrick listed for one year chosen at random, 1881, is illustrative. The Most Illustrious Order of St Patrick, an Irish Order of Chivalry comparable to the Scottish Knights of the Thistle, was instituted by King George III in 1783. Its membership consisted of the monarch, and twenty-two knights, of whom two or three were usually also members of the royal family. Members of the order were listed by Mrs Robertson for automatic inclusion in her *Row A*. In 1881 there were twenty-two non-royal knights, all partially or wholly resident in Ireland. A trawl through the 1980 edition of *Who's Who* gives the following geographical breakdown of the addresses of their descendants one hundred years later. Republic of Ireland: 3. Northern Ireland: 2, but both also with houses in England. England: 6. Australia: 1. Kenya: 1. Canada: 1. Switzerland: 1. Two gave no addresses in their *Who's Who* entry, and two have no entry at all, presumably either because the line is extinct or because they declined to be listed.

The Order of St Patrick has long ceased to exist. Other Anglo-Irish institutions or structures survive, modified, adapted or unchanged. The Church of Ireland is small, but the views of its leaders are listened to with respect. The Catholic hierarchy's ban on attendance by Catholics at Trinity was lifted in 1959. About ninety per cent of the student body are now Catholics. So are more than half of the academic staff. The Kildare Street Club amalgamated with the University Club in the 1970s, in the premises of the latter in St Stephen's Green. The old building in Kildare Street, where so many Unionist issues were discussed, and decisions (usually the wrong ones) taken, still stands, its outward appearance unaltered, its internal use considerably so. A placard in its windows facing Nassau Street reads 'Teas'. Despite the best efforts of the property developers, the lovely old squares, and the solid Victorian houses in the southern inner suburbs of Dublin, are still elegantly in place, their names, Fitzwilliam Square, Merrion Square, Leeson Street, Wellington Road, Waterloo Road, Raglan Road, commemorating bygone Anglo-Irish heroes and magnates, or British heroes and events honoured by the Anglo-Irish. A translation into Irish is placed below them on their nameplates. The Royal Dublin Society continues to make an admired and valuable contribution to Irish life. The Royal Irish Academy does the same to Irish learning. And the live, human, legacy, the problem of the divided people of the six counties of Northern Ireland, remains unresolved.

APPENDIX

For obvious historical reasons Irish nationalism and Irish Catholicism became so tightly enmeshed with one another that from the time of the Treaty of Limerick the two terms became almost synonymous. The grafting of an exclusively Gaelic identity on to the synonym was a much later development, dating from the revived popular enthusiasm for Gaelic Irish culture and history in the latter part of the nineteenth century.

Long before this revival, the Old English had been absorbed by intermarriage with the Gaelic Irish into a cultural whole. The ancestry of the Old English component of Catholic Ireland was ignored when the new patriotism came into fashion. The belief grew, and was fostered by the Gaelic League, the Gaelic Athletic Association, Republican politicians and some of the Catholic clergy, that the only true Irishman was a Catholic and that all Irish Catholics were by definition of Gaelic origin.

A closer approximation to the truth, in so far as it is susceptible of establishment, would be that most Irish Catholics probably have a proportion of Gaelic genes, most have a lesser proportion of English, Norse and Norman genes, and some are genetically more English than Irish. The unifying factors are religious and cultural, not racial. An unscientific look at patronymics, culled from arbitrarily chosen sources, casts a certain indecisive light on the matter.

The 1980s Irish telephone directory is issued in two parts, one

267

covering Dublin and its neighbourhood, and one dealing with the rest of Ireland excluding Northern Ireland. As source material for the determination of the ethnic roots of the inhabitants of modern Ireland the two volumes have their limitations, but conclusions of broad interest can be drawn.

In the two volumes combined, there are 2,600 Doyles (the name is of Norse origin), 4,450 Walshes (Welsh men-at-arms, followers of the Normans) and 3,850 names with the prefix Fitz (Fitzgerald, Fitzgibbon and so on. Fitz is a corruption of the Norman-French *fils* meaning son.) Other Norman names include Joyce, Purcell, Barry, Blake and Synnott. Sweeneys and Sheehys are descendants of the Gallowglasses, while the sons of Olaf are represented by MacAuliffe.

It is of course a possibility, perhaps a certainty, that some families have changed their names in the past for reasons of convenience or conformity or protective colouration, but the majority would not have done so. The systematic use of patronymics has continued from the tenth century, when the Mac's and O's (son of, grandson of) were first adopted to simplify nomenclature and to establish family identity. Although there have undoubtedly been distortions of surnames, often brought about by English-speaking compilers of records giving phonetic renderings of names proffered orally, there is a remarkable consistency. For example, a large number of McCarthys and O'Briens still live in Munster, and a large number of O'Reillys live in County Cavan, areas that were their ancestral lands from the earliest Gaelic times.

A further excursion into this rough and ready line of ethnology can be made by looking at the names of people involved in what are regarded in the twentieth century as unarguably patriotic activities, conducted by people of impeccably Gaelic credentials. The Easter 1916 Proclamation of Independence, addressed to the People of Ireland by the Provisional Government of the Irish Republic, and the source of the authenticity of all Irish independent governments since the establishment of the Irish Free State in 1922, had seven signatories. Their surnames were Clarke, MacDiarmada, Macdonagh, Pearse, Ceannt (originally Kent), Connolly and Plunkett. Of these only MacDiarmada, MacDonagh and Connolly (who was born and brought up in Scotland) are of Gaelic origin. The paternal ancestors of the other four must first have come to Ireland as agents or beneficiaries of the 'foreign people' denounced in the Proclamation for their long usurpation of the right of the people of Ireland to its ownership.

The 1984 All-Ireland Hurling Final, an event played under the auspices of the Gaelic Athletic Association, was contested between county teams representing Cork and Offaly. The game is played by teams fielding fifteen players each, and each side has seven nominated substitutes. Out of the total of forty-four listed participants on this occasion, seventeen and a half (the half was the hyphenated, by the *Irish Times* at any rate, Barry-Murphy) bore names of identifiably Norse, Norman or Anglo-Saxon origin.

The proportion of non-Gaelic names among elected representatives sitting in Dail Eireann, the parliament of the Republic, has consistently been about fifty per cent, rather higher than that of the 1984 hurling contenders. So, for that matter, has been the proportion of non-Gaelic names in the leadership of the Irish Republican Army, for whom the implementation of their policy of 'Brits Out' would, if pressed to its logical conclusion in an historical context, result in a crippling manpower shortage.

None of this proves very much, other than that the shorthand of racial rhetoric delivered in Ireland as elsewhere can be misleading. One of the unplanned achievements of the Anglo-Irish was to unite into a cultural-religious whole people of varying roots who responded to a common oppression, and took shelter under the common umbrella of nationhood.

SELECT BIBLIOGRAPHY

Books

Andrews, C.S., *Dublin Made Me*, Cork, 1979

Beckett, J.C., *The Making of Modern Ireland 1603–1923*, London, 1966

Beckett, J.C., *The Anglo-Irish Tradition*, Belfast, 1982

Berleth, Richard, *The Twilight Lords*, London, 1979

Beresford-Ellis, P., *The Boyne Water*, London, 1976

Craig, Maurice, *Dublin 1680–1860*, Dublin, 1980

Curtis, Edmund, *A History of Ireland*, London, 1936

Gwyn, Denis, *Edward Martyn and the Irish Revival*, London, 1930

Kee, Robert, *The Green Flag*, London, 1972

Lynam, Shevawn, *Humanity Dick*, London, 1975

Lyons, F.S., *Parnell*, London, 1977

Maxwell, Constantia, *A History of Trinity College, Dublin, 1591–1892*, Dublin, 1946

O'Brien, Conor Cruise and Maire, *Concise History of Ireland*, London, 1972

Petrie, Sir Charles, *The Great Tyrconnel*, Cork, 1972

Robertson, Nora, *Crowned Harp*, Dublin, 1960

Somerville-Large, Peter, *Irish Eccentrics*, London, 1975

Woodham-Smith, C., *The Reason Why*, London, 1953

Woodham-Smith, C., *The Great Hunger*, London, 1962

Journals and Periodicals

The Irish Sword (Journal of the Military History Society of Ireland)
Irish Historical Studies
Sunday Tribune
Irish Times

Pamphlet

The Influence of the Potato upon Irish History

INDEX

272

Clare, Viscount 112
Clare Island
  de Mendoza's crew slaughtered at 51
Clarendon, Earl of
  successor to Ormonde 110
  replaced by Tyrconnel 111
  and the Famine 224, 237
Clarke, Captain Chichester 262
Cleveland, Duchess of 102
Clew Bay 157, 158
Clontarf
  defeat of Danes at 12
Clontibret
  a trouncing for the English at 62
Colclough, John
  executed in 1798 Rebellion 192
Coleraine (now Londonderry)
  land settlement in 75, 76
Confederacy, the 87, 88, 89, 90
Congreve, William
  at Trinity College 145
Connacht 16, 184, 188
  Normans in 20
  Fitzgeralds and 23
  slaughter of Armada survivors in 50–1
  and English authority 53–4
  engagements at with Hugh Roe
    O'Donnell 62–3, 65
  and transplantation 95, 98
  Protestants in 139
  French land in 192
Conolly, William
  history of 127–8, 137
Constantinople
  Whaley received royally at 161
Coote, Sir Charles
  and rebellion 86, 91, 93
  and land allocation 95
  and Charles II 96
Coote, Sir Eyre
  Lally beaten by 210, 211
Cork 53, 65, 86, 121
  and Norsemen 12, 18
  and colonization 26, 30
  allocation of land in 46
  commerce in 49
  English forces in 66
  surrenders to William 118
  and Treaty of Limerick 119
  Protestants in 139
Cork, Lord 53, 75

Cornwall 6, 26
Cornwallis, Lord
  and 1798 Rebellion 192
  Humbert surrenders to 193
  as Viceroy 200
Corps of Volunteers 176–7
  disbanded 185
Costello, John A. 92n.
Court of Claims 98, 106
  new Court formed 123
Courtenay, Thomas 36
Courtenays, the
  become penniless 65
Courtney, Sir William
  acquires land in Limerick 46
Crommelin, Louis 168
Cromwell, Oliver 138
  defeats Charles I 89
  and Ireland 90, 91–6
Crown and Harp (Mrs Nora Robertson)
  an analysis of Anglo-Irish social life 247
Cuffe, Hugh
  allocated land in Cork 46, 53
Culmore
  O'Doherty attacks 73
Curran, John Philpot
  at Trinity College 146

Dail Eireann (lower chamber of Irish
    parliament)
  and Leinster House 134, 151
Daly's – a Dublin gambling establishment
    160
Danes in Ireland 12, 16
Dangan 90
Davells, Sir Henry
  at Munster 36
Davis, Thomas 7n.
  a Young Irelander 235
Davitt, Michael
  and Land League 245
De Burgos, the (later Burke q.v.)
  of Ulster 16
Declaration of Indulgence 111
Delaney, Patrick
  a success story 128
Denny, Lady
  despatches some Armada sailors 51
Denny, Sir Edward
  allocated land in Kerry 46
Derry 10, 54

276

277

Mary I, Queen (Mary Tudor) 21
Maynooth
  and Lord Dunboyne's bequest 163-4
  and a government grant 184
  parish clergy educated at 217
  and some Church of Ireland funds 243
Mayo, County
  and Treaty of Limerick 119
Mayo Volunteers
  Fighting Fitzgerald takes action against
    Colonel of 158
Meagher, Thomas
  a Young Irelander 235, 236n.
Meath, County 121
Mellifont Abbey
  O'Neill submits to Mountjoy at 69
Mendozo, Don Pedro de
  his Armada crew slaughtered 51
Mitchel, John
  a Young Irelander 235, 236n.
'Modest Proposal, A' (Jonathan Swift) 145
Molesworth, Lord 164
  his influential pamphlet on agriculture
    150
Monaghan, County 54
  Hugh Roe O'Donnell and 61-2
  land settlement in 75
Monasternenagh
  and a tribute to Irish fighters 38
Monmouth, Duke of 102
Monroe, Henry
  and the 1798 Rebellion 189
Montgomery, Hugh
  and a dubious land transaction 74
  his enterprises prosperous 76
Montgomery of Alamein, Field-Marshal
    the Viscount 250
Moore, George 193
Moore, Henry
  commemorated in Dublin 133
Moore, Captain Hugh
  with Whaley to Acre 161
Moore, John
  and French in Connacht 193
Moore, Dr Michael
  and Trinity College 144
Moore, Thomas
  at Trinity College 146
  and Robert Emmet 216
Moriarty (farmer)
  destruction and revenge 43

Mornington, Lord 212
Morocco
  Fitzmaurice's men demolished at 33
Moryson, Fynes
  describes devastation in Munster 69
Mountcashel, Viscount 112, 113
Mount Charles, Lord 265
Mountgarret, Lord
  and rebellion 86
Mountjoy, Viscount
  victorious against O'Neill 67-9, 112
  his army makes donation to Trinity
    College 143
  death of 191
Mountrath, Earl of (see: Coote)
Mount's Bay 26
Mulgrave, Lord Lieutenant of Ireland 220
Munro, General
  and rebellion 86, 87, 89
Munster 188
  Normans in 20
  Papal troops for 22
  Fitzgeralds and 22-3
  First Plantation of 24-32, 36, 39-44, 46
  Second Plantation of 48-50, 65, 75
  settlement of land in 45-7
  devastation in 69
  rebellion in 86-7
  and Protestantism 139
Murphy, Father John of Boolavogue 190,
    192
Murphy, Father Michael
  killed in 1798 Rebellion 191

Napoleon Bonaparte 187 and Note
Naseby
  Charles I defeated at 89
Nassau, Henry, Count
  Williamite commander in Ireland 114
Navigation Acts 173
Nelson, Lord 185n., 187n.
Newgrange, County Meath
  ancient cemetery at 4, 5
New Ross
  and rebellion 88, 190-1
Newry 59, 61, 62
Newtownbarry 190
Newtown Butler, South Fermanagh 113
Nicolson, John 212
NORAID 240
Normans

282

Prior, Thomas
  founding member of Royal Dublin
    Society 149
Proclamation 1916 196, 198
Protestant Ascendancy 99, 122, 127, 128,
    139, 144, 181, 201
Protestants in Ireland
  in England 21
  in Ireland 78–84, 136–7, 139–41, 257–8
  establishment of an Ascendancy of 122
  and Corps of Volunteers 176
  in 1798 Rebellion 190
Puritans, the 80

Quakers
  and famine relief in Ireland 226, 237–8
  reports on famine 231
Quebec
  and emigrants 224–5

Raleigh, Sir Walter 47, 48
  and Ireland 26, 31, 32
  and atrocities at Smerwick 42
  acquires Youghal and other lands 46
  introduces potatoes and tobacco to
    Ireland 49
Reagan, Ronald 240
Redmond, John Edward
  and Home Rule 257, 260, 262
Resumption Bill 123
Richelieu, Cardinal
  and revolt in Ulster 85, 87
Rinuccinni, Papal Nuncio
  in Irish rebellion 88–91
Roberts, Abraham 211
Roberts, Frederick ('Bobs Bahadur')
  a distinguished career 211
Robertson, Mrs Nora
  her analysis of Anglo-Irish social life
    247–52, 265
Roches, the
  and fight against Munster Plantation 29
Roche, Sir Boyle
  some sayings of 154–5 and Note
Roche, Maurice, Lord Fermoy 52–3
Romans
  and Celts 5
  Ireland immune from 6
Roscommon, County 206
Rosse, Richard, 1st Earl of
  a sinful life 164–5

Rosse, Earl of (present) 48
Rossmore, Lord
  a good landlord 241
Routh, Sir Randolph 228
Royal College of Physicians 208
Royal College of Surgeons 208
Royal Dublin Society 134, 208, 266
  founding of 149–52
Royal Hospital, Kilmainham 102
Royal Irish Academy 266
  founding of 152
Royal Irish Constabulary 220, 243, 257
Royal Navy 185 and Note
Royal Society for the Prevention of Cruelty
    to Animals 155
Russell, George ('AE') 256
Russell, Lord John (Prime Minister) 237

Saintfield
  and the 1798 Rebellion 189
St Leger, Sir Warham
  Earl of Desmond (Gerald Fitzgerald)
    under house arrest at home of 24
  and colonization of Munster 26, 27, 32
  allocated land in Cork 46
St Patrick
  in Ireland 8, 9
St Ruth, Marshal
  in Ireland 118
Salterstown 76
Sanders, Father Nicolas
  as ally of Fitzmaurice 33, 35, 37
  Gerald Fitzgerald ready to hand over 39
  no pardon for 40, 52
  death of 42
  and Society of Jesus 80
Sandwich Islands, Pacific Ocean
  Tone as governor of 195
Sarsfield, Patrick 132
  quoted on Battle of the Boyne 116
  in battle 118–20
Schomberg, Duke of, Marshal
  King William's commander in Ireland
    113, 114
Schomberg, Meinhard
  in William's army in Ireland 114
Schull, County Kerry 231
Scotland 6
  Vikings in 12
Sebastian, King of Portugal
  conscripts Fitzmaurice's army 33

285

288